About the Author

Moustafa Gadalla is an Egyptian-American independent Egyptologist, who was born in Cairo, Egypt in 1944. He holds a Bachelor of Science degree in civil engineering from Cairo University.

Gadalla is the author of eleven internationally acclaimed books about the various aspects of the Ancient Egyptian history and civilization and its influences worldwide. He is the chairman of the Tehuti Research Foundation—an international, U.S.-based, non-profit organization, dedicated to Ancient Egyptian studies.

From his early childhood, Gadalla pursued his Ancient Egyptian roots with passion, through continuous study and research. Since 1990, he has dedicated and concentrated all his time to researching and writing.

Other Books By The Author

[See details on pages 268-272]

Egyptian Mystics: Seekers of the Way

Egyptian Cosmology: The Animated Universe - 2nd ed.

Egyptian Divinities: The All Who Are THE ONE

Egyptian Harmony: The Visual Music

Historical Deception: The Untold Story of Ancient Egypt - 2nd ed.

Egyptian Rhythm: The Heavenly Melodies

Exiled Egyptians: The Heart of Africa

Pyramid Handbook - 2nd ed.

Tut-Ankh-Amen: The Living Image of the Lord

Egypt: A Practical Guide

This Book is Dedicated to

The Baladi People of Egypt and Hispania

Acknowledgement

We appreciate the ability to display charts and tables from various references, as noted in the book.

The title of this book refers to the *Romany*, which is one of several names given to these people (others being *Gypsies*, *Bohemians*, etc). The term *Romany* is preferred because it does not have an unjustifyably negative connotation like the terms "Gypsies" and "Bohemians" do. The term *Romany* is derived from the Ancient Egyptian word, **Rom-at**, which means *Egyptian people*. This book will show that all these different names have meaning only in Egyptian context.

Book Cover (Front): **Ausar** (Osiris) is shown in the form of a bull, bearing a mummy of the deceased on his back. [From a coffin in the British Museum (No. 29,888).]

Book Cover (Back): An Ancient Egyptian flamenco dancer is accompanied by hand clappers.

Book Cover Artwork by: K&D Design, North East, PA, USA

Book Production by: Moustafa Gadalla and Faith Cross

Egyptian Romany

The Essence of Hispania

Moustafa Gadalla

Maa Kheru (True of Voice)

Tehuti Research Foundation

International Head Office: Greensboro, NC, U.S.A.

Egyptian Romany

The Essence of Hispania

by Moustafa Gadalla

Published by:

Tehuti Research Foundation
P.O. Box 39406
Greensboro, NC 27438-9406, U.S.A.

Printed in the United States of America, 2004

Publisher's Cataloging-in-Publication

Gadalla, Moustafa, 1944-
Egyptian romany : the essence of hispania / Moustafa Gadalla.
p. cm.
Includes bibliographical references and index.
LCCN 2004095121
ISBN-13 978-1-931446-19-9
ISBN-10 1-931446-19-9
ISBN-13 978-1-931446-20-2 (E-book)
ISBN-10 1-931446-20-2 (E-book)

1. Gypsies--Their Egyptian origin. 2. Gypsies--Influences in Hispania. 3. Ethnology--Hispania. 4. Hispania--Social life and customs. 5. Iberia--Antiquities. 6. Egyptian language--Influence on European languages. 7. Egypt--Religion--Influence. 8. Egypt--Civilization. I. Title

Manufactured in the United States of America
Published 2004

Table of Contents

Dedication and Acknowledgment 2
Table of Contents 5
Preface 9
Standards and Terminology 14
Map of the Mediterranean Basin 16
Map of Ancient Egypt 17
Map of the Iberian Peninsula 18

1. The Romany (Gypsy) Essence of Hispania 21
The Egipcianos of Hispania
The Egyptian-Iberian Fugitives
The Cultured Romany/Gitanos
The Most Religious
The Timeless Egyptian-Hispanic Culture

2. Our Heavenly Mother 37
The Ascension of the Queen
Lady of Sorrow
The Virgin Mother with the 10,000 Names
Matrilineal/Matriarchal Society
The Ama Rules
The Revered Ama
The Bull of His Mother

3. Out of Egypt 55
The Mirages of Iberia
The Egyptian Romany Colonies
The Egyptian Influence in the Eastern Mediterranean
The Spread of the Egyptian Religion
The Twin Sisters

4. The Egyptian-Hispanic Alloys 67
Who Needed Iberian Minerals?
The Egyptian Knowledge of Metallurgy and Metalworking
The Golden Silver Alloy (Electrum)
The Copper and Bronze Alloys
The Glazing Alloys
The Egyptian Mining Experience
Fortifications of Isolated Communities

5. In the Beginning – Almeria 83
The Sirets and Petrie Archeological Connections
The Telling Tombs
Dry Weather Farming
The Early (New) Settlers

6. Masters of the Seas 93
The Egyptian Ships
Egyptian Goods
The Egyptian Geodesy
Patrons and Shrines of the Seafarers
Our (Holy) Mother of the Sea

7. Merchants of the Seas 107
The Phoenicians' Homeland
The Egyptian-Phoenician Connection
The Egyptianized Phoenicians
The Seafaring Phoenician/Carthaginians
The (Non-) Phoenician Iberian Colonies

8. Canopus and Cádiz: A Tale of Two Harbors 117
The Gitano Dancers of Cádiz
Egyptian Fishing Techniques at Cádiz
The Many (Egyptian) Names of Cádiz
The Immortal Hercules: The Egyptian Lord of Travel
The Greater Canopus Harbor (Alexandria before Alexander): Maiden of the Seas
The Foundation of Cádiz

The Lost Temples of Cádiz

9. The Assyrian Devastation and Aftershocks 133
The Assyrian Assaults
The Egyptian Exodus
Turdetania Urbanization
The Persian Rampage of Egypt

10. Romanticizing the Romans 141
Romanticizing the Romans
The Fictional Romanization of Iberia
The (Non-) Roman Temples and Tombs

11. The Moors and the Egyptians 149
The Identification of the "Moors" (The Moabi Brothers)
The Nomadic Moorish Rulers
The Civilized Populace
The Egyptian Green Revolution
The Egyptian Hispanic Arts and Crafts
The Egyptian Housing and Gardens of Iberia

12. The Origin of the Hispanic Languages/Dialects 167
The Egyptian Source of the Arabic Language
Sound Shifts and Linguistic Studies
The Distinction of a Language
The Intimate Egyptian-Hispanic Tongue
The Divine Mother Language
Romancing the Mother Tongue
Writing Variations and Linguistic Studies

13. The Animated Religious Traditions 191
The Animated Cosmic Order
The Role of Saints
The Cyclical Renewal Festivals
Egyptian Mysticism in Galicia (Priscillianism)

Santiago de Compostela
The Egyptian/Iberian Mystical Societies

14. The Egyptian-Hispanic Musical Heritage 207
The Egyptian Romany Muses
The Music of Civilization
The Heavenly Musical Forms
Love Conquers All
Singing and Poetry
The Musical Instruments
Rhythmic Dancing
The Musical Activities
The Heavenly Muses

Glossary 237
Selected Bibliography 240
Sources and Notes 249
Index 258
About TRF Books 268
Order Form 272

Preface

It has been said that history is "written" (more correctly *dictated/colored*) by the winner(s) of the latest conflict. This is very true in the case of Hispania (Spain and Portugal), where the history books are tailored by the descendants of the northern "winners" of the Reconquest. The true builders of the Hispanic society were pushed out of their lands by the northern "winners". Subsequently, these homeless people of non-European stock were called "nomadic" and "uncultured". This silent and peaceful majority—the truly civilized—were called by many names—Mossarabs (***Mozarabs***), Gypsies (***Gitanos***), Romany, ***Moriscos***, Mudehars (***Mudejars***), . . .etc. The true voices of Hispania—such as the poet Federico Garcia Lorca—highlighted and celebrated these people of non-European stock as the true people of culture in Hispania. Lorca wrote in his book, ***Gitano Ballads*** [1928],

> ***. . . . .the gitano is the most distinguished, profound and aristocratic element in my country****, the one that most represents its way of being and best preserves the fire, the blood and the alphabet of Andalusian and universal truth. . .*

To further humiliate these people of culture—the Romany—western academicians denied their Egyptian heritage and arbitrarily and forcefully assigned/imposed an Indian ethnicity on them.

The essence of Hispania—namely the people known as the Romany, ***Gitano***, etc—will be the centerpiece of this book, which will show the neglected historical evidence about the Egyptian roots of the Romany of Hispania and the intimate relationship between Ancient Egypt and Iberia. The role of the Egyptians in the Iberian history was credited to others, such as the Phoenicians, Romans, Arabs, Berbers, etc. These commonly held views are without supporting evidence and are mostly (if not totally) based on the repetitive assertions of unfounded views—sheer repetition and nothing else makes them appear to be "unquestionable facts".

This book will contradict most of the present common theories and will provide the evidence that shows the intimate relationship between Egypt and Hispania—archeologically, historically, culturally, ethnologically, linguistically, etc.

Chapter one, *The Romany (Gypsy) Essence of Hispania*, sorts through the subject of the Gypsies and differentiates the Egyptian Romany from non-Egyptian nomadic groups. It highlights their Egyptian characteristics and relates them to the ***Gitanos***, ***Moriscos***, ***Mozarabs***, ***Mudejars***, etc.

Chapter two, *Our Heavenly Mother*, shows how Ancient Egypt and Iberia share the intense love for the Virgin Mother (known in Ancient Egypt as **Auset** (*Isis*) and in Christianity as *Mary/Maria*). A shortened version of the story of **Auset** and **Ausar** is presented, so as to draw parallels between the Ancient Egyptian **Auset** and the Virgin Mary. The role of Mary/**Auset** formed the basis for the matrilineal/matriarchal societal framework. This chapter also shows the role of the bull in Ancient Egypt and Iberia, and that the practices of bullfights and running of the bulls in Iberia can only be found in Ancient Egypt, since at least 5,000 years ago.

Chapter three, *Out of Egypt*, gives an overview of the major pitfalls in the common theories about the history of Iberia. It highlights the false chronology and dating in most references. It also highlights the incredible silence in most references about the role of the most populous, wealthiest, and prominent civilization in the ancient world—namely Egypt. It provides the accounts of early Egyptian immigration to other countries, and accounts of some of their early settlements in Asia and Europe. It also provides the general consensus on the population characteristics in Iberia and how the Ancient Egyptians (of all nations in the world) match these characteristics exactly.

Chapter four, *The Egyptian-Hispanic Alloys*, describes the Ancient Egyptian knowledge of metallurgy, and their ability to make numerous metallic alloys. It will show how Ancient Egypt lacked certain minerals to make specific alloys (such as electrum, copper, and bronze), the high demand for metals in Egypt, and how the fluctuation in the production of such goods in Ancient Egypt correlated to the rise and fall of mining activities in Iberia. It also shows the Ancient Egyptian history of organization and management of large mining sites, settlement fortifications, etc.

Chapter five, *In the Beginning—Almeria*, highlights the archeological findings at the early settlements in several Iberian regions—beginning at Almeria, and correlates these activities in Iberia with Ancient Egypt—to show unique similarities and affinities between Ancient Egypt (in pre- and early dynastic times) and Iberia, in all aspects of religion, architecture, farming, metalworking, etc.

Chapter six, *Masters of the Seas*, shows the supremacy of the Ancient Egypt ships, their sizes, types, and functions. It provides an overview of the Egyptian goods that were sought worldwide. It identifies the patrons (deities) of travel and how they were adopted 100 % by others, such as the Phoenicians.

Chapter seven, *Merchants of the Seas*, evaluates the common theory about the role of the Phoenicians/Punics in the history of Iberia, by describing the archeological and historical evidence in the Phoenicians' homeland. The evidence is overwhelming that Phoenicia was a vassal of Ancient

Egypt and that the Phoenicians copied all aspects of the Ancient Egyptian culture. It shows that Phoenicians were experienced seafarers and traders and nothing else. The Phoenicians did not have the number of people (or the talent) for the farming, art, industry, and building skills necessary to establish new settlements in Iberia or elsewhere.

Chapter eight, *Canopus and Cádiz: A Tale of Two Harbors*, provides a clear history of Cádiz and its role as the western gateway to western Iberia, northern Europe, and the African continent. It shows that the reported fishing and salting techniques as well as its famed dancers were duplicates of the same in Ancient Egypt. It highlights the significance of the Canopus harbors (Alexandria before Alexander), as the center of commerce in the whole world, for thousands of years. It describes the role of the (Egyptian) Hercules/Herakles at Egyptian harbors and how other countries imitated Egypt in this regard. It shows the similarities between the Cádiz harbor with its temples and the harbor at Canopus with its temples.

Chapter nine, *The Assyrian Devastation and Aftershocks*, correlates the rise of power of the Assyrians (and later the Persians), to the waves of mass migration from Ancient Egypt, which coincided with the increase in population and the number of settlements in Iberia.

Chapter ten, *Romanticizing the Romans*, addresses the lack of merit of Romans' influence in Iberia—in all aspects of Iberian life, such as culture, government, religion, language, society, buildings, etc.

Chapter eleven, *The Moors and the Egyptians*, addresses the falsehoods of credits given to the Moors/Moslems/Arabs. It identifies the true origin of these invaders and how they were removed from the civilized aspects in Iberia, such as farming, housing, gardens, arts, crafts, etc, and how all these aspects and activities were only found in Egypt, before they appeared in Iberia. It also shows the huge number of Egyptian settlers in the areas that are the best farmed in Iberia, such as Algarve and Murcia.

Chapter twelve, *The Origin of the Hispanic Languages/ Dialects*, defines the role of the Ancient Egypt language as the mother of all Semitic languages, as well as all other languages/dialects in the Mediterranean Basin and beyond.

Chapter thirteen, *The Animated Religious Traditions*, shows how the people of both Egypt and the Iberian Peninsula share the same concept of Animism, the power of saints, religious pilgrimages, festivals, etc. It also describes the role of Ancient Egypt in Priscillianism, which was (and continues to be) widespread. It also relates the fate of Priscillian to the pilgrimage and traditions at Santiago de Compostela. It shows that the history and practices of confraternities in Catholic-ruled Iberia (and southern Italy) coincide exactly with "Sufi" Orders in Islamized countries, and that the fundamentals and practices of these mystical groups under Islamic and Christian rules are of Ancient Egyptian origin.

Chapter fourteen, *The Egyptian-Hispanic Musical Heritage*, shows the intimacy between the Egyptians and Iberian heritage as it relates to music, poetry, song, and dance. It shows that the Ancient Egyptians—not the Moors—are the source of music, singing, dancing, and poetry in the Iberian Peninsula. It highlights the role of the (Egyptian) Romany as the performers of these activities in the Iberian Peninsula. It describes the major celebratory musical activities in both Egypt and the Iberian Peninsula.

Moustafa Gadalla
Abib 19, 13002 (Ancient Egyptian Calendar)
July 27, 2004 CE

Standards and Terminology

1. Words and terms have different meanings for different people, at different times in history. Here are a few examples:

a. North Africans are sometimes called *Libyans*, the name given to them by the Greeks of the first millennium BCE. North Africans are called *Berbers*, by the Moslem Arabs who entered North Africa from Syria and Arabia, from the 7th century CE onward.

b. The people who presently speak Arabic are called Arabs. Arabs, as an ethnic group, are the people living in present-day Saudi Arabia. Calling everyone who was forced to speak Arabic by the Moslem invaders is a common error.

So, the terms, *Libyans, Berbers, Arabs*, ...etc., should be treated very carefully, because the meanings vary from person to person, from region to region, and from one era to another. Most references, however, are very careless in using such terms, and omit adequate explanation.

2. You may find variations in writing the same Ancient Egyptian term, such as **Amen/Amon/Amun** or **Pir/Per**. This is because the vowels you see in translated Egyptian texts are only approximations of sounds, which are used by Egyptologists to help them pronounce the Ancient Egyptian terms/words.

3. The Ancient Egyptian word, **neter**, and its feminine form **netert**, have been wrongly, and possibly intentionally, translated to *god* and *goddess*, by almost all academicians.
Neteru (plural of **neter/netert**) are the divine principles and functions of the One Supreme God.

4. When referring to the names of cities, Pharaohs, **neteru**, etc., if the commonly used Greek name is different than the true Egyptian name, we will show the correct Egyptian name **in this font**, followed by the "Westernized common" Greek rendering between parentheses.

5. The term *Baladi* will be used throughout this book to denote the present silent majority of Egyptians, who adhere to the Ancient Egyptian traditions, under a thin exterior layer of Islam.
The same term—*Baladi*—was used to describe the native people of Iberia, since the arrival of the Syrians in 741 CE.

6. When using the Latin calendar, we will use the following terms:
BCE - **B**efore **C**ommon **E**ra. Noted in many references as BC.
CE - **C**ommon **E**ra. Noted in many references as AD.

7. Throughout this book, the fonting of quotations varies depending on the source of quotation. There are generally three types of fonting:

This font is used to refer to Ancient Egyptian sources.
This font is used to refer to Hispanic terms/quotes.
This font is used to refer to quotes from other sources.

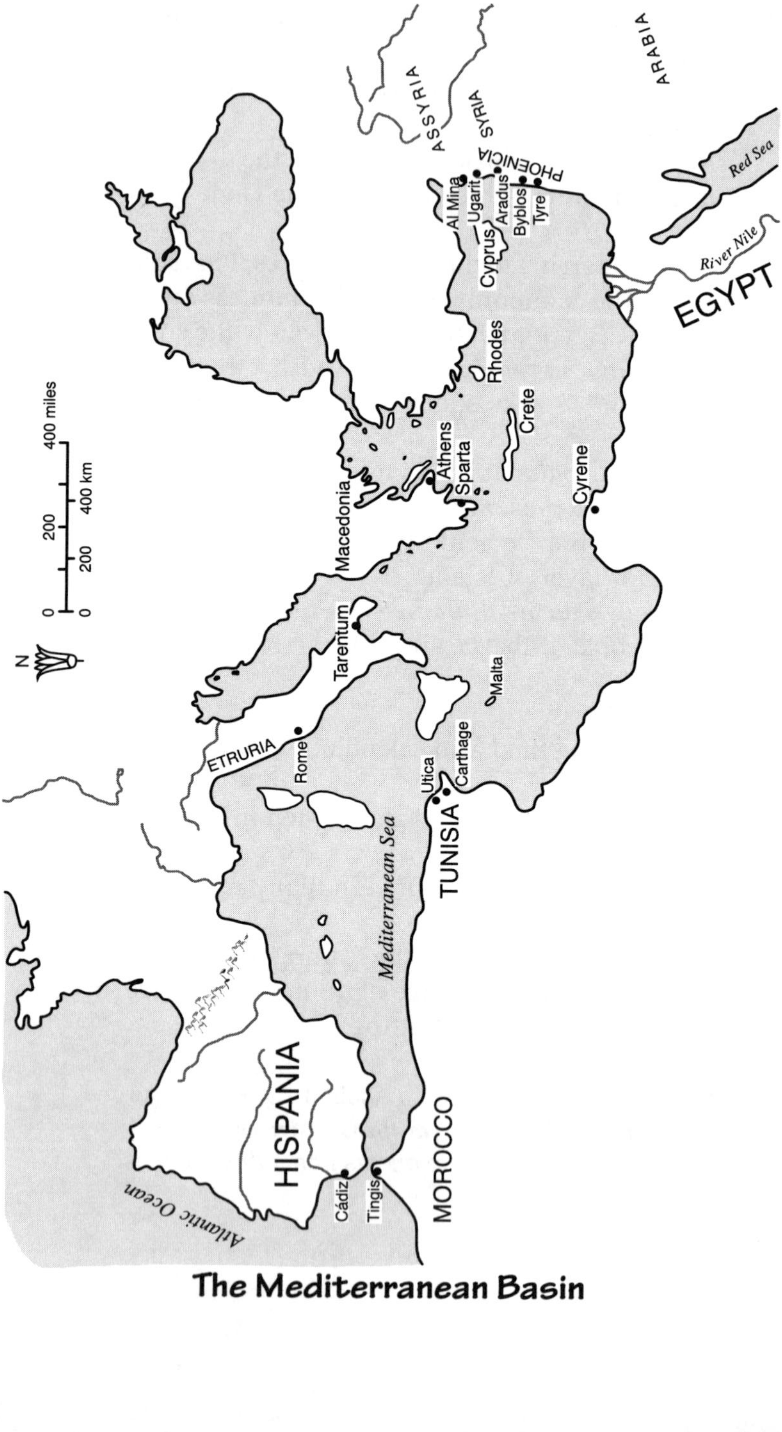

The Mediterranean Basin

Map of Ancient Egypt

The Iberian Peninsula - West

The Iberian Peninsula - East

1

The Romany (Gypsy) Essence of Hispania

The Egipcianos of Iberia

The people commonly referred to as *Romany* (Gypsy, ***Gitano***, Bohemian, etc) are consistently found in (or near to) ancient settlement sites of the Iberian Peninsula, especially in the southern and central regions. Their Egyptian heritage is clearly recognized in the furthermost areas of Iberia, such as the Basque provinces, where they are called ***Egipcioac***, or Egyptians. The ***Egipcioac/Egipcianos*** of Iberia are proud of their heritage as the descendants of the Egyptian Pharaohs. They were/are fond of talking of Egypt and its former greatness. Unfortunately, the spirit of a post-Reconquest "purified" Spain lingers on, and as a result, the Romany of Hispania's insistence of Egyptian heritage has been arbitrarily and capriciously denied by most of academia.

The Reconquest has created total demographic chaos, where the native people were forced to become refugees in their own land. Antonio Dominguez Ortiz points out that the word ***Gitano*** (after the Reconquest) came to be applied not just to the ***Egipcianos*** *(people of Egyptian origin)* but also to other marginal groups: runaway slaves fearful of expulsion, as well as the ***hungaros*** (Hungarians) from central Europe, who live an entirely nomadic lifestyle. A detailed discussion of the various facets of this diverse nomadic group, which was/is carelessly called *gypsies* (***Gitanos***), is beyond the scope of this book. It is these un-Egyptian nomadic and sometimes criminal elements that give the ***Egipcianos*** a bad name.

It is interesting to note that the word *gypsy/gipsy* is derived from the Spanish word ***Egipci-anos***. All other names that describe the ***Egipcianos*** are, as expected, Ancient Egyptian names. The Hispanic ***Egipcianos*** are known as **Roma-ny**, **Bohem-ian**, ***Gitanos***, etc. All such terms are Ancient Egyptian.

- **Roma** is an Ancient Egyptian word meaning *(Egyptian) people/men*. The Egyptian people alone were termed **romat**; other nations were Negroes, Asiatics, or Libyans, but never **romat**. In the Egyptian and most Semitic tongues, the letter *t* at the end of the word is silent, and hence the common word, **Roma**. **Rom** is a recognizable Hispanic ***Gitano*** word meaning *man*. The word *man* in Sanskrit is *domba*. This is a strong linguistic confirmation of the falsehood publicized by western academia that the *Roma-ny* are of Indian origin, despite the Hispanic Romany insistence of their Egyptian heritage.

- The word **Bohem-ian** is also an Egyptian word. The verb-stem of this word is **Bohem/Bahm**, which means to *be/make obscure* or *dark/black/mysterious/mystical*. *Bohem-ian* will thus mean *mystical*, which describes the mystical nature of the Hispanic Romany religious practices.

- The word ***Gitano*** is also of Egyptian origin. **Git/Ghit** means *tillable land*, in the Egyptian tongue. The term, **La Tina** also means *fertile soil/land* in Egypt. The Ancient Egyptian word **Kemet** also means *black (fertile) soil*. The conservatism of the Egyptians and Iberians is rooted in the earth/land. As such, these above-mentioned terms that are associated with the ***(Egipcianos) Gitanos*** are likewise related to the earth/land.

In this book, we will not (and have no right to) deny the Egyptian heritage and descendancy of the Romany. We therefore will refer to these very ancient natives of Iberia throughout this book as (Egyptian) Romany, who are different than European nomadic groups. The heritage of the (Egyptian) Romany is totally credible from their physical characteristics and demeanor, as well as linguistically, historically and culturally—as will unfold throughout this book.

A significant number of the Romany are most noted for their traditional metalworking. They are usually found at the outer limits of most major Spanish cities. Just like in ancient times, industrial factories, in our modern times, are usually located at the outer perimeters of the cities.

In Ancient Egypt, the Pharaoh himself, as well as other spiritual leaders and spiritual intermediaries were/are identified with the mysterious craft of the smith. The smiths in Egypt were/are highly revered and sometimes feared, because of their supernatural powers in handling, controlling, and manipulating the four elements of creation. These four elements are always present at the smith's forge: fire, the air of the bellows to tease fire, water to tame fire, and earth, as the provider of raw materials. These sons of earth are Animistic, and therefore they are noted for their spiritual powers.

As in Ancient and Baladi Egypt, the Romany craftsmen

in Jerez (nicknamed the *City of Gitanos*)—including coopers, tinsmiths, hat manufacturers, and belt makers—were/are organized into strong guilds. By 1870, there were approximately 50 different societies of artisans, small proprietors, and workers in Jerez. The members of these confraternities are active participants in the numerous festivals [more about festivals later in this chapter, and in chapter 13].

The borough of Triana, on the other side of the river by Seville, has from time immemorial been noted as a favorite residence of the (Egyptian) Romany; and here, at the present day, they are found in greater number than in any other town in Spain. They are also recognizable at Cádiz and Córdoba, which contain a dozen Romany/***Gitano*** extended families, as well as in Extremadura, Catalonia, Murcia, and Valencia.

Once the racial and cultural biases that lead to the arbitrary wrong premise about an Indian origin or nomadic style of the (Egyptian) Romany/***Gitanos*** are set aside, the facts become clearer (as some academic circles began to realize) that the Romany/***Gitanos***/Gypsies have been in Iberia much longer than the nomadic groups that arrived from central Europe a few centuries ago. The (Egyptian) Romany/***Gitanos*** are what Andalusia is—they are the Andalusian way of life. [See affirming statements from the famed Andalusian Federico Garcia Lorca, later in this chapter.]

Immigration from Egypt to Iberia occurred in several waves. They were closely related to the events in Ancient Egypt. [Earlier waves during the 3rd and 2nd millennium BCE will be discussed in chapter 5.] Some came in prosperous times to pursue business contacts. The majority came in stressful times. The next major immigration wave was due to the Assyrian invasion of Egypt [as will be discussed in chapter 9]. Another major immigration wave occurred during the 9th century CE [as will be discussed in chapter 11].

The Egyptian-Iberian Fugitives

Another word that is associated with the (Egyptian) Romany is the word *flamenco*, which appears to be a mispronunciation of the "Arabic" words *felag* and *mengu* (*felag-mengu*), which means *fugitive peasant*. This term is actually Egyptian (the origin of the Arabic language), and is pronounced in the Egyptian way—hard *g* and not the soft Arabic *g* (as in the English letter *j*). In any event, the term *felag-mengu* applied to all of the persecuted people who fled to the mountains, when the land was appropriated by the "winners" from the north, who defeated the Moorish rulers. The "winners" destroyed Spain—in "saving" it. Their actions went far beyond the elimination of a few thousand Moorish rulers, their families, and mercenary armies.

The Reconquest created waves of refugees that became nomadic by force—not by choice. The dispersions were caused by three subsequent decisions by the northern "winners".

1. New land policy, where much of the land was colonized rather than settled by Castilians.

Previously, under and prior to the Moorish rule, the rulers did not own that much land. They mostly acted as overlords who collected exactions (taxes) from the working people. The concept of land for the working people (as is the case in Ancient Egypt) doesn't accept the premise that land is a property that can be owned. For them, people have the right to occupy a land, only if they work it, and they can only own the fruit of their labor. The Ancient Egyptians had no verb meaning *to possess*, *to have*, nor any verb meaning *to belong to*. On the other hand, for the non-agrarian "winners" of the Spanish Reconquest, a land without documented ownership is "ownerless" (i.e. "up for grabs"). Furthermore, as a result of the Reconquest, people whose lives were threatened naturally escaped for their lives. Leaving their land vacant, the marching army considered the vacated land (by default) to be "ownerless". The victorious Castilian monarchs considered land to be a property that is owned, and as a result made lavish grants of land to loyal soldiers and to the military orders that had collaborated in the campaigns. Many farmers agreed to become tenant farmers, but others escaped to the mountains or left Spain for other countries.

2. Religious cleansing of non-Catholics.

As a consequence of the Reconquest, Catholicism became the only official religion of the land. The northern winners considered any non-Caucasian European to be of a "Moorish" descent. To compound this wrong assumption, they assumed that these people were Moslems. The confusion of terms of categorizing a person as an Arab, Moslem, Moor, etc. began under the Arab-Berber rule, whose "tax" system was based on the religion of the taxpayer. Under Islamic rule, a person must officially announce his religion, since Islamic law imposes additional special "tax" (known as *Jizya*) on Christians and Jews. The Iberian population, controlled or threatened by the Moorish invaders, had to declare one of the three "approved" religions [Islam, Christianity, and Judaism]. Such declaration was a necessary and pragmatic announcement and never a conversion. As a result, we therefore have arbitrary categorization of people and their beliefs.

The confusion was compounded by the aftermath of the Reconquest and the violent actions to "purify" Iberia, which resulted in confusing terms, such as *Mossarabs* (**Mozarabs**), **Moriscos**, *Mudehars* (**Mudejars**), *Gypsies* (**Gitanos**), etc. Yet when the dust settles, we will find that such categorizations are arbitrary and careless. All these artificial categories are descriptions of one ethnic group—*Baladi*—simply the natives—the silent, peaceful, and truly civilized majority. There are absolutely no distinctions in the race or physical characteristics between these four arbitrarily-named "groups"—***Mozarabs, Mudejars, Moriscos, and Gitanos***—which means that they are one and the same.

The term, ***Mozarabs*** (Mossarabs), was given to those who *"were considered Christians, but who adopted Arabic/Islamic manners and attire"*. This is a capricious and wrong distinction, since Islamic law insists that Dhimmis [Christians and Jews living in Moslem lands] must be discriminated from Moslems in their attire. Furthermore, the evidence shows non-Christian practices among this group of people. It is reported that the Church in 1076 forbade the "***Mozarabic*** rites", and despite the official suppression of such rites, they persisted in many of the Spanish churches. One must then conclude that the ***Mozarabic*** rites were contrary to Catholicism. In other words, such rites reflected the populous' Animistic beliefs. [See later in this chapter and chapter 13 re. Animistic beliefs.] Actually, the term, ***Mozarab***, refers to Egyptian, since ***Mozarabic*** is pronounced *Mossarabic/Moss-arabic*, meaning *Egyptian Arab / Egyptian dialect of Arabic*, and hence referred to by confused writers as "vulgar Arabic" or "Hispano-Arabic". *Mossr/Massr* is the name of Egypt—known to Arabs and other countries ever since Pharaonic times.

The term ***Moriscos*** was given to peasants and farmers in south, southeast, and central Spain. This term applies generally to settlers who arrived during the Moorish rule (mostly Egyptians [as detailed in chapter 11]). The ***Moriscos*** are arbitrarily categorized as Moslems, based on their physical features of non-European Caucasian stock.

The term ***Mudejars*** (Mudehars) applies generally to settlers who were already present in the Iberian Peninsula prior to the Moorish rule. Like the ***Moriscos***, the ***Mudejars*** are also arbitrarily categorized as Moslems, based on their physical features of non-European Caucasian stock. The word ***Mudejars*** was explained as to come from the "Arabic"-sounding word that means *settled* or *tamed*. In other words, the term ***Mudejars*** means *baladi—native of the land.* **Mudejar** also means *darkish/tanned/blackish.* The apparent two meanings (*settled* and *darkish/tanned/blackish*) are related—in an Egyptian (not Arabic) context—to mean *a dark-skinned settler.* The Ancient Egyptian term, **Kemet**, has the same double meaning(s) as ***Mudejars***—the *blackish land* as well as the *people of this land.* The people described as ***Mudejars*** are recognized as skilled craftsmen, masons, builders, and farmers mostly in central and northeastern Spain, as well as in Andalusia, in the Ebro valley, and the Levant, and in the big cities like Córdoba, Saragossa, Valencia, and Seville.

It was claimed that the ***Moriscos/Mudejars/Gitanos*** converted to Christianity and attempted to live under Christian rule. As will be explained later, they never really "converted", since their Ancient Egyptian Animistic religious beliefs are consistent with the spiritual message of Christianity [as will be explained later in this chapter].

3. Racial/ethnic cleansing of non-European Caucasians.

After 1525, all residents of Spain were officially Christian, but forced conversion and nominal orthodoxy were not sufficient for complete "integration" into Spanish society. Purity of blood (***limpieza de sangre***) regulations were enacted. Many of Spain's oldest and freest families scrambled to reconstruct family trees, and forged documents in the process.

Between September 1609 and January 1610, an estimated total of 135,000 tan-skinned ***Moriscos/Mudejars*** were ordered to be deported from the kingdom of Valencia. Then more expulsion orders followed from Castile, Extremadura, La Mancha, Andalusia, Murcia, Catalonia and Aragón. By the end of March 1611, a total of 300,000 tan-skinned ***Moriscos/Mudejars*** had been ordered to leave Spain. Some left for Egypt, France, and North Africa, but most formed clandestine groups and hid out, living their lives in a kind of hybrid underground culture. These forcefully transient people are generally known as ***Gitanos***. To add insult to injury, the northern Catholic "winners" denied the ***Gitanos*** their Egyptian heritage, and imposed an "Indian" identity on them. The facts however remain that there were/are no distinctive or different physical characteristics between the "***Gitanos***" and either the "***Moriscos***" or the "***Mudejars***". In other words, the Indian origin of ***Gitanos*** is nullified, since the ***Moriscos*** are recognized to come from non-Indian origin, namely North Africa.

The shared origin of "***Gitanos***" and "***Moriscos***" is being recognized more and more in academic circles. George Borrow in his book, *The Zincali: An Account of the Gypsies of Spain* [1923, page 317], acknowledged that the "***Gitanos***",

> ***. . . . . are the descendants of the Moriscos who remained in Spain, wandering about amongst the mountains and wildernesses, after the expulsion of the great body of the nation from the country in the time of Philip the Third.***

So, now we are dealing with the same people when referring to ***Gitanos*** and/or ***Moriscos***.

It is implied that the ***Moriscos*** are the immigrants from North Africa. This is partially true, because they came from the North African country of Egypt. However, the implication of non-Egyptian North African origin—namely the nomadic Berbers—is incorrect for several reasons. Berber men had white skin, and they frequently had light colored eyes and blond hair. They are distinctly very different than Egyptians who are tanned/brown/dark, with dark-colored eyes and hair. Most importantly, Egyptians are un-warlike, and have relied exclusively throughout their history on foreign mercenaries for their military forces. When we review the writings of Ibn Khaldun—a Spaniard of North African Berber origin—he states that his people are nomads who abhor farming, industry, etc. [See chapter 11 for specific references.] The North

African Berbers also speak a particular Berber tongue, with distinctly different sounds of the alphabet, than both Egyptian and Hispanic languages—such as the letter *g*, which is always pronounced as the hard sound *g*, in the Egyptian/Hispanic tongues. However, the Berbers never pronounce the hard *g*, but always a soft *g*, equivalent to the English letter *j*.

Additionally, by comparing the spoken language of the ***Gitanos*** and the North African Berber (or Arabic) language(s), we find a lack of affinity. Yet there is a strong affinity between the Egyptian and ***Gitano/Morisco/Mudejar*** tongue, which again leads to the real origin of ***Gitano/Morisco/Mudejar***—Egypt. [More about linguistic affinities throughout this book and in chapter 12.]

The Cultured Romany/Gitanos

The historian J.H. Elliot wrote the following about the consequence of the Reconquest,

> *Spanish society drove itself on a ruthless, ultimately self-defeating quest for an unattainable purity.*

But these very same people who were pushed out or into hiding are the essence, soul, and root of Hispania. This fact was publicized by the famed Andalusian poet, Federico Garcia Lorca, who saw the ***(Egipciano) Gitano*** as the perfect embodiment of his country, as stated in ***Gitano Ballads***, a volume of poetry published to great acclaim in 1928. In commenting on the significance of the (Egyptian) Romany/***Gitano*** in his poems, Lorca observed:

> *Although it is called **gitano**, the book as a whole is the poem of Andalusia, and I have called it **gitano** because **the gitano is the most distinguished, profound and aristocratic element in my country**, the one that most represents its Way of being and best preserves the fire, the blood and the alphabet of Andalusian and universal truth. . . . .*

The Egyptian origin of the Romany/***Gitanos*** was noted by Voltaire, who could easily see the figurative relationship between the ancient dancers of Cádiz and the ***Gitanos***. In his *Essai sur les moeurs*, Voltaire maintained that *"**the gitanos were the descendants of the priests and priestesses of Isis, whose castanets and tambourines derived directly from antiquity.**"* [Vaux de Foletier pgs. 25 and 238].

Lorca called Jerez the *City of the (Egyptian) Gitanos*, where its quarters of Santiago and Puerta del Sol are heavily populated by the ***Gitanos***. Jerez is located in the very heart of the flamenco country and has nourished some monumental figures in the history of ***cante jondo***—a great example being the legendary Pharaonic Manuel Torres, ***Niño de Jerez***. Lorca dedicated his series of ***Viñetas flamencas*** in the ***Poema del cante jondo*** [I: 201-08] to this (Egyptian) Romany (***Gitano***) singer. Even though Manuel Torres, perhaps the greatest flamenco singer of all time, was an "illiterate", Lorca nonetheless called him, "*the man with the greatest culture of blood I have ever known*" [I:1098]. Lorca related that the Andalusian ***Gitanos*** are the quintessential Andalusians. About his ***Gitano Romances*** he once commented that the book was ***Gitano*** because it was Andalusian: "***The gitano is the purest and most authentic thing in Andalusia***." Then he made an extremely important qualification, *"not the filthy beggars in rags **who wandered from town to town—they were Húngaros, that is, they were not Andalusian gitanos**. The true gitano were people who had never stolen and who never wore rags"* [I:1121-22].

In a 1933 interview, Lorca referred to some facts: "*From Jerez to Cádiz, ten family clans (extended families) of absolutely pure blood are guarding the glorious tradition of flamenco.*" Jerez is an Egyptian name meaning *guard*. It is a short distance from Jerez to Cádiz. The (Egyptian) Romany/***Gitanos*** are also found in the mountain towns above Jerez as far as Ronda, and in Triana, and many other places throughout the Iberian Peninsula. These ten extended families of ***Gitanos*** represent the tip of the iceberg of Andalusian art, and they were the source and substance of much of Lorca's poetry.

The Most Religious

Herodotus, the father of history, described the Ancient Egyptians as the "*most religious of all the nations of the world*". Likewise, it is well known that the (Egyptian) Romany of Hispania are intensely religious—as Animists and not by attending church services. Their Ancient Egyptian beliefs agree with the spiritual message of the Gospels, but not with its "historicity". The British Egyptologist Sir E. A. Wallis Budge wrote in his book, *The Gods of the Egyptians* [1969],

> *The new religion (Christianity) which was preached by St. Mark and his immediate followers, in all essentials so closely resembled that which was the outcome of the worship of Osiris, Isis, and Horus.*

The similarities, noted by Budge and everyone who has compared the Egyptian **Auset/Ausar/Heru** (Isis/Osiris/Horus) allegory to the Gospel story, are powerful. Both accounts are practically the same, e.g. the supernatural conception, the divine birth, the struggles against the enemy in the wilderness, and the resurrection from the dead to eternal life. The main difference between the two accounts is that the Gospel tale must be accepted by the Christian faithful as historical "truth" and the **Auset/Ausar/Heru** story is considered by the Egyptians to be an allegory. The spiritual message of the **Auset/Ausar/Heru** allegory and the Christian revelation are exactly the same. [An abbreviated version of the Ancient Egyptian allegory is found in chapter 2 of this book.]

As stated earlier, the Animistic people of Iberia (Romany, ***Gitanos, Moriscos, Mudejars, Mozarabs***, etc) never converted to Islam (or Christianity). Their (apparent) Christian beliefs, together with their Animistic practices, appear as "Paganistic-Christian" practices and traditions. Their religious traditions and practices match exactly the cosmological and Animistic concepts found in Ancient (and present-day Baladi) Egypt [detailed in chapter 13].

The Romany people of Hispania, like their fellow Egyptians (Ancient and Baladi), believe in the powers of the folk saints. This special relationship is manifested in the ***romería*** (derived from the Ancient Egyptian term, **Rom**, meaning *Egyptian man/person*), which can be defined as a small-scale pilgrimage in which the inhabitants of a given locality journey in a body to a sanctuary to celebrate the festivity of the supernatural protector housed therein. The same practice is found in both Ancient and present-day Baladi Egypt.

Like Ancient and present-day Egypt, ***romertias*** (or pilgrimages) take place all over Hispania. Countless pilgrims still wind their way through the northern passes to Santiago de Compostela, or to the shrine of the little **black Virgin** (***La Moreneta***) of Montserrat in the rough terrain of the mountains above Barcelona. But the most extraordinary ***romertia***, which is practically a duplicate of an Ancient Egyptian festival and described by some as "the most pagan", is without doubt the pilgrimage to the edge of the great marsh of the Guadalquivir Delta for the Pentecost festival celebrating ***La Blanca Paloma*** (*the White Dove*), ***La Reina de las Marismas*** (*Queen of the Marshes*), ***La Virgen del Rocio***, (*the Virgin of the Dew*).

Over half a million (Egyptian) Romany of Hispania celebrate this festival of ***la Reina y Madre de Andalucia*** (*the Queen and Mother of Andalucia*), 50 days after Easter Saturday.

This beautiful Romany/***Gitano*** festival at the Guadalquiver Delta has its ancient counterpart in the Nile Delta. Ancient texts from various sources described the Egyptian ***Romerias*** to **Auset** (Isis) in the delta of the Nile, when more wine was drunk than at any other time, with a great number of people traveling in each boat, some of the women playing flutes and rattles, others dancing, and the men keeping time by clapping [Herodotus 2.59-60]. We cannot help being reminded of the ***Romeria del Rocio***, when we read about this Ancient Egyptian festival describing the meticulous dressing of **Auset** and of her procession with crowds of men, women, and children marching at night with candles and torches to the accompaniment of flutes and drums and timbrels [Apuleius *The Golden Ass* 11.8-10]; to celebrate by dancing, by singing their songs and beating out the rhythm with handclaps, by drinking vast quantities of wine and camping out under the open sky [Ovid Fasti 3.523-42].

Likewise in present-day Egypt, the *Apostles (Prophets) Festival* in Egypt is held 50 days after Easter Saturday. This festival is of Ancient Egyptian origin. Pentecost signifies the period of the **Khamaseen** (meaning *the Fifty*), when the southerly hot and reddish sandstorms and winds are of frequent occurrence. This annual event commences on the day immediately following Good Friday, i.e. Easter (Light) Saturday, and ceases on the Day of Pentecost (or Whitesunday)—an interval of 50 days.

This Pentecostal event is related to the Ancient Egyptian allegory about **Auset** (Isis) and **Ausar** (Osiris), that after **Ausar** (Osiris) was killed, **Set** (Seth) became the king of Egypt and he ruled oppressively until he was dethroned 50 "days" later. **Set** represents the color red and the oppressive weather that is dry, fiery, and arid. In other words, **Set** represents the red, hot cloud of dust—**Khamaseen**. The festival commemorates the end of the oppressive weather. The skies are no longer dusty and red. The skies are clear—white, thus ***La Blanca Paloma***. During the oppressive 50 days, **Auset** (Isis) hid with her baby son in the marshes. As such, she is the *Queen of the Marshes*.

The birth of **Heru** (Horus) in the papyrus swamps.

The Timeless Egyptian-Hispanic Culture

As noted by Lorca, the (Egyptian) Romany are the essence of Hispania. The cultural characteristics of the natives of Hispania and Egypt are one and the same—intensely religious, un-warlike, and traditionalist to a fault.

Richard Ford, in his *Hand-book for Travellers in Spain* (which brilliantly described the Spain of the 1830s), frequently highlighted and emphasized the Oriental, "pagan", and ancient nature of its culture. He described Spain as *"a land bottled for antiquarians"*. On several occasions he quoted Livy, who described the people of southern Iberia about 2000 years ago as *"Of all the Spaniards the most unwarlike,"* to which Ford added: *"nor are they at all changed"*.

In the Mediterranean Basin, Egypt is the only other country that is un-warlike. As a result of their peaceful nature, both Egypt and Iberia were invaded many times by other people. Only Egyptians and Iberians hold to their old traditions, no matter what.

Throughout the history of Egypt, the emphasis was the adherence to traditions and they were NEVER to deviate from such a principle. In the oldest text of the world (5000 years ago), the Egyptian scribe, **Ptah Hotep**, states:

> **Don't modify/change anything from your father's (ancestor's) teachings/instructions—not even a single word. And let this principle be the cornerstone for teachings to future generations.**

The Ancient (and present-day Baladi) Egyptians never deviated from this principle. The Egyptians are remarkably traditionalists to a fault. Early historians have attested to this fact, such as Herodotus, in *The Histories, Book Two, [79]*:

The Egyptians keep to their native customs and never adopt any from abroad.

Herodotus, in *The Histories, Book Two, [91]*:

The Egyptians are unwilling to adopt Greek customs, or, to speak generally, those of any other country.

Plato and other writers affirmed the complete adherence of the Egyptians to their own traditions. Nothing has changed with this attitude since then, for each traveler to Egypt, since that time, has confirmed the allegiance to such conservatism.

Because the Romany of Hispania are of Ancient Egyptian descent, the cultures of both Egypt and Hispania are deeply rooted in the land/soil [see earlier in this chapter for several examples—***Gitano***, ***Latina***, **Kemet**, and ***Mudejar***]. This earthy (of the earth) quality is of the utmost importance, since it is the basis for their radical conservatism. The Iberian history is comparable to Egyptian history, for both were invaded over and again by practically all other Mediterranean countries, without ever putting up any real resistance. Yet both the Egyptians and the people of southern Iberia, by their superior, more refined culture, successfully "conquered" their invaders by receiving them passively. Both peoples learned to maintain their ancient traditions under a thin layer of Islam/Christianity.

This ancient culture is/was passive, absorptive, and conservative, and as such is a timeless culture, so much of which has come down virtually unscathed from antiquity. With all the false claims of how the Ancient Egyptians/Iberians changed their ways, languages, religions, traditions, etc, careful study will show that such claims are mere mirages.

2

Our Heavenly Mother

The Ascension of the Queen

Across the Mediterranean Sea from Egypt, every year on the eve of the 15th of August, a sacred musical drama is sung in the cathedral of Elche—a "mystery" on the death and Assumption of the Virgin Mary, with the same words and music and the same stage properties that have been used since at least the 15th century. The very ancient town of Elche is located in the heartland of the people known as ***Moriscos***—another name for the (Egyptian) Romany.

The solemn procession is held on 15 August. It has been acknowledged by all that neither the procession nor the Mystery Play are purely church festivals, and that they pre-date Christianity.

The 15th day of August is a national holiday in the Iberian Peninsula and many other countries, commemorating the Ascension of the Virgin Mary to the heavens, after her death. On the very same day—15 August, across the Mediterranean Sea, in Egypt, the Egyptians have been commemorating a festival called *Bride of the Nile*, since ancient times.

In the Ancient Egyptian context, the *Bride of the Nile* is **Auset** (Isis)—the Virgin Mother—and the River Nile is her soul mate—**Ausar** (Osiris). On 15 August, the Ancient Egyptian festival commemorates the end of the 50-day rainy period in Ethiopia, which causes the annual flooding of the Nile.

The Egyptians have been associating the beginning of the annual flood season with **Auset** (Isis), who began to weep after her soul mate, namely **Ausar** (Osiris), ascended to heaven 40 days after his death. Egyptians associated **Auset's** first teardrop with the beginning of the rise of the Nile. **Auset** continued to weep, wishing for the dead **Ausar** to rise again. The *Weeping Widow* became for the Egyptians the *Lady of Sorrow*.

Auset (Isis) **Ausar** (Osiris)

One of the most compelling parts of this Egyptian popular folktale is how these two symbols relate to the flood season in Egypt. The beauty here is that **Auset** (Isis) is wishing for **Ausar** (symbolizing the water) to rise from the dead, and the water of the Nile is consequently rising as a result of her weeping.

Auset (Isis) therefore recreates/regenerates **Ausar** from her tears every year. Her tears are blood-red in color, which is the same color of the floodwaters, since this water comes as a result of the rainy season in Ethiopia, which erodes the silt of the Ethiopian highlands, and carries it towards Egypt along the Blue Nile and other tributaries. So, **Auset's** tears represent this reddish color of the water during the flood season. In essence, **Auset** (Isis) is crying a river—so to speak. The Iberians follow the same Ancient Egyptian traditions in their presentations of the statues of Mary with bloody teardrops coming out of her eyes.

In this popular Egyptian folktale, **Auset** (Isis) finished her crying over her soul mate, **Ausar** (Osiris), in about the middle of August, which means that **Auset** has cried all the tears she had. It is at this point in time that the Egyptians (both ancient and modern) hold a festival, signifying the last teardrop from **Auset** (Isis), which will cause the peak of the flood level. It is during this celebration that the Egyptians throw an effigy of **Auset** into the waters, to symbolize that **Auset** (Isis) drowned in her own tears—the River Nile itself.

The "historical" tradition associated with the Elche festival is very interesting. They say that in May 1266, or (as others say) in December 1370, an "ark" drifted to the coast of Spain. It was labeled "for Elche", and was found to contain an image of the Virgin Mary as well as the words, music and ceremonial of a liturgical drama.

The Mystery of Elche begins with the entry of the Blessed Virgin, accompanied, prominently and throughout the Mystery and Procession, by the "Two Maries/Marias" dressed like herself, in white lace. The Two Beloved (Marys) are the Ancient Egyptian twin sisters—**Auset** and **Nebt-Het** (Nephthys). In Ancient Egyptian traditions, the two sisters—**Auset** and **Nebt-Het**—represent each individual's accompanying guiding angels.

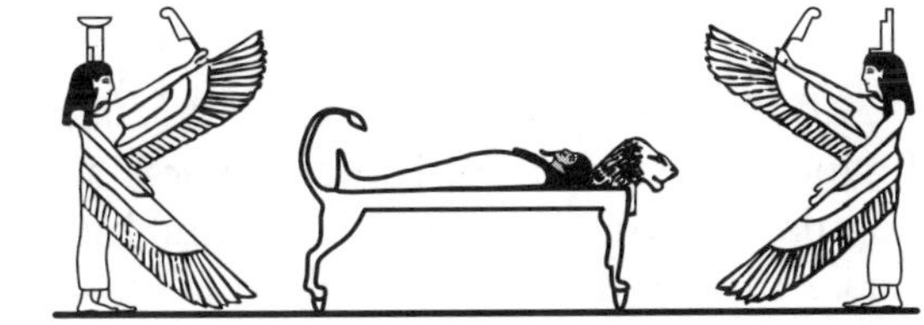

Nebt-Het (Nephthys) The deceased **Auset** (Isis)

The Elche Mystery play has three "Marias". The origin of the name ***Mary/Maria*** lies in Ancient Egypt, where the root of the word, as represented in its consonants, means *the beloved*. The term **Ma**ry/**Me**ry/**Ma**ria is one of the most repeated words in Ancient Egyptian texts.

The Virgin Mother, who wept in sorrow, is more intensely revered in Egypt and the Iberian Peninsula than any other place on earth.

Lady of Sorrow

The most common story to all Egyptians was that of **Auset** (Isis) and her family. A shortened version of this story goes as follows:

The union of **Nut** (the sky/spirit) and ***Geb*** (the earth/ matter) produced four children: **Auset** (Isis), **Ausar** (Osiris), **Nebt-Het** (Nephthys), and **Set** (Seth).

The story goes that **Ausar** (Osiris) married **Auset**, and **Set** married **Nebt-Het** (Nephthys). **Ausar** became King of the land (Egypt) after marrying **Auset**.

- The story sets the basis for the matrilineal/matriarchal society. **Auset** is the legal heiress—whoever marries her, becomes the legitimate ruler.

Both **Ausar** (Osiris) and **Auset** (Isis) were adored by the Egyptians. But **Set** (Seth) hated **Ausar** and was jealous of his popularity. One day, the evil **Set** and his accomplices tricked **Ausar** into lying down inside a makeshift coffin. The evil group quickly closed and sealed the chest, and threw it into the Nile. **Ausar** died and his coffin flowed into the Mediterranean Sea, to the shoreline of a foreign land (Byblos). Meanwhile, **Auset**, upon receiving the news of **Ausar's** death and disappearance, was in grief and searched everywhere. After searching near and far, and after traveling to a foreign land (Byblos), she finally found and returned back to Egypt with the chest containing **Ausar's** dead body. She hid the body in the marshes of the Nile Delta. **Auset** used her magical powers to transform herself into a bird. Drawing **Ausar's** essence from him, she conceived a child—**Heru** (Horus). In other words, **Auset** was impregnated by the holy ghost of **Ausar**.

- **Auset's** conception of **Heru** (Horus) by no living man is the oldest version of immaculate conception. The *supernatural conception* and the *virgin birth* of **Heru** (Horus) found their way into Christianity.

Auset (Isis) later gave birth in secret to **Heru** (Horus), in the swamps of the Nile Delta. When **Set** (Seth) heard about the newly born child, he set out to kill him. Hearing that the evil **Set** (Seth) was coming after her baby, **Auset** (Isis) hid him in the marshes of the Nile Delta and raised him secretly there.

- This is the source of the biblical story in which Herod, on hearing about the birth of Jesus, sets out to destroy all the newborn males, and how as a result, Mary and her baby boy went into hiding in Egypt.

The story continues that one night when the moon was full, the evil **Set** (Seth) and his accomplices found the chest containing the dead body of **Ausar** (Osiris) and cut him into 14 pieces, and scattered them all over Egypt. **Auset** (Isis), with the help of others, such as **Anbu** (Anubis) and **Tehuti** (Thoth), collected all the pieces... all except the phallus, which had been swallowed by a fish in the Nile. She then reunited the dismembered body of **Ausar** and, with the help of others, wrapped it in linen bandages and mummified it.

Egyptians of all periods regard **Auset** (Isis) as the role model of the faithful wife and loving mother, who bore pain and suffering, sorrow and solitude, and endured untold persecutions. The sorrows of **Auset** (Isis), the search for her husband's body, her weary wanderings, her loneliness when she brought forth **Heru** (Horus), the death of the child, etc., formed the subjects of scenes that were re-enacted in the **Ausar** (Osiris) play, which was performed annually at the Ancient Egyptian temples at Mendes (in the Nile Delta), **Abtu** (Abydos), and throughout the country.

The Virgin Mother With the 10,000 Names

Auset's (Isis') role in the Egyptian Model Story and the story of the Virgin Mary are strikingly similar, for both were able to conceive without male impregnation. **Heru** (Horus) was conceived and born after the death of **Auset's** husband, and, as such, **Auset** (Isis) was revered as the *Virgin Mother*. The ideal of virginity was a cornerstone of the Ancient Egyptian traditions.

The 6th century BCE statue of **Auset** and her son, now in the Turin Museum, inspired the 15th century painter Masaccio, in his presentation of The Virgin and Child.

This image was plentiful in the Ancient Egyptian artifacts. We can easily find one or several such Egyptian statues in museums throughout the world.

Auset (Isis) as the *Queen of **Ausar** (Osiris)*, and *Mother of the God* (i.e., **Heru**), and her loving care made her *Queen of Heaven*. Her protection was eagerly sought throughout Egypt. She became the great and beneficent **netert** (goddess) and mother, whose influence and love pervaded all heaven and earth and the Other World, and she became the personification of the great feminine, creative power that conceived and brought forth every living creature and thing—from the deities in heaven to man on the earth and insects on the ground. She was the personification of all tilled lands, the benevolent spirit of the fields, and the **netert** of the harvest. What she brought forth she protected and cared for, fed and nourished, and she employed her life in using her power graciously and successfully—not only in creating new beings, but in restoring to life those who were dead. Throughout the *Book of the Coming Forth by Day/Light* [known mistakenly as the *Book of* *the Dead*], **Auset** is spoken of as a giver of life and food for the dead. Her countless attributes inspired the Ancient Egyptians to call her ***Auset*** *With the 10,000 Names/Attributes.*

Likewise, the many aspects of Mary in the Iberian Peninsula are found in her various titles, among them: ***Santa Maria de la Vega, Santa Maria del Val de Mora, Santa Maria del Caño, and Santa Maria de la Cabaña.*** Other epithets attached to her name singled out special events in her life (such as the Annunciation, the Purification, and the Visitation), or identified prized attributes (***la Santa Caridad, la Misericordia, la Piedad***). Across the Iberian Peninsula, hundreds of confraternities became Mary's children by adopting her various matronymics into their titles. Through language, they fulfilled their wishes to develop intimate relationships with the *Mother of God.*

Matrilineal/Matriarchal Society

The (Egyptian) Romany of Hispania love the Virgin very intensely. They, like the Ancient Egyptians of Hispania, strictly follow the matrilineal practices in their society.

Auset, in Egyptian, means *seat/ throne*. It is therefore that **Auset** (Isis) is always shown wearing a throne upon her head. The throne of **Auset** represents the principle of legitimacy, as a female-based (feminine) principle. Such a principle is the basis for the matrilineal/matriarchal societies of both Ancient Egypt and the Iberian Peninsula.

Throughout Egyptian history, it was the queen who transmitted the solar blood. The queen was the true sovereign, landowner, keeper of the royalty, and guardian of the purity of the lineage. The man who married the eldest Egyptian princess claimed a right to the throne. Through marriage, she transmitted the legitimacy to her husband to become the next Pharaoh—he only acted as her executive agent. This social/political law was incorporated into the Egyptian Model Story, whereby **Ausar** became the first Pharaoh of Egypt, as a result of his marrying **Auset**. She (**Auset**) is the sun—source of energy/light/power, and he (**Ausar**) is the moon—the reflection of the sun (**Auset**)/light/authority.

Ancient Egyptian texts attest to the fact that the queen mother was practically the most powerful person in Egypt. It was not mere influence that the eldest daughter possessed, it was a right acknowledged by law, both in private and public life. Since women were the legal heirs to the throne, they played an important part in the affairs of state, performing as a kind of power broker. The Queens of Egypt wielded exceptional influence, as advisors to the Pharaohs.

The Pharaohs, as well as the leaders of smaller localities, adhered to this matriarchal system. If the Pharaoh/leader had no daughters, a dynasty ended and a new dynasty began, with a new revered woman as a new seed for a new dynasty.

It should be noted that a careful observation of historical events in the Iberian Peninsula shows how Visigoth, Moor, and Catholic rulers gained the legitimate right to rule, throughout different eras, after marrying the daughter of the sitting king.

The matrilineal practices in Egypt also applied to the whole society, as evident from the funerary stelae of all kinds of people throughout the known recorded history of Egypt, where it is the usual custom to trace the descent of the deceased on the mother's side, and not on that of the father. The person's mother is specified, but not the father, or he is only mentioned incidentally. This tradition is still enduring secretly (because it is contrary to Islam) among the Baladi Egyptians.

The system of naming in the Iberian Peninsula (like Ancient and Baladi Egypt) follows the same principle. Each person is identified by his given name and dual surnames of the father and the mother, such as the famous author, Federico Garcia Lorca. When he is referred to by one name, it is Lorca—the surname of his mother.

The Ama Rules

The matriarchal system was the basis of the social organization in Ancient Egypt, where the queen (wife) and queen mother had positions of great respect and potentially much authority. Likewise, the famed alliance/bond in Baladi Egyptian and the Iberian societies is between the wife and her mother. As a result, Baladi Egyptians, Spanish and Portuguese married couples live with the wife's family, so mother and daughter are not separated. Consequently, there is a distinct tendency toward matrilocal residence among extended families. Because of these community-wide preferences, the ***pueblo's*** extended families show a strong matrilateral tendency.

Living with the bride's parents is the preferred rule. Even when the young woman leaves the maternal hearth, she settles nearby in a pattern that might be called matrivicinal. That is, the newlyweds try to move into a house next to or nearby the mother of the bride, so the women are rarely separated. This arrangement magnifies the social influence of women since it brings wife and mother into close contact.

The men in Spain refer to their wives as the *masters* of

their homes. The woman rules the house, and within it she rules the man as she rules her children. The woman is the *ama* (the master).

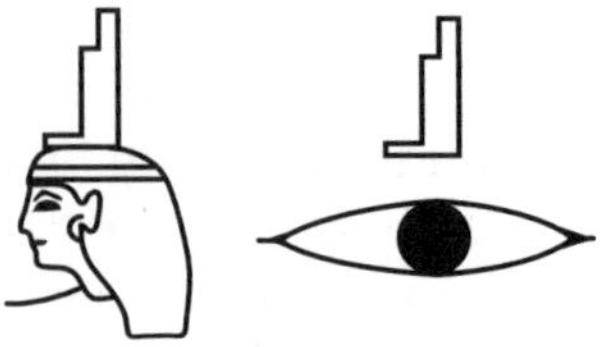

Auset (Isis) (Seat on top) **Ausar** (Osiris) (Seat & Eye)

The relationship between the husband and wife is shown symbolically in the Ancient Egyptian symbol for the wife (**Auset**) being the throne—the source of legitimacy. The husband (**Ausar**) is the overseer (the eye) that sits below the throne. It never escaped the Egyptians to notice that on the human face, the eye is located below the eyebrow. An Egyptian proverb states, *"The eye never overtops the eyebrow"*, signifying the hierarchical order in the family and the society as a whole.

The historian, Diodorus of Sicily, reported that part of the agreement entered into at the time of marriage in Egypt was that the wife should have control over her husband, and that no objection should be made to her commands.

An instruction from the New Kingdom (c. 1500 BCE) affirms Diodorus' account:

Do not control your wife in her house,
When you know she is efficient;
Don't say to her: "Where is it? Get it!"
When she has put it in the right place.
Let your eye observe in silence,
Then you recognize her skill:
It is joy when your hand is with her,
There are many who don't know this.

The above-mentioned matrilineal/matriarchal traditions are contrary to the doctrines of Islam and Christianity, as well as to the traditions of the foreign invaders of the Iberian Peninsula—Romans and Moors.

The Revered Ama

The Iberians, and most noticeably the (Egyptian) Romany, have brought the Mother Goddess into prominence in Christiandom. It was in the Iberian Peninsula that the concept of the Virgin Mother was initiated in a movement of popular support for her cause, which finally forced the papacy to admit the Immaculate Conception into dogma in 1854. There is no other place with such fierce devotion to the virgin principle except in Ancient Egypt.

The populace of Egypt and the Iberian Peninsula looked upon the Virgin as a patroness whose solicitude extended over the entire range of human needs. She bestowed her own divine favors, and was indiscriminate in the way that she gave to all who asked. To those in need, no other divine figure equaled the status of the Virgin Mother and no other sacred symbol so calmed their anxieties and indulged their fantasies. She was the guarantee of man's soul, for having refused to admit his body.

Diodorus of Sicily, in *Book I,* [25. 2-6], describes the same qualities of the (Egyptian) Virgin—**Auset**/Maria:

> *As for Isis, the Egyptians say that she was the discoverer of many health-giving drugs and was* ***greatly versed in the science of healing****; consequently, now that she has attained immortality,* ***she finds her greatest delight in the healing of mankind and gives aid in their sleep to those who call upon her****, plainly manifesting both her very presence and her beneficence towards men who ask for her help. In proof of this, as they say, they advance not legends, as the Greeks do, but manifest facts; for practically the entire inhabited world is their witness, in that it eagerly contributes to the honours of Isis because she manifests herself in healings. For* ***standing above the sick in their sleep she gives them aid*** *for their diseases and works remarkable cures upon such as submit themselves to her; and many who have been despaired of by their physicians because of the difficult nature of their malady*

> *are restored to health by her, while numbers who have altogether lost the use of their eyes or of some other part of their body, whenever they turn for help to this goddess, are restored to their previous condition. Furthermore, she discovered also the drug which gives immortality, by means of which she not only* ***raised from the dead her son Horus****, . . .*

In the Iberian Peninsula, Mary was considered to be a more dependable ally to salvation than Christ, for her mercy softened the justice of her son. Despite attempts beginning in the 12th century to render the figure of Christ in a more human and compassionate form, he frequently displayed the traditional appearance of a stern judge almost as unapproachable as God the Father. Mary stood closer to human frailty and weakness and received the first requests for assistance among the mediators with God.

The intense and sole veneration of Mary/Maria in the Iberian Peninsula was (and continues to be) resisted by the Church. To attempt to change the "Marian beliefs" among the laity, the Catholic hierarchy sought to place the Virgin's status beneath Christ. As a result, during the Counter Reformation, the iconography of the radiant young mother holding a baby and breast-feeding him in her arms [such as **Auset** breast-feeding her baby depicted here from Ancient Egypt] was changed to the ***Pietá*** image of a sorrowful mother bracing the somewhat unwieldy figure of the mature, martyred redeemer across her lap. The Tridentine "reformers" sought to re-direct attention towards the redemption of Christ by emphasizing her emotional submission to the ordeals of Christ and, like the rosary devotions, made her part of the crucifixion. They intentionally presented the Virgin Mother in a lower status than her son. This attempt never worked, for in the people's hearts, she continued to be the essence of all, and the populace continues to give lip service to the authorities when they must.

The Bull of His Mother

In Ancient Egypt, the Mother-Goddess, **Auset** (Isis), had a son who, in the form of a bull, was sacrificed annually in order to assure the cycle of the seasons and the continuity of Nature. Similarly in the Iberian Peninsula, the bull appears to have been venerated from pre-Roman times, and the ritual killing of the bull was common practice. Here, clearly, was the source of modern bullfighting in which the matador assumes the role of a priest as the bull is ritualistically slaughtered.

The Ancient Egyptian **Apis**—the Bull (**neter**) god

As per present practices, ancient writers asserted that it was the mother who was chosen to produce a calf with particular qualities—he was *The Bull of His Mother*—so to speak. Herodotus, in describing him, says,

> *Apis, also called Epaphus, is a young bull, whose mother can have no other offspring, and who is reported by the Egyptians to conceive from lightning sent from heaven, and thus to produce the bull-god Apis.*

The religious connotations of this sacrifice, as well as its dramatic and even theatrical character, is an echo of a sacrifice in the sacrament, where we are reminded of Christ's death so that mankind might be saved. In essence, the bullfight is a genuine religious drama in which, as in the Catholic Mass, a god is worshipped and sacrificed.

This practice is reminiscent of the Ancient Egyptian annual **Heb-Sed** festival (which was regularly held towards the end of December), where the Pharaoh's power was renewed in a series of rituals including ritual sacrifice. The renewal rituals aimed at bringing a new life force to the King—a (figurative) death and a (figurative) rebirth of the reigning King. This gives more meaning to the phrase: *The*

King is dead—Long live the King.

All Egyptian Pharaohs identified themselves with **Heru** (Horus)—as a living King, and with the soul of **Ausar** (Osiris)—as a dead King. Since the bull represents the bodily image of the soul of **Ausar**, the Kings of Egypt were frequently called *bulls*, such as the *young bull*, or the *mighty bull.*

Diodorus, in *Book I,* [85, 3-5], explains the rejuvenation powers of the King at the **Heb-Sed** festival,

> *Some explain the origin of the honour accorded this bull in this way, saying that at the death of Osiris his soul passed into this animal, and therefore up to this day **he always passed into its successors at the times of the manifestation of Osiris**.*

The bulls were/are also associated with fertility rites, as explained by Diodorus, *Book I,* [21, 8-22],

> *The consecration to Osiris, however, of the sacred bulls, which are given the name of Apis and Mnevis, and the worship of them as gods were observed generally among all the Egyptians, since these animals had, more than any others, rendered aid to those who discovered the fruit of the grain, in connection with both the sowing of the seed and with every agricultural labour from which mankind profits.*

Fertility was/is represented by **Auset** (Isis)—who represents Mother Earth. Planting is the burying of seed into earth. As such, planting is associated with burial—death that leads to a resurrection, i.e. sprouting. This beautiful analogy was described by Plutarch, in his *Moralia* Vol V, [377, 65], where we read:

> *. . . the Egyptians say that Osiris is being buried at the time when the grain is sown and covered in the earth and that he comes to life and reappears when plants begin to sprout. For this reason also it is said that Isis, when she perceived that she was pregnant, put upon herself an amulet on the sixth day of the month Phaophi* [equivalent to 17 October in the Latin calendar]. . . .

Ausar (Osiris) represents the process, growth, and the underlying cyclical aspects of the universe—the principle that makes life come from apparent death.

Ausar represents the rejuvenation/renewal principle in the universe. Therefore, in the Ancient Egypt context, the bull had to suffer a sacrificial death to ensure the life of the community. The sacrifice of the holy animal, and the eating of his flesh, brought about a state of grace.

Small tablets in Ancient Egyptian tombs sometimes represent a black bull, bearing the corpse of a man to its final abode in the regions of the dead. The name of this bull is shown to be **Apis**, because **Ausar** (Osiris) represents the state of death in everyone/thing—the divine in mortal form.

Ausar (Osiris) in the form of a bull, bearing a mummy of the deceased on his back. [From an Egyptian coffin in the British Museum (No. 29,888).]

It continues to be a common practice in present-day Egypt—that young bulls are sacrificed upon the death of a person. The same practice continues in the thousands of annual folk saints' festivals in Egypt.

The traditions of bull rituals and sacrifices were observed in Egypt, prior to any other country, as testified by classical Greek and Roman writers. Greek tradition asserts that the Bull-god **Apis** was held in the greatest honor in Egypt, in the time of King Menes (5,000 years ago) [as reported by Aelian, in *De Natura Animalium, XI, 10*].

The Ancient Egyptians practiced bullfights. They were sometimes exhibited in the dromos (or avenues), leading to the temples, as at **Men-Nefer** *(Memphis) before the temple of* **Ptah** *(Vulcan). This was a serious and solemn ritual.*

The first professional bullfighters in Ancient Egypt were the smiths (butchers) who specialized in such rituals and who already knew a lot about bull behavior and the release of energies associated with the sacrificial process. Likewise in the Iberian Peninsula, specialized guild(s) are assigned to this solemn task. They continue to follow the original profession's training, practices, and traditions.

In the Iberian Peninsula, on the day before the sacrifice (fight), the bulls destined for their fate are brought to a site outside the town. The bulls are enticed by tame oxen, ***cabestros***, onto a road that is barricaded on each side, and then they are driven full speed by the mounted ***conocedores*** into the ***Plaza***. This is reminiscent of the Ancient Egyptian ritual of the *Running of the Bulls*, as referred to in the Palermo Stele, about 4500 years ago.

Toreo is an unmistakably "religious" experience, in which, just as in the Mass, there is adoration and sacrifice of a God. The "god" sacrificed in ***toreo*** is clearly an allusion to the Ancient Egyptian pre-Christian rituals that in so many ways prefigured or foreshadowed the rituals that the Church would later employ. The bullfight is a true ritual, like the Catholic Mass, where the officiant and the communicants are engaged in deliberately symbolic activity; their every word and action have an agreed upon spiritual referent; moreover, everything is rigidly predetermined—nothing is left to chance. Drinking wine in Mass is like drinking the blood of the ***toro***.

The ritual sacrifice consists of three acts, and they are called in Spanish ***los tres tercios de la lidia***, or the three thirds of the combat. This scheme is consistent with Ancient Egyptian traditions. The bull represents the soul of **Ausar** (Osiris). **Ausar's** number is/was three. The bullfights last three rounds to match **Ausar's** number. In mystical Egypt, three signifies the cyclical number of death/rebirth. The last (third) death is when one achieves immortality like **Ausar** did/represented. [Read more details in *Egyptian Mystics: Seekers of the Way*, by same author.]

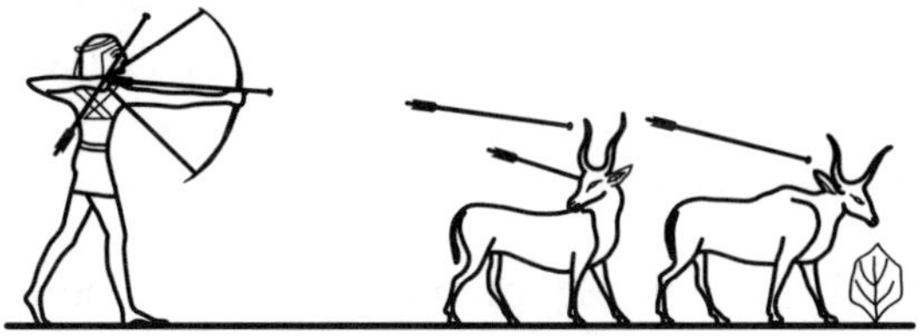

A chasseur shooting at the wild oxen. Beni Hassan.

The second act of the ***toreo***—the ***banderillas***—is reminiscent of a scene in a tomb in Beni Hassan (in Middle Egypt), where a man uses archery to shoot several arrows at the neck of the bull, to slow up the bull and regulate the carriage of his head, in order to tire his neck muscles and carry his head lower before the final blow of the third act.

Great care was taken in training the fighting bulls for this purpose. Like Ancient Egypt, the Hispanic bulls learn to use their horns by fighting among themselves [shown below], and sometimes the ***ganadero***, the breeder, toughens them by making them walk miles every day for their feed.

A bullfight depicted in a Theban tomb.

As is the case in Iberia, the Ancient Egyptian breeder was rewarded, as per Aelian, who stated,

The man from whose herd the divine beast has sprung, is the happiest of mortals, and is looked upon with admiration by all people.

This is consistent with the respect paid to the possessor of the favored herd, in which the "sacred" bull had been discovered. Additionally, and as affirmed by Aelian,

Apis is an excellent interpretation of futurity.

Accordingly, the Egyptians also drew omens respecting the welfare of their country, at these breeding sites.

There were numerous sites for breeding wild (sacrificial) bulls in Ancient Egypt. The most prominent breeding sites were in the marshes of the Delta, as reported in *Strabo,* [XVII, I, 22].

The ***toros bravos*** of Andalusia, the descendants of the mythical herds of Geryon, have pastured in the rich delta of the Guadalquivir, much as the Egyptian bulls hunted by the Pharaohs in the delta of the Nile, from the remotest past. And, what is more important, only by way of Andalusia has the ***toro bravo*** survived up to our time. The delta of the Guadalquivir is the place of residence and center of the most colorful festivals in Iberia. The (Egyptian) Romany at the delta of Guadalquivir share the same exact traditions with their kin at the delta of the River Nile.

3

Out of Egypt

The Mirages of Iberia

The powerful similarities between the civilized people of Ancient Egypt and Hispania were (and continue to be) ignored by western academicians. Even the true identity (Egyptian) of the civilized people who settled in Hispania, throughout its history, is arbitrarily and capriciously denied. Instead, the countless books written about the history and culture of the Iberian Peninsula consist of nothing more than repeated deceptive assertions. Just like a mirage—the closer you approach/study the credibility of a statement, any possible factual basis disappears from sight. Here are a few and preliminary examples of the carelessness and biases in history writing about the Iberian Peninsula:

1. Certain "chosen" groups (Phoenicians, Romans, Arabs, etc) are credited with many things, such as introducing highly productive farming techniques, numerous settlements, crafts, organizational government, arts, etc. into the Iberian Peninsula. Yet none of these groups have a history of such "talents" in their home countries. In later chapters, we will show the background of each group (Phoenicians, Romans, Moors, etc), in each's home country, because one cannot teach/contribute what one has never known and practiced in their home country.

2. A certain artistic design/style of a temple, column, glassware, mosaic, ...etc., is given a Latin/Roman/Greek/Phoenician/Islamic name, even though that same design was used in Ancient Egypt thousands of years earlier. Any item that appears to resemble this particular design is then automatically credited to one of these "chosen" groups, and as a result we keep reading of "Phoenician" settlements, "Roman" temples, "Roman" mosaics, etc, with no supporting archeological/historical evidence whatsoever.
To compound the wrong assertion that something is "Phoenician"/ "Roman"/ "Moorish", based on a style, we find the authors have given arbitrary dates based on their arbitrary premise of the origin of such a finding.

3. Because there was no accurate calendar outside Egypt in the ancient world, dating of most archeological findings in the Iberian Peninsula (and elsewhere) is based on the arbitrary status of metal "developments" (Copper, Bronze, Iron, etc. Ages). As such, if a bronze item is found in a tomb, then the tomb is arbitrarily assigned a date within the "Bronze Age".

This arbitrary and chaotic "metal development" dating has caused an error in judgment by 1,000 years in the history writing of the Iberian Peninsula. Castro, in *Iberia in Prehistory* [1995, on page 12], explains the radiocarbon dating method that has shattered the arbitrary accreditation to the Aegeans, in the ancient history of the Iberian Peninsula:

> *The concept of Aegean colonies in the western Mediterranean during the Copper Age began to lose ground with the impact of the radiocarbon dating 'revolution' in the Aegean. . . The so-called 'Millares culture' is considered to have lasted from 2600 BC to 1800 BC, peaking between 2400 BC and 2200 BC. Such data implies that* ***the modern chronology for the Copper Age in southeastern Spain has been pushed back by at least 1000 years*** *since the days in which 'colonists' were considered to have been in command of Los Millares.*

The old idea of an Aegean migration to the coast of Almeria in the third millennium BC was promptly discarded, and all possible affinities of Los Millares with Anatolian or Cycladic settlements then began to sound pointless.

Once the proper dating was accurately determined for the archeological findings in the Iberian Peninsula, the Aegean mirage completely disappeared, and the Ancient Egyptian reality in the Iberian Peninsula becomes ever clearer—as will unfold throughout the book.

The Egyptian Romany Colonies

Superficially, Ancient Egypt seems isolated and distinct from the rest of the world, isolated by the deserts that hem in the narrow valley of the Nile. Yet the Egyptians were in constant contact with other countries. Classical writers such as Plutarch, Herodotus, and Diodorus told how Ancient Egypt had colonies throughout the world. Diodorus of Sicily, *Book I,* [29, 5], states:

> *In general, the Egyptians say that their ancestors* ***sent forth numerous colonies to many parts of the inhabited world, by reason of the pre-eminence of their former kings and their excessive population****;*

Diodorus, *Book I,* [31, 6-9], affirms that Egypt was the most populous country in the ancient world:

> ***In density of population it (Egypt) far surpassed of old all known regions of the inhabited world, and even in our own day is thought to be second to none other****; . . .*
> *. . .The total population, they say, was of old about seven million and the number has remained no less down to our day.*

Diodorus, *Book I,* [28, 1-4], tells of some Egyptian colonies that were reported to him in Asia and Europe:

Now the Egyptians say that also after these events (Osiris' travel around the world) ***a great number of colonies were spread from Egypt over all the inhabited world****. To Babylon, for instance, colonists were led by Belus, who was held to be the son of Poseidon and Libya; . . . . .*

. . . . . They say also that those who set forth with Danaus, likewise ***from Egypt, settled what is practically the oldest city of Greece, Argos****, and that the nation of the Colchi in Pontus and that of the Jews, which lies between Arabia and Syria, were founded as colonies by certain emigrants from their country. . . . .*

By virtue of the eminence of the Egyptian colonists in Asia and Europe, they played a major role in their new settlements. Diodorus, *Book I,* [28,6-7], discusses the significant role of the Egyptian colonists as rulers of these new colonies:

Moreover, ***certain of the rulers of Athens were originally Egyptians****, they say. Petes,* [Called Peteus in Iliad 2. 552.] *for instance, the father of that Menestheus who took part in the expedition against Troy, having clearly been an Egyptian, later obtained citizenship at Athens and the kingship.*

Diodorus, *Book I,* [29, 1-5], also states:

In the same way, they continue, ***Erechtheus also, who was by birth an Egyptian, became king of Athens****. . . . . Erechtheus, through his racial connection with Egypt, brought from there to Athens a great supply of grain, and in return those who had enjoyed this aid made their benefactor king.* ***After he had secured the throne he instituted the initiatory rites of Demeter in Eleusis and established the mysteries, transferring their ritual from Egypt****. . . . .* ***And. their sacrifices as well as their ancient ceremonies are observed by the Athenians in the same way as by the Egyptians****. . . . .*

. . . . . in charge of the more important religious ceremonies of Attica; the pastophoroi were those Egyptian priests who carried in processions small shrines of the gods. They are also the only Greeks who swear by Isis, and they closely resemble the Egyptians in both their appearance and manners.

Herodotus (500 BCE) stated that he came from

Halicarnassus, a **Dorian** town. He clearly stated the connection between the **Dorians** and Egypt, in *The Histories, Book 6,* [Sections 53-55]:

> *[53] . . . if one were to trace back, generation by generation, the lineage of Danaë the daughter of Acrisius,* ***the chiefs of the Dorians would turn out to be true-born Egyptians****.*
>
> *[55] Enough has been said about all this. Others have explained how and through what achievements* ***they became kings over the Dorians, despite being Egyptians****, and so I will not go into that. I will record things that others have not picked up.*

Herodotus, in [55] above, stated that such a fact was common knowledge at his time (500 BCE) and needed no elaboration.

Other connections between the **Dorians** and Egyptians were made reference to several times by Herodotus, such as in *The Histories, Book 2,* [Section 91].

The Egyptian **Dorian** influence extended throughout the Mediterranean Basin. At Tarentum in southern Italy, the celebrated Pythagorean center was established by Pythagoras and his followers, after he spent 20 years studying in Egypt, in the 5th century BCE. The center became their great cultural and philosophical headquarters. The Doric language of the **Dorians** was spoken in the Peloponnese, various Greek islands, and in Magna Graecia, in southern Italy, where Tarentum was established. Magna Graecia was a haven for refugees from the Greek Isles and Egypt.

Magna Graecia has/had everlasting influences on the history and culture of Italy. Magna Graecia played a major role during the Punic wars and its inhabitants fled and resettled in the Iberian Levant.

Lastly, it should be noted that Ancient Egyptian records (as well as records in other areas) have countless names of places in the world that are not recognizable in our present time. Names of places, ethnic groups, and countries keep on changing. The country names of Europe just 100 years ago, for example, are unrecognizable to most present-day Europeans. When these records disappear, a few centuries from now, the names of such countries will be totally unrecognizable.

The Egyptian Influence in the Eastern Mediterranean

For the ancient world, Egypt was heaven on earth—the true center of the world. In the *Hermetic Texts* [25 BCE], Ascleptus III stated,

> *...in Egypt all the operations of the powers which rule and work in heaven have been transferred to earth below...it should rather be said that the whole cosmos dwells in [Egypt] as in its sanctuary...*

In addition to the influential Egyptian colonies throughout the world, Egypt itself was opened to foreign visitors for learning. Practically all notable Greeks went to Egypt for education, as noted by Diodorus of Sicily, *Book I,* [96, 1-2]:

> *But now that we have examined these matters, we must enumerate what Greeks, who have won fame for their wisdom and learning, visited Egypt in ancient times, in order to become acquainted with its customs and learning...*
> *. . .Homer and Lycurgus of Sparta, and Plato, and that there also came Pythagoras of Samos and the mathematician Eudoxus* [The famous astronomer, geographer, and mathematician of Cnidus, pupil of Plato.]... [For instance, according to Strabo (17. 1. 29), he was able to see the houses in Heliopolis where Plato and Eudoxus had stopped.].

Homer, more than 3,000 years ago, made references to Egypt that indicated his high esteem. In the *Odyssey*, for example, he refers to the good reputation Egypt enjoyed in the ancient world of Asia, Africa and Europe. In other passages, Homer relates the events of the Greek King Manelaus' journey to Egypt, his arrival at Pharos Island (present-day Alexandria), and his 20-day sojourn in Egypt.

Herodotus visited Egypt during the 5th century BCE. He devoted the second volume of his history to accounts about Egypt. Herodotus spoke highly of Egypt, and stressed Greece's indebtedness to it. Herodotus stated that the Egyptians culturally and scientifically surpassed all other societies of the world. Herodotus began his account of Egypt in his *Histories*, by stating,

> *Now, let me talk more of Egypt for it has a lot of admirable things and what one sees there is superior to any other country.*

Crete was also indebted to the Egyptian civilization. The name **Keftiu** (present-day Crete) is found in Egyptian texts at least since the 12th century BCE. A passage in the *Odyssey* tells of King Odysseus' journey to Egypt from Crete. He tells how the northerly wind helped his nine boats sail easily for five days until they reached the Nile. According to Homer, the Egyptians were extremely hospitable to the king and his entourage, and he greatly enjoyed **his seven-year sojourn** there.

Trade and other cultural developments linked the Cretans with Egypt, and they adopted many aspects of Egyptian civilization. Many Egyptian-made relics have been uncovered in Crete.

In time, the Greeks spread into the Balkan Peninsula and adopted many aspects of Cretan civilization that were influenced by Egypt.

The Egyptian influence on the Phoenicians will be detailed in chapter 7.

The Spread of the Egyptian Religion

The basis of the Egyptian religion is described in chapters 2, 13, and throughout this book. The most identifiable aspect of the Ancient Egyptian religion is the role of **Auset** (Isis) and **Ausar** (Osiris) in the cosmological order of the world. The most significant (but not all) aspects of **Auset** and **Ausar** are best described by Diodorus of Sicily, *Book I,* [11, 5-6],

> *These two gods, they hold, regulate the entire universe, giving both nourishment and increase to all things . . . .*

These two (and other) Egyptian deities were adopted throughout the Mediterranean Basin and beyond. For example, the bas-reliefs, coins, and other antiquities that have been found in Thessaly, Epirus, Megara, Corinth, Argos, and many other places prove that the worship of **Auset** was widespread, and that **Ausar**, **Anbu** (Anubis), **Heru-p-Khart** (Harpokrates), and **Nebt-Het** (Nephthys), were associated with her in votive inscriptions. The coins of Malta of the 2nd or 1st century BCE show that the concept of **Auset** (Isis) and **Ausar** (Osiris) was of importance in the island.

In Magna Graecia, the monuments found in Catania in Sicily show that this city was a center of the worship of Egyptian deities. Southern Italy contained many temples of **Auset** (Isis), and the remains of statues, etc., found in Reggio, Puteoli, Pompeii, and Herculaneum prove that the worship of Egyptian deities must have been common.

From Egypt, **Auset** (Isis) and the bull-god of **Sarapis** (**Sar-Apis**, meaning *Lord Apis*) passed to Asia Minor and to the Islands of the Mediterranean, (e.g., Cyprus, Rhodes, Samos, Chios, Lesbos, Delos, Crete, etc). To affirm Herodotus'

reports of the Greek adoption of Egyptian deities, archeological evidence in the 4th century BCE shows that Athens was basically a center of the Egyptian religion, and shrines to **Auset** (Isis), both public and private, were erected in many parts of Greece at this period.

On Greece, for example, Herodotus in the *Histories, Book 2,* [107], wrote:

> ***It was the Egyptians too who originated, and taught the Greeks to use ceremonial meetings, processions, and processional offerings****: a fact that can be inferred from the obvious antiquity of such ceremonies in Egypt, compared with Greece, where they have been only recently introduced. The Egyptians meet in solemn assembly not once a year only, but on a number of occasions.*

Affirming Herodotus' statement, Plutarch states in *Moralia, Isis and Osiris*, [378-9, 69],

> *Among the Greeks also many things are done which are similar to the Egyptian ceremonies in the shrines of Isis, and they do them at about the same time.*

In Rome, in the 1st century BCE, **Auset** (Isis)was regarded as the principal **netert** (goddess) of the city. Great buildings and temples were set up in her honor, filled with Egyptian objects, obelisks, altars, statues, lavers, etc., which were brought from Egypt in order to make the shrines of **Auset** (Isis) resemble those of her native country. Priestesses, who professed to be well acquainted with the "mysteries" of **Auset**, dwelt in or near these temples, and assisted in performing services and ceremonies in which large congregations participated. From Rome, the reverence for **Auset** (Isis) naturally spread to the provinces and beyond.

In the Ancient Egyptian cosmology, **Auset** represents the power responsible for the creation of all living creatures. Accordingly, Ancient Egyptians called her ***Auset** (Isis) with* *the 10,000 Names/Attributes*. Plutarch took note of that and wrote in his *Moralia Vol V*,

> *Isis is, in fact, the female principle of Nature, and is receptive of every form of generation, in accord with which she is called by Plato the gentle nurse and the all-receptive, and by most people **has been called by countless names**, since, because of the force of Reason. she turns herself to this thing or that and is receptive of all manner of shapes and forms.*

The "many names" of **Auset** (Isis) were adopted throughout Greece and in Italy, and beyond. Thus the Greeks and Romans identified her frequently as Selene, Demeter, Ceres, and with several goddesses of crops and of the harvest in general. She was also regarded as an Earth-goddess, and as such was the mother of all fertility and abundance. Some of her attributes caused her to be identified as Aphrodite, Juno, Nemesis, Fortuna, and Panthea.

The Ancient Egyptian religious practices associated with **Auset** (Isis) and **Ausar** (Osiris) had made major strides in Italy. In Campania, an inscription, dated at 105 BCE, was found in a temple of the Ancient Egyptian **Sarapis (Sar-Apis)**, at Puteoli, which is evidence that the temple existed prior to that date. About 80 BCE, a College of the Servants of **Auset**, or Pastophori, was founded in Rome in the time of Sulla, and a temple was built in the city. In 44 BCE, a temple was built in Rome to honor **Auset** (Isis) and **Ausar** (Osiris), and a few decades later, the festival of these Egyptian deities was recognized in the public calendar.

The main festival in Italy corresponded exactly to the Ancient Egyptian festival that commemorated the murder of **Ausar** (Osiris) and the finding of his body by **Auset** (Isis). As in Ancient Egypt, it opened in November with the singing of dirges and heartbreaking lamentations for the death of **Ausar** (Osiris), which were, no doubt, based upon the compositions that were sung in Egypt about the same time. Then, on the second day, scenes that represented the frantic grief and anxiety of those who went about searching for the body of **Ausar** were enacted. On the third day **Auset** found the body of her husband, and there was great rejoicing in the temple. Grief gave place to gladness and tears to laughter, musicians of all kinds assembled and played their instruments, and men and women danced, and everyone celebrated.

[For more information on the Ancient Egyptian festivals, dates, practices, etc, see *Egyptian Mystics: Seekers of the Way*, by Moustafa Gadalla.]

The Ancient Egyptian religious practices, as they relate to the model story of **Auset** (Isis) and **Ausar** (Osiris), spread all over southern Europe, and into many parts of North Africa, and it continued to be a religious power in these regions until the close of the 4th century CE. These Ancient Egyptian ideas and beliefs survived in Christianity, whereby Mary the Virgin assumed the attributes of **Auset** (Isis) the Everlasting Mother, and to the Babe Jesus those of **Heru** (Horus). [More about such comparison in chapters 1 and 2.]

The religious practices in present-day Iberia are described by most writers as more "pagan" than "Christian". Such beliefs and practices correspond almost exactly with the Ancient Egyptians' beliefs and practices, as will unfold throughout this book.

The Twin Sisters

Out of Egypt, many Egyptians departed to form numerous colonies—yet no place in the Mediterranean Basin was (and continues to be) of the highest kinship as Hispania. The relationship between Ancient Egypt and the Iberian Peninsula was much more than influence by a prominent Egypt. The relationship was a grass-root extension. As we study the many aspects of the Egyptian and Iberian cultures, we will find that Egypt and the Iberian Peninsula are basically twin sisters. If we look at the cultural characteristics in the Iberian Peninsula, all agree that the people who caused the enlightenment in the Iberian Peninsula:

1. had "oriental" characteristics.
2. were un-warlike and settled peacefully among the local population.
3. had advanced knowledge of metallurgy, and manufactured large quantities of metal products.
4. were highly organized and were very talented in management.
5. had knowledge of dry weather farming, irrigation, etc.
6. were experienced builders and artisans, and who built megalithic tombs, etc.
7. were very religious people who had Animistic beliefs.

The above descriptions can only apply to one country—Egypt. By combining oral traditions, ethno-history, and archeological evidence (dating of major settlements, tombs, mining activities, ...etc.) of all the people in the Mediterranean Basin, one can see that the civilized newcomers could come only from the Nile Valley.

The characteristics of the newcomers to the Iberian Peninsula match the Ancient Egyptians, in all aspects. The (Egyptian) Romany of Hispania represent the special Egyptian-Hispanic alloy.

4

The Egyptian-Hispanic Alloys

Who Needed Iberian Minerals?

It is no coincidence that the (Egyptian) Romany of Hispania are always found in (or in close proximity to) the ancient mining sites. Furthermore, the (Egyptian) Romany/ ***Gitanos*** are recognized throughout history for their excellence in metalworking. Ancient Egyptians sought the minerals of Hispania, a long time ago. The mineral wealth of Iberia was renowned worldwide, as reported by Strabo, in his *Geography*, [3.2.8],

> *. . .up to the present moment, in fact, neither gold nor silver, nor yet copper, nor iron, has been found anywhere in the world, in a natural state, either in such quantity or of such good quality.*

Such minerals were in short supply in the eastern Mediterranean. As a consequence, the early settlements of prehistoric Iberia were located in those regions in which copper and silver were either available or accessible: the provinces of Almeria, Granada and Murcia in the southeast, and the areas of Huelva, Algarve, Baixo Alentejo and Extremadura in the southwest. These are the very same regions where the (Egyptian) Romany have lived since time immemorial.

The question is, which country in the eastern Mediterranean Basin was using these large quantities of Iberia's mineral ores? The consuming country must meet the following necessary criteria:

1. has the wealth to pay the native Iberians for the ore metals, in valuable or consumable goods,

2. has a large demand for such ores, i.e. has a large rich population that consumes the manufactured goods made from such mineral ores,

3. has the technology in metallurgy and has the records and evidence to show such knowledge, and

4. has the means and knowledge to explore for the needed mineral ores, establish mining processes, and transport heavy loads for long distances.

Logic and evidence show that:

1. Ancient Egypt was the most populous and wealthiest country in the ancient world.

2. Ancient Egypt was the only country in ancient history that had knowledge of metallurgy, and was able to produce numerous metallic alloys in large quantities, such as electrum, arsenic copper, and bronze objects—since pre-dynastic times (more than 5,000 years ago).

3. Ancient Egypt did not have copper, tin, lead, ..., even though they produced large quantities of copper and bronze alloys. Ancient Egypt also produced electrum—an alloy of gold and silver. Ancient Egypt lacked silver, which is found abundantly in the Iberian Peninsula.

4. Ancient Egypt had records of mining activities and for-

tified settlements that looks exactly like pre-historic Iberian fortified settlements.

5. Ancient Egypt had the mining knowledge and experience and the means to transport heavy weights for long distances, by land and sea.

6. The increase/decrease in mining activities in the Iberian Peninsula (such as silver, copper, tin, etc) corresponded exactly with increased/decreased volume of products in Ancient Egypt, which always correlated to the ups and downs in Ancient Egyptian history. [More details in this chapter, chapter 5, and throughout the book.]

The Egyptian Knowledge of Metallurgy and Metalworking

The Egyptians possessed considerable knowledge of chemistry and the use of metallic oxides, as manifested in their ability to produce glass and porcelain in a variety of natural colors. The Ancient Egyptians also produced beautiful colors from copper, which reflects their knowledge of the composition of various metals, and the knowledge of the effects produced on different substances by the earth's salts.

The methods of metalworking: melting, forging, soldering, and chasing of metal, were not only much practiced, but also most highly developed. The frequent references in Ancient Egyptian records of metalworking gives us a truer concept of the importance of this industry in Ancient Egypt.

Most of the techniques employed by the Egyptian craftsman can be traced back to pre-dynastic times (more than 5000 years ago). By the Old Kingdom (2575-2040 BCE), Egypt had already reached a standard of material culture that remained basically unchanged until the Roman Period.

The Golden Silver Alloy (Electrum)

The Ancient Egyptians utilized gold, which was mined in Egypt. They also used silver, which was/is not found in Egypt. They used silver individually or combined in the golden-silver alloy known as electrum. Ancient Egyptian records indicate that the **neteru** (gods/goddesses) are *made from electrum*—as the source of energy in the universe. In addition to making religious objects such as statues, amulets, etc, this amalgam was much used for personal adornment and for ornamental vases. The proportion of the gold to the silver was generally that of two to three. An Ancient Egyptian papyrus from the time of Tuthomosis III (1490-1436 BCE) indicates that an official received a "great heap" of electrum, which weighed 36,392 uten, i.e. 3311 kilograms 672 grams.

Gold and silver were also cast to make small statues in the same manner as copper and bronze. The two metals are first found early in the Gerzean Period (Naqada II), about 6,000 years ago, mostly in the form of solid beads.

Despite the absence of silver ore in Egypt, the Egyptians regarded silver as the most valuable of all precious metals; it stood before gold in all the old inscriptions, and in fact, silver objects are much rarer than gold ones, in the tombs. Importation of silver ore reached a peak, which led to a fall in the value of silver under the New Kingdom (1550-1070 BCE), especially the 18th Dynasty (1575-1335 BCE), for later texts usually mention gold first in the same way that we do.

The Copper and Bronze Alloys

It is an undisputed fact that the eastern Mediterranean

areas (including Ancient Egypt) lacked mineral ores to produce copper and bronze alloys—copper, arsenic, and tin, which were obtained from abroad. The Ancient Egyptians manufactured large quantities of these alloys, more than 5,000 years ago.

Egyptian copper was hardened by the addition of arsenic. The content of arsenic in the copper alloy varied depending on the intended use. Variation in composition has been observed between some types: for example, daggers and halberds had stronger cutting edges, and contained 4% arsenical copper, while axes and points contained 2% arsenical copper. Arsenical copper was employed from the Pre-Dynastic Period (c. 5000 BCE) right up to and including the Middle Kingdom (2040-1783 BCE).

The Ancient Egyptian stone that is housed in the Palermo Museum is known as the "Palermo Stone". This Ancient Egyptian stone records the making of a copper statue of Khasekhemwy of the 2nd Dynasty (c. 2890-2649 BCE). A copper statue of Pepi I (2289-2255 BCE) is the earliest surviving example of metal sculpture, and is presently displayed in the Cairo Museum.

In addition to manufacturing arsenic copper, the Ancient Egyptians also manufactured bronze products. The addition of a small proportion of tin to copper produces bronze, and results in a lower melting point, an increased hardness, and a greater ease in casting. The content of tin varies widely between 0.1% and 10% or more. Many bronzes of a very early period have been found. A cylinder bearing the name of Pepi I (2289-2255 BCE), showing clean-cut lines as well as other bronze articles of the same period, indicates that the molding of bronze items dates to earlier than 2200 BCE.

The bronze industry was very important for the country. Bronze was employed in Egypt for large vessels a well as for tools and weapons, and this metal work was perfected.

There are numerous examples of perfected bronzes that come from all periods since the Old Kingdom (2575–2150 BCE), such as the Posno Collection, which is now housed at the Louvre in Paris.

The Egyptians employed various kinds of bronze alloys, as we learn from the texts of the New Kingdom, where there is frequent mention of *"black bronze"*, and the *"bronze in the combination of six"*, i.e. a six-fold alloy. Such variations produced different colors. Yellow brass was a compound of zinc and copper. A white (and finer) kind of brass had a mixture of silver, which was used for mirrors, and is also known as "Corinthian brass". Adding copper to the compound produced a yellow, almost gold, appearance.

Copper and bronze provided material for a wide range of domestic utensils, such as cauldrons, pitchers, basins, and ladles, in addition to a wide range of tools and weapons—daggers, swords, spears, and axes, as well as battle-axes. In the Old and Middle Kingdoms, rounded and semicircular forms of battle-axes predominated.

Records from the middle Kingdom Period (2040–1783 BCE)—such as those depicted in Beni Hassan tombs, show the variety of Ancient Egyptian weapons such as the various shields [depicted herein], with several variations of riveting.

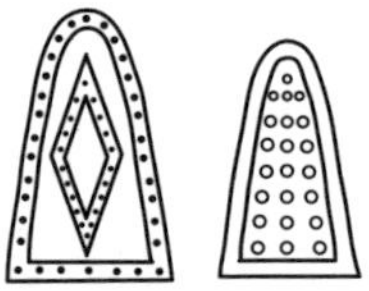

During the New Kingdom Era (1550–1070 BCE), the Ancient Egyptians raised a large military in order to protect their borders. The Egyptians hired mercenaries for their military forces. The Egyptians manufactured their necessary fighting equipment.

A secure and prosperous Egypt was able to produce large quantities of metal goods from the 18th Dynasty (1575–1335 BCE). This increase in number of goods corresponded to the increase in mining activities and the increase in number of copper and bronze items in Iberian tombs of the same period, as is referenced in the next chapter.

The Ancient Egyptian demand for large quantities of copper, arsenic, and tin developed more than 5,000 years ago. The three mineral ores were imported from the only source known in the ancient world—Iberia. Archeological records show the early utilization of the mineral wealth in southern Iberia for copper and arsenic. As for the tin, we are aware of the "Tin Route", which ran along the western coast of the Iberian Peninsula, where the tin came from Galicia and possibly Cornwall. Strabo, in Vol 3 of his *Geography*, tells us that:

> *Tin . . . is dug up; and it is produced both in the country of the barbarians who live beyond Lusitania, and in the Cassiterides Islands; and tin is brought to Massilia from the British Islands.*

Evidence of early contacts along the "Tin Route" that came from the eastern Mediterranean region—namely Ancient Egypt—will unfold throughout this book.

The Glazing Alloys

The Ancient Egyptians produced numerous types of glazed articles as early as the Pre-Dynastic Period (c. 5000 BCE). Glazed objects from this early time were mostly beads, with solid quartz or steatite being used as a core. Steatite was used for carving small objects like amulets, pendants, and small figures of **neteru** (gods/goddesses), as well as a few larger articles, and it proved an ideal base for glazing. Glazed steatite objects are found throughout the Dynastic Period

(3050-343 BCE), and it is by far the most common material for scarabs. The same glazing techniques were used to mass-produce funerary equipment (amulets, shabti-figures) and house decoration (tiles, inlays of floral patterns).

The variety and high quality of the Ancient Egyptian glazing articles are indicative of the Ancient Egyptian knowledge of metallurgy. The most common colors of the Egyptian glaze were blue, green, or greenish-blue. The color is the result of adding a copper compound. More brilliant results were achieved by using a mixture of copper and silver, which were both imported.

The Ancient Egyptian glass was formed by strongly heating quartz sand and natron with a small mixture of coloring agents such as a copper compound, or malachite to produce both green and blue glass. Cobalt, which would have been imported, was also used. After the ingredients were fused into a molten mass, the heating ceased when the mass reached the desired properties. As the mass cooled, it was poured into molds, rolled out into thin rods or canes, or other desired forms.

Egyptian glass bottles are shown on monuments of the 4th Dynasty (2575-2465 BCE). The transparent substance shows the red wine they contained. Egyptian glass bottles of various colors were exported into other countries such as Greece, Etruria, Italy, and beyond.

The Ancient Egyptians displayed their excellent knowledge of the various properties of materials in the art of staining glass with diverse colors, as evident from the numerous fragments found in the tombs at **Ta-Apet** (Thebes).

Glass mosaics were made of various parts, which were made separately, and then united by heat by applying a flux. The Ancient Egyptian glass mosaics have wonderful, brilliant colors.

Glass is frequently found in what is commonly called Egyptian cloisonné-work, a term used to describe an inlay consisting of pieces of glass, faience, or stone set in metal cells—the cloisons—and fixed with cement. The process consisted of putting powdered glass in the cloison and applying enough heat to melt the powder until it became a compact mass.

Glazed pottery, tiles, and other ceramics were major industries in Ancient Egypt. Some tiles had high glazes and designs in an intense blue. They also produced ceramics with an iridescent metallic sheen.

Some tiles were painted in pigments made by mixing metallic oxides (of copper, manganese, cobalt, etc.) and alkaline silicates with water. Glazed tiles of the highest quality are to be found in Egypt from about 4,500 years ago in Sakkara. The "Southern Tomb", only 700ft [300m] from the Step Pyramid, was discovered unmolested at Sakkara by Lauer and Firth in 1924-26. It consists of several chambers lined with blue tiles exactly like the burial chambers of the Step Pyramid.

The Egyptian quality of glazed products is also found in "Moorish" Iberia. The Moorish rulers brought Egyptian craftsmen and masons in order to provide the same Egyptian glazed products for their palaces and mosques. These talented craftsmen were later known as *Mudehars*/**Moriscos**. [More about the *Mudehars*/**Moriscos** in chapters 1 and 11.]

The Egyptian Mining Experience

In the organized nature of the Ancient Egyptian civilization, they maintained written records, showing the nature of their expeditions and the organization of their mining activities. The surviving Ancient Egyptian records show a tremendous organization of mining activities more than 5,000 years ago, in numerous sites throughout Egypt and beyond.

The turquoise mines at Serabit el Khadem in the Sinai Peninsula show a typical Ancient Egyptian mining quarry, consisting of a network of caverns and horizontal and vertical passages carefully cut with proper corners—as were the quarries of the Ancient Egyptians in all periods. The Ancient Egyptians were able to cut deep and long into the mountains with proper shoring and support of excavated shafts and tunnels. The underground water seepage into the tunnels and shafts were safely pumped out to ground level. These Egyptian pumps were famed worldwide, and were used in the mining activities in Iberia, as per the following testimony of Strabo, in his *Geography* [3. 2. 9]:

> *So Poseidonius implies that the energy and industry of the Turdetanian miners is similar, since they cut their shafts aslant and deep, and, as regards* ***the streams that meet them in the shafts, oftentimes draw them off with the Egyptian screw****.*

The very religious Egyptians have always built temples/shrines along with commemorative stelae near/at each mining site. The same exact practice was found in the Iberian Peninsula in prehistoric times. [More about such temples in chapter 10.]

The Ancient Egyptian mining site at Serabit el Khadem provides a typical mining site, with its small temple of **Het-Heru** (Hathor), called "*the Lady of the Turquoise*", which stood on a high rocky terrace that dominates the valley, since the 4th Dynasty (2575–2465 BCE), or possibly much earlier. This temple was afterwards enlarged by the kings of the New Kingdom, especially by Tuthomosis III. In front of the temple, for at least a half mile, is a kind of avenue that was arranged through numerous massive stelae covered on four sides with inscriptions commemorating mining expeditions. Inscribed stelae are also found at other mines throughout Egypt describing the work at each mining site.

At the mines of Wadi Maghara, in Sinai, there still stand the stone huts of the workmen as well as a small fort, built to protect the Egyptians stationed there from the attacks of the Sinai bedouins. There was a water well not far from these mines, and sizeable cisterns in the fortress to hold water. The mines of the Wadi Maghara were actively worked all throughout the dynastic era (3050–343 BCE).

The ore metals were treated on site before transporting by land and water, under heavy security, to the populated areas of Egypt by the Nile Valley. The capability of the Ancient Egyptians to transport tremendous loads by land and water is evident in the case of granite. The quarries of Aswan were the only sources in Ancient Egypt to obtain the beautiful red Egyptian granite. This granite was worked even under the Old Kingdom (2575–2465 BCE). Huge blocks were carved and transported by heavy-duty means on land, water, and land again, for several hundred miles, from Aswan to the Nile Delta and Canopus (Old Alexandria). In other words, Ancient Egypt had a strong road system and impressive navigable canals throughout the country.

Some of the blocks in the temple of King **Khafra** (2520–2494 BCE) not far from the great Sphinx, measure 14 ft [4.26m] in length, and those under the architraves in the sanctuary of **Sebek** in the Fayoum, built by Amenemhet III (1844–1797 BCE), are even more than 26 ft [7.9m] long. Among the Theban obelisks there is one more than 107 ft [32.6m] high, while a papyrus speaks of an obelisk of some kind from the quarries of Aswan, which measured 120 cubits, i.e. nearly 200 ft [61m]. These again are surpassed in bulk by the colossal seated statue of red granite, which lies shattered in the Ramesseum (1304–1237 BCE) at **Ta-Apet** (Thebes); this colossus was hewn out of a single block 55 ft [16.75m] high and correspondingly broad.

From the above accounts, the reader will understand how the Egyptians were able to move even the heaviest of their monuments. The weights concerned were immense. The statue of Ramses II in the Ramesseum weighed, according to one reckoning, more than 1,000 tons. In other words, complete handling and transportation modes were used on land and water, to transport material from the mines in Sinai and the Eastern and Western Deserts to the Nile Valley.

Ancient Egyptian records since the Old Kingdom (2575–2150 BCE) show that good roads were built and provided with frequent intermediate aid stations. Inscriptions of the 19th Dynasty in the desert temple of Redesieh, relate that King Seti I (1333–1304 BCE) commissioned stonemasons to dig a water well to provide water for both the mining operations as well as the mining workers. When the well was finished, a station and "**a town with a temple**" were built. Ramses II (1304–1237 BCE), his successor, mediated plans to provide for boring additional water wells along the roads to mining sites, which were in need of water.

Each mining site was conceived and planned for, with actual plans drawn up. Two Ancient Egyptian papyri were found, which include site maps,

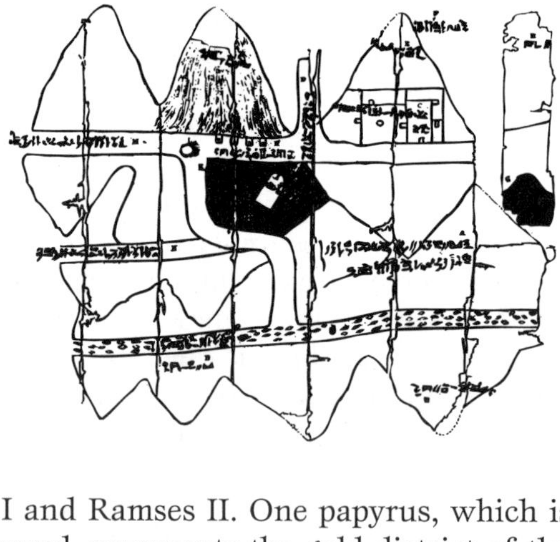

related to mining for gold during the reigns of the two Pharaohs Seti I and Ramses II. One papyrus, which is only partially preserved, represents the gold district of the mountain Bechen, and belongs to the time of Ramses II. The illustration on the found papyrus [shown herein] depicts two valleys running parallel to each other between the mountains. One of these valleys, like many of the larger valleys of the desert, is covered with underwood and blocks of stone to control the soil erosion as a result of stormwater runoff. The prepared site plan shows the major details of the site, such as the road network within the mining site and its connection to the outer roadway system, and "**routes leading to the sea**". The site plan also shows treatment areas of ore metals (such as washing, etc), small houses, storage areas, various buildings, a temple with a sanctuary to **Amon**, a water tank, etc. The area surrounding the mining site shows cultivated ground, to provide the food needed for the mining site colony.

The Ancient Egyptian records also show the various division and specialties of the manpower at mining sites. Ancient Egyptian surviving records show the names and titles of various officials who, under the Old and the Middle Kingdom, directed the works at Hammamat, at Bechen mines. They included treasurers, ship captains, masons, architects, and artists. Under the Ancient Egyptian King Pepi I (2289–2255 BCE), the records show the name of the director of the quarries and the names and titles of the higher officials who conducted inspection visits to the site. Inscriptions mention many titles, such as: "**the superintendent of all the works of the king**", and "**the chief architect in the two departments**". This great man paid two visits of inspection to Hammamat—once accompanied by his son, and once, when it was a question of the religious texts on the walls of a temple, with a superintendent of the commissions of the sacrificial estates of the two departments. The Ancient Egyptian records show the structure of the mining organization. For example, we find that the site manager had subordinates, such as "**deputy artists**", to whom he could occasionally delegate his office, and one or two architects, who were usually subordinate to him, but who are also mentioned in one place as acting independently.

Egyptian mining activities were very organized with

people traveling back and forth to check the site work, to ensure proper efficiency of operation, and to provide amenities to these fortified sites. Under the reign of Ramses IV (1163–1156 BCE), Egyptian records report of an expedition to the mountain of Bechen, under the direction of the "**superintendent of the works**". Altogether the expedition consisted of 8368 people. The men under his command were at least 110 officers of each military rank. With them were more than 50 civil officials and ecclesiastics, and the superintendents of oxen, the high priests of various temples, etc. The technical work was carried out by stonemasons, painters, and certifying engravers, who worked under three chiefs of the stonemasons, and "**the superintendent of the artists**". The labor work was carried out by 5000 miners, 200 officers of various departments, 800 men of the barbarian mercenaries, and 2000 various types of labor. The management of this large number of people is extraordinary. 8368 people is the size of a large community, even nowadays.

Fortification of Isolated Communities

Ancient Egyptian mining sites and other remote sites were provided with adequate protection to ensure the security needs of each individual settlement. Egyptians were experts in building new settlements. An example is found south of the Egyptian frontier, where there is archeological evidence of major public work projects in Kush, which were built in order to establish a permanent presence in the area during the Middle Kingdom. King **Senwasert** III (1878–1844 BCE) established (present-day) Semna as a natural strong point, with three fortresses, in order to provide security for the African trade caravans.

A system of regular fortification was adopted in the earliest times, and the form of the fortresses was quadrangular.

The outer walls were typically formed of crude brick 15 ft [4.5m] thick, and often 50 ft [15.2m] high, with square towers at intervals along each face. Some of the walls were buttresses; and sometimes the whole wall was doubled by an outer casing, leaving a space between the two, filled in here and there by a solid buttress, which strengthened and united them, and prevented anyone from passing freely around the inner wall when the outer one was broken through.

The towers, like the rest of the walls, consisted of a rampart and parapet. The parapet was crowned by the usual round-headed battlements, in imitation of Egyptian shields, like those on their stone walls. Two towers were placed at each side of the very angle, which remained recessed between them, and was slightly rounded off.

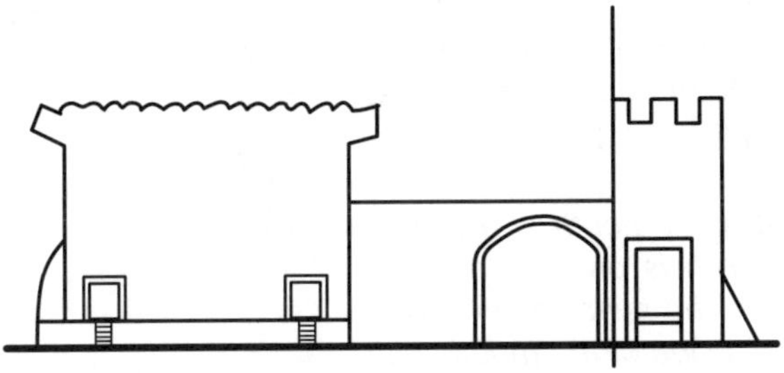

A fort from a Beni Hassan tomb. (Middle Kingdom)

Large fortresses were each typically provided with a long wall, on the side most exposed to attack, projecting from 70 to 100 ft [21 to 30m], at right angles from, and at the same height as, the main wall, upon which the besieged were able to run out and sweep the faces, or curtains, by what we should call a "flanking fire." In order to keep the enemy as far from the main wall as possible, the wall was raised on a broad terrace or basement, or was provided with an outer circuit, or low wall of circumvallation, parallel to the main wall, and distant from it, on every side, from 13 to 20 ft [4 to 6m]; and a tower stood at each side of the entrance, which was towards one corner of the least exposed face.

Whenever it was possible, the fortress was square, with one (or occasionally two) entrances, and a sally port (or a water gate, if near the river). For an irregularly-shaped landscape, the fortress was made to conform to the contours of the ground. Another more effective defense used with larger fortifications, was a huge ditch surrounding the fortress. A continuous stone wall was built along the center of the ditch. Over the ditch was a wooden bridge that was removed during a siege. The fortress stood on a platform on the scarp in the center.

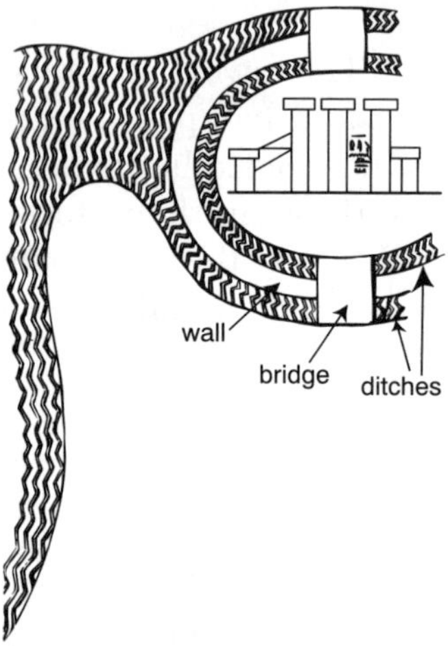

The fortified town, surrounded by double ditches, over which are bridges.

Diodorus of Sicily describes such a defensive arrangement, which was provided at the seven mouths of the Nile Delta and its branches, in his *Book I,* [33.5-8]:

> *. . . At each mouth is a walled city, which is divided into two parts by the river and provided on each side of the mouth with pontoon bridges and guard-houses at suitable points.*

In this chapter, we have shown the Ancient Egyptian knowledge and practices in mining and metalworking activities. The archeological evidence in the Iberian Peninsula will show the correlation and effects of such activities between Ancient Egypt and the Iberian Peninsula. The first stop is **Almeria**—which is an Ancient Egyptian name, meaning *harbor*—signifying the (first) landing in Iberia.

5

In The Beginning – Almeria

The Sirets and Petrie Archeological Connections

The Ancient Egyptian connection to the Iberian history became a solid reality when two Belgian mining engineers, Louis and Henri Siret, began working in the region of Almeria in the later part of the 19th century. They located, excavated, and recorded several hundred tombs and settlements dating from the Middle Palaeolithic to the Classical period. They uncovered a wealth of evidence, including different types of megalithic tombs, nucleated and defended settlements and wealthy burials containing objects of copper, bronze, gold, silver and ivory. During the period 1880–1887 they excavated the settlement sites of El Argar (after which the local Bronze Age culture was named), El Garcel, Gerundia, Campos, Tres Cabezos, El Oficio, Gatas, Lugarico Viejo, Fuente Vermeja, Parazuelos, Ifre and Zapata, as well as many communal tombs and cave sites. Subsequently they undertook excavations on the famous Copper Age settlements and tombs at Los Millares and Almizaraque.

The two communities of Los Millares (c. 2600–1800 BCE) and El Argar (c. 1700–1400 BCE) represent the Copper Age and the early Bronze Age respectively. The area of southeastern Spain is recognized as containing one of the key sequences for the study of the emergence of more complex cultures in the 3rd and 2nd millennia BCE, because of the wealth acquired from mining activities. Metallurgical and agricultural activities were undertaken simultaneously, as evident from the archeological findings.

The most extensive source of copper in the Iberian Peninsula is located in the southwest. The territories of the provinces of Huelva and Badajoz in Spain, and Algarve and Baixo Alentejo in Portugal, are broadly included in this zone. The Copper Age settlements of the Iberian Atlantic seaboard are remarkably similar to the communities in the southeast. Both Copper Age groups lived in fortified settlements, built corbel-type tombs for their ancestors, and appear to have made full use of the available agricultural resources. In both areas the prelude to metallurgy seems to have emerged quite suddenly, before the end of the 4th millennium. Furthermore, in both regions, the Copper Age communities feature communal graves constructed by megalithic builders. For all these reasons, therefore, Portugal integrates easily into the study of prehistoric Spain. Three Portuguese regions—Estremadura, Alentejo, and Algarve—share the characteristics and the issues of the period, and those of the southern regions of the Iberian Peninsula. Also in central and southern Portugal, at the time of the high Copper Age (2600–1800 BCE), and similar to southwestern Spain, early metallurgists enclosed their settlements within fortifications. The comparatively close similarities between these two major groups, in distinctly different locations, points to a common source.

In addition to the archeological findings at the regions stated above, the archeological registry suggests that regular contacts were made through organized navigation through the Strait of Gibraltar as early as the 4th millennium BCE, along the "Tin Route", along Iberia's western coast.

Tin was needed to manufacture bronze alloys since predynastic times (5000 BCE) in Ancient Egypt. The advantages of a tin-bronze alloy in the production of cutting tools

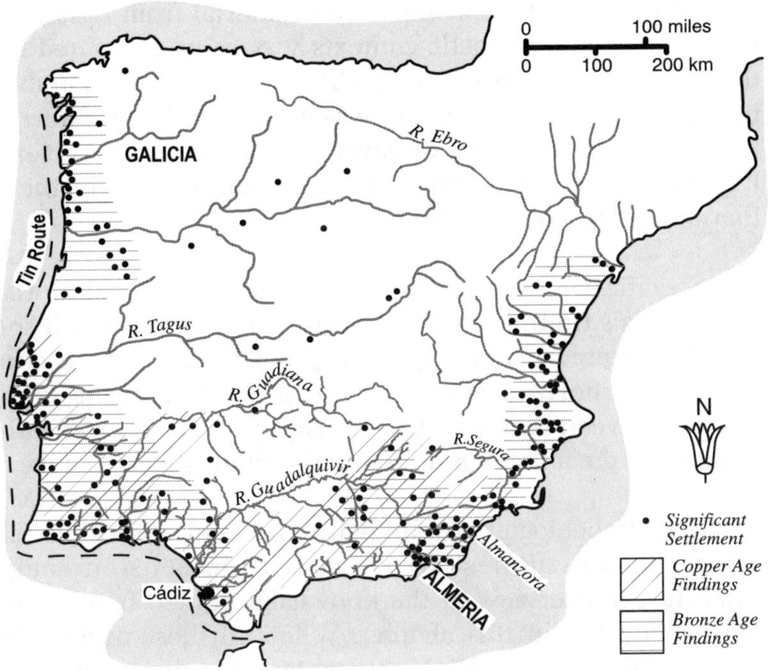

Map showing the sites discussed in this text

and weapons are essential. Such demand was satisfied from northwest Iberia (and beyond). The abundant tin resources of northwest Iberia were little exploited until the end of the 2nd millennium BCE, coinciding with the time of the prosperous Ancient Egyptian Middle Kingdom (2040–1783 BCE), when mining activities increased in Ancient Egypt.

Given the absence of a similar body of later prehistoric cultural material from elsewhere in the peninsula, the Siret brothers were faced with the problem of dating and explaining this concentration of settlements and tombs. As there was insufficient comparative material within the peninsula, it had to be assumed that the cultures and peoples represented by these assemblages originated in other areas.

At the same time, comparative material from Egyptian pre-dynastic and dynastic contexts was being excavated by the British Egyptologist, Flinders Petrie. No such comparable material from later prehistory was known in the Mediterranean Basin, so the newly discovered materials from Ancient Egypt gave the Sirets the means to date and explain their Iberian cultural assemblages.

Specific comparisons between Ancient Egypt and southwest Iberia's findings noted countless similarities, in all societal, economical, and religious aspects. When we count on our cultural horizon as a whole, the proportion of the similarities between both the Ancient Egyptian and Iberian cultures are so great that it is difficult to attribute them to chance.

The archeological findings in Almerian and other regional Iberian cultures provide us with insights on many subjects. An overview of the knowledge gained from them will be covered in this chapter. When all these aspects of analysis are considered, it becomes clear that they (individually and collectively) point overwhelmingly to Ancient Egypt as the cause of the sudden changes in the Iberian Peninsula.

The Telling Tombs

The hundreds of tombs and their contents found in Iberia, from the 3rd and 2nd millennia BCE, tell us a lot of information about the people, society, religious beliefs, burial customs, form/style of architectural construction, general activities, type and level (technological and artistic) of crafts and industries, farming, etc.

The similarities between the Iberian archeological and Ancient Egyptian tomb findings, as a result of the work of the Siret brothers in Iberia and Petrie in Egypt, are exactly the same, as noted below in a few examples.

1. *The various types of megalithic tombs and their architectural features.* Like Ancient Egypt, the Iberian Copper Age tomb constructional materials and methods had the following features: dry-stone corbelled and vaulted (and false-vaulted) structures. [See examples below.] The tomb forms varied from tombs with chambers and entrance passages, to those at Los Millares with their side-chambers and segmented passages.

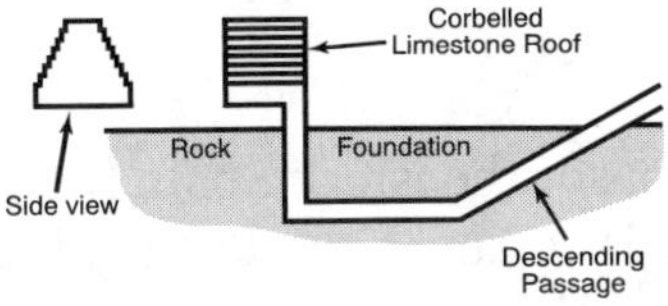

Dry-stone corbelled room in Snefru's Meidum Pyramid (2575-2551 BCE)

False-vaulted roof in the main underground room in Menkaura's Pyramid (2494-2472 BCE).

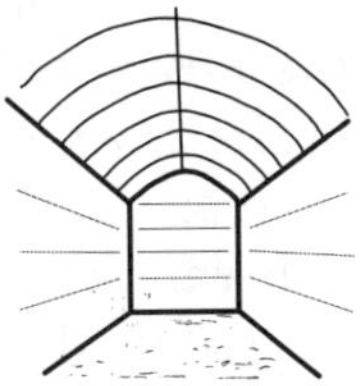

2. *Burial customs that included burial of personal goods with the deceased.* Like Ancient Egyptian tombs, Iberian tomb contents included: funerary adzes, the axe symbol, numerous motifs, female figurines, biradial flint tools, ivory combs, hippopotamus ivory, ostrich-egg-shell beads, stone vases, painted pottery and bone phalanges.
Close parallels in jewelry, swords, daggers, and other pieces establish, beyond a doubt, strong contacts between early Iberian and Ancient Egyptian cultures.

3. *Similarities in religious beliefs.* Iberian tombs and artifacts show Egyptian design motifs and symbolism. Both expected life after death. Several Iberian tablets detail the voyage of the soul or spirit, which is very much like Ancient Egyptian texts, as found in Egyptian tombs.

4. *Technological skills of the manufactured goods* found in the tombs and the chronological coinciding quality and quantity of such goods in both Ancient Egypt and Hispanic archeological sites.

Dry-Weather Farming

The archeological evidence in prehistoric Iberia supports that both metallurgical and agricultural activities were undertaken simultaneously at hundreds of excavated settlements, in Los Millares, El Argar, as well as in central and southern Portugal, at the time of the high Copper Age (2600–1800 BCE).

The region extending from southeastern Spain (in which the Los Millares site is located) to southern Portugal is one of the most arid in the whole of Europe. At Los Millares, the increase in demographic growth, more efficient methods of cultivating the land, and improvements in trade contacts, have contributed greatly to significant social change in such communities. Residents of Los Millares were able to utilize the available water resources efficiently. Communities in the southeastern region had organized methods of water conservation and diversion.

Ancient Egypt was renowned worldwide for its dry-weather irrigation and farming techniques. A highly organized communal irrigation system was developed since prehistoric times. [For more details, see chapter 11, subchapter *The Egyptian Green Revolution*.]

Like Ancient Egypt, the social consequences of successful and efficient dry-farming practices in southern and eastern Iberia were far reaching, since the more efficient farming is, the more dependent the society becomes on leaders, chiefdoms or commanding groups. A ranked society was postulated, the leaders of which coordinated the various activities of the society. This promoted a more efficient distribution of the workforce, with various interactive specialized groups. This may have been the reason behind the establishment of large control centers, such as the great Los Millares site, as evident by the fortified settlements and the monumental tombs of the Copper Age in southeast Spain.

The Early (New) Settlers

The archeological findings indicate that in both areas of Los Millares and El Argar, the prelude to metallurgy seems to have emerged quite suddenly, before the end of the 4th millennium. The sudden emergence of complex societies leads us to investigate the origin of these new settlers.

The ethnic and political development of the region was closely correlated on the Peninsula as a rich source of metals, the most prolific zone being the 'pyrite arc' extending from the copper- and silver-rich Sierra Morena in the south to Galicia and the Cantabrian Mountains in the northwest where tin and gold are concentrated. The figures for copper objects in the Almeria lowlands (and in the uplands of eastern Granada) support the hypothesis that 3rd millennium BCE copper metallurgy in southeast Spain was small scale in production and organization. The variety and quantity of the finds do not support the inference of a high frequency of copper production and deposition. The same argument can be applied to the copper object finds at Almizaraque.

The evidence shows that certain Early Bronze Age sites in the Iberian Peninsula are actually colonies established by people coming from the eastern Mediterranean. The Copper Age settlements such as Los Millares, Vila Nova de Sao Pedro and Zambujal are known to have been constructed around 2700 BCE—2,000 years before the arrival of Phoenician traders. They have been described as solitary, heavily-defended settlements situated in a culturally foreign environment, i.e. for the purpose of mining—similar to Ancient Egyptian mining sites [as described in chapter 4].

The fluctuation in the rate of mining activities and size of settlements correlate exactly with events and use of ore materials in Ancient Egypt. Such parallels can be drawn between the metallurgical production in Ancient Egypt—as noted in chapter 4—and the following archeological evidence, during the same periods in the Iberian Peninsula.

- Copper was in use in Egypt in pre-dynastic times (c. 6,000 years ago), and the early settlements of prehistoric Iberia were located in those regions in which copper and silver were either available or accessible: the provinces of Almeria, Granada and Murcia in the southeast, and the areas of Huelva, Algarve, Baixo Alentejo and Estremadura in the southwest.

- The walled and bastioned forts, as well as the mining activities and the frequency of metal objects of Almeria and the Lower Tagus, dropped sharply (c. 2200 BCE), which coincided with the collapse of the Old Kingdom in Ancient Egypt. As a consequence, the Millaran culture met a similar fate.

- Archeological records indicate that there was negligible or non-existent silver working, anywhere in the Iberian Peninsula in the pre-Bronze Age. Radiocarbon dates show that the fortified sites known as 'colonies' in southeast Spain and central Portugal were constructed and occupied by the second half of the 3rd millennium BCE. But we know that silver was not exploited in Iberia before c. 1800 BCE. As indicated in chapter 4, silver usage was rare in Ancient Egypt at that time as well.

- The low frequency of tin bronzes and their variation in composition, during the Argaric Period, has been attributed to the occurrence of tin in small pockets in one area—La Union, near Cartagena, in southern Murcia. Likewise, there was a limited production of tin-bronze in pre-dynastic and early dynastic eras of Ancient Egypt.

- More mining of copper and tin resources of northwest Iberia began in earnest at the end of the 2nd millennium BCE. Judging by the number of known necropoles of the early Bronze Age in the southwest, it can be assumed that there was a considerable increase in the population by the second half of the 2nd millennium BCE, which coincides with the very active Egyptian economy during the Middle Kingdom Era (2040–1783 BCE).

- At the end of the Argaric culture, and after the initial phase of the Later Bronze Age, there is a marked break in metal types and frequencies. In Almeria and Granada there is a dramatic fall in the frequency of metal objects. This corresponds to the turmoil in Egypt during and after Akhenaton's rule.

To summarize the archeological findings, all references agree that the new settlements were generally located in good defensive positions, close to rivers, with access to both the mining sites for metal ores and the sea, and that the early (new) colonists:

1. came from the eastern Mediterranean region,

2. sought mineral ores that were lacking in their homeland (copper, silver, tin, etc),

3. have knowledge of metallurgy and produced large amounts of metal products,

4. have knowledge and excelled in dry-weather farming and irrigation techniques,

5. built fortified settlements,

6. have religious beliefs and motifs that correspond with the Ancient Egyptians,

7. built the same type of megalithic tombs as in Ancient Egypt,

8. co-existed in peace with the sparse native population. In order to obtain these metal resources, the settlers would have exchanged some material trinkets and religious ideas with the indigenous population. Thus the colony sites served as the intermediaries between the natives and the metal ore seekers, and

9. caused the "orientalization" of Iberian culture.

The only people that have these main characteristics are the Ancient Egyptians, and nobody else. The archeological evidence does not support a Phoenician presence in Iberia before the 7th century BCE. [More about the Phoenicians in chapter 7.]

Early Ancient Egyptians began arriving at **Almería** (an Ancient Egyptian word meaning *harbor*) in the 4th or 5th millennium. During the 2nd millennium, trade strengthened since Iberia was, and is, very rich in copper and silver—commodities scarce in the eastern Mediterranean region.

A large group of people, who still live in the same archeological sites that were mentioned in this chapter, look, act, and declare themselves to be descendants of the Land of the Pharaohs. They continue to be expert metallurgists and excellent farmers in the same old areas. These people are called by many names: ***Gitanos, Moriscos, Mudejars, Mozarabs***, and Romany. All these names deal with a race of people of the same origin—Egypt, who arrived to the shores of the Iberian Peninsula in several immigration waves.

6

Masters of the Seas

The Egyptian Ships

Transferring people, minerals, and goods between Ancient Egypt and other faraway places like the Iberian Peninsula was much more extensive and common than is generally imagined. The seas were not barriers, but high roads for active international commerce. Traveling by water has been (and continues to be) the most effective, economical, and safest way to travel for both people and goods. Travel by land complements travel by water for major/large goods.

As shown earlier, Ancient Egyptians consumed large amounts of mineral ore, which were unavailable in the eastern Mediterranean region, and were only available in Iberia. The needs of a civilized society, such as the Ancient Egyptians, are not fully satisfied with the produce of its homeland. Thus, trade routes were developed to faraway places. The Nile was navigable throughout the length of Egypt. The Red Sea gave access to Africa and the Far East. The Mediterranean Sea gave them access to countries in Europe and even to northern Europe and the Americas.

Ancient Egypt had the means, knowledge, material, and experience to transport people and goods by sea and land. The quality of the Ancient Egyptian ships were truly recognized and appreciated when the Khufu (Cheops) boat (4500 years old) was found next to the Great Pyramid in Giza, during the 1970s. That boat, now housed in a museum next to the Great Pyramid, is superior and much more seaworthy than Columbus' Santa Maria, The Mayflower, or the Vikings' ships. The physical evidence is clear that the Egyptians had the means to travel on the high seas. Sizes of even larger ships than Khufu's will be detailed later.

Khufu's boat is one of the largest ancient boats found to date. The extreme length of Viking boats found in Europe was not more than 98.5 ft [30m], while Khufu's boat is 142.5ft [43.4m] long. It is about 19.4ft [5.9m] wide and 5.75ft [1.75m] deep and has a displacement of over 40 tons. The prow, formed in the shape of a papyrus-bundle, is about 20ft [6m] tall. Its stern rises to 23ft [7m]. Its rudder consists of two massive oars. The boat has several cabins on its deck. There is some evidence that Khufu's boat was actually used in water. Marks caused by abrasion between the ropes, which shrink when wet, and the wood of the vessel, which expands when wet, are still clearly visible in many places.

The boat consists of several pieces of wood that are held together with ropes, which shrink when wet, and the wood of the vessel, which expands when wet. Such shrinkage and expansion provided tight, secure seals, and eliminated any need for metal nails. This method of boat construction allowed the Ancient Egyptians to carry the pieces of the boat, while traveling on land, until they reached a safe and navigable waterway. This ingenious construction technique allowed the Ancient Egyptians to travel deeper inland.

The Ancient Egyptians were famed for their shipbuilding throughout the Mediterranean Basin, even though the timber necessary for large-scale carpentry and for boat building was unavailable in Egypt. The Ancient Egyptians had a large fleet, as evident from the huge quantities of timber that they had imported from Phoenicia.

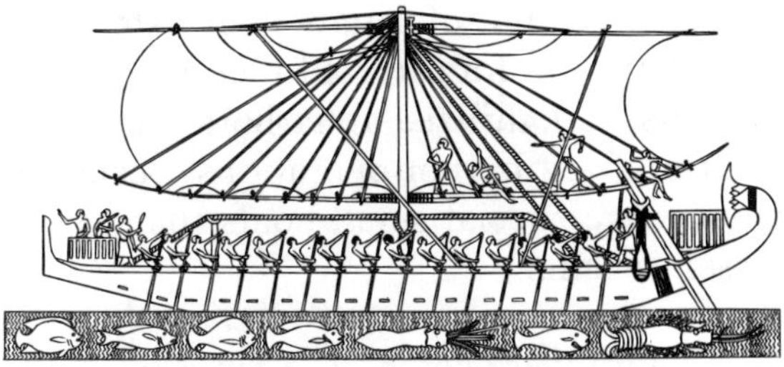

Sailing boat of Queen Hatshepsut on the voyage to Punt.

The Egyptians built a whole range of practical boats, well adapted to different uses and to the geography and climate for the transportation of both passengers and freight. The Egyptian ships traveled the waters of the Nile and the high seas, since the most ancient times. Ships varied enormously in size. Some of them were huge. Diodorus mentioned one, made of cedar, built during Sesostris' reign, which measured about 450ft [140m].

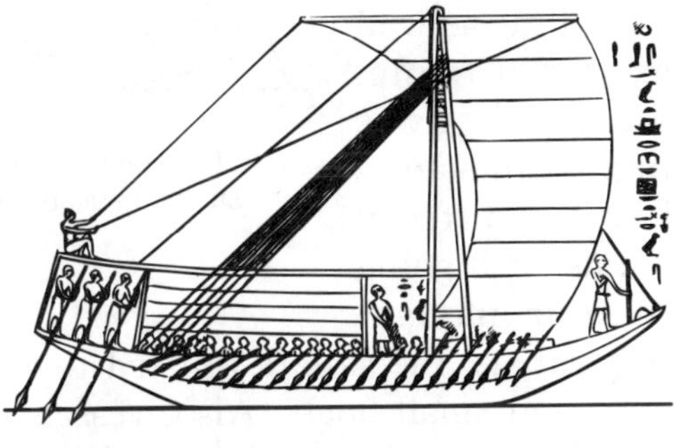

Large boat with sail, a double mast, and many rowers. In a tomb at Kom Ahmar, above Minya.

All types of commercial and military vessels were known, more than 5,000 years ago, before the Phoenicians became seafarers in the 1st millennium BCE—transporting goods to the Iberian Peninsula.

In very early times, boat building was carried on extensively. Even under the Old Kingdom (2575–2150 BCE), boats were built of large dimensions and of considerable port; thus we hear of a "**broad ship of acacia wood, 60 cubits long and 30 cubits broad**" , i.e. nearly 100ft [30.5m] long and 50ft [15.25m] across, and a boat of this immense size "**was put together in 17 days only**".

The pictures under the Old Kingdom represent several different types of boats, the inscriptions also do not speak of *boats* simply, but of square boats, stern boats, towboats, etc. Each type is fit for certain functions/situations. Several types of boats were utilized at harbors such as Canopus (pre-Alexandria), to fit harbor operations. Besides the freight vessels, there were special small boats that were used for carrying lesser weights.

There were some very large freighters, used for transporting grain, stone, bricks and even the gigantic obelisks, which were hewn out of a single block in the quarries of Aswan, and then carried on the river to the site of the temple in **Ta-Apet** (Thebes/Luxor), and elsewhere.

Nearly all the boats seem to have been adapted for sailing as well as for rowing. When sailing was impossible—owing to contrary winds, or if going in calm navigation canals, the sailors utilized towing techniques of towlines and small boats. Also, vessels that were intended to carry large freight seem to have been towed either by men or by other vessels, because they were too heavy for independent movement. Therefore, even during the Old Kingdom, most vessels were provided with a strong post on which to tie a towing rope. Many towboats were provided with short perpendicular posts at both ends for the towline. They were steered, like all vessels of the Old Kingdom, by means of long oars. This kind of vessel was employed in the transport of blocks (i.e. can carry tremendous weights) from the quarries.

Towboat [c. 2400 BCE], The lath-crate stores breakable items during transport.

The rudders of most Ancient Egyptian ships, since the Old Kingdom era, consisted of two massive (steering) oars.

Throughout the Egyptian history, most boats were decorated and were adorned in the fore part with large paintings; the stern resembles a gigantic lotus flower; the blade of the rudder-oar resembles a bouquet of flowers, whilst the knob at the top is fashioned into the head of a deity.

Egyptian Boat from the Middle Kingdom

The Ancient Egyptians also had a naval fleet, the size of which varied according to defensive needs on the high seas, during the different eras of the Ancient Egyptian history. Special boats were built purposely for war. Herodotus and Diodorus both mention the fleet of long vessels, or ships of war, fitted out by **Senwasert** I (Sesostris I) on the Arabian Gulf. They were 400 in number; and there is every reason to believe that the trade, and the means of protecting it by ships of war, existed there at least as early as the 12th Dynasty, about 2,000 years before our era.

The galleys—or ships of war, used in their wars outside of Egypt—differed from those of the Nile. They were less raised at the head and stern; and on each side, throughout the whole length of the vessel, a wooden bulwark, rising considerably above the gunwale, sheltered the rowers, who sat behind it, from the missiles of the enemy; the handles of the oars passing through an aperture at the lower part.

These commercial and naval ships were served with several ports, guiding landmarks, water markers, loading and unloading facilities. Several roads, along with supply stations, were provided between the seaports and the populated centers along the Nile.

Egyptian Goods

Egyptian agricultural and manufactured goods of all kinds were sought worldwide. Indigenous products, most notably glass, textiles, luxury goods and papyrus, found ready markets in the east and the west and the latter, at least, continued to do so for centuries after the Arab invasion of Egypt in 639 CE.

Bottles and vases of various kinds—glass, porcelain, alabaster, and other materials—many containing numerous colors—were frequently exported from Egypt to other countries. The Greeks, the Etruscans, and the Romans received them as articles of luxury—prized as ornaments for the table because of their remarkable quality. When Egypt became a Roman province, part of the tribute annually paid to the conquerors consisted of Egyptian-made glass vases. It is careless and wrong to consider items possessed by the Romans (as a result of "spoils of war" and tribute), as "Roman made"!!

The Egyptian glassware, in particular, was of the finest quality, as noted by Strabo. Glass bottles of various colors were eagerly bought from Egypt, and exported into other countries; and the manufacture, as well as the patterns of many of those found in Greece, Etruria, and Rome, show that they were of Egyptian work.

Other high quality exports included stained glass of various hues, counterfeited emeralds, amethysts, and other precious stones.

The exported Ancient Egyptian vases were very numerous, and varied in shape, size, and materials; being of hard stone, alabaster, glass, ivory, bone, porcelain, bronze, brass, silver, gold, glazed pottery, or common earthenware, which had beautiful shapes, ornamental designs, and superior quality of the material. The design patterns of their vases and painted pottery had different styles of: floral decoration, figurative, harmonically geometric, or combinations of two or all three types—as shown in examples below:

Gold vases of the time of Tuthomoses III. Ta-Apet (Thebes).

Vase ornamented with two heads. Ta-Apet (Thebes).

Gold and silver cups were often beautifully engraved, and studded with precious stones. Among these we readily distinguish the green emerald, the purple amethyst, and other gems; and when an animal's head adorned their handles, the eyes were frequently composed of these gems, except when enamel, or some colored composition, was employed as a substitute. Many of their ornamental vases, as well as those in ordinary use, were of the most elegant shape. They bear a strong resemblance to the productions of the best epochs of ancient Greece, both in their shape and in the fancy devices upon them, that some might even suppose them borrowed from Greek patterns. But they were purely Egyptian, and had been manufactured in the valley of the Nile, long before they were known in Greece; a fact invariably acknowledged by those who are acquainted with the remote age of Egyptian monuments, and of the paintings that represent them.

The Egyptian Geodesy

The Ancient Egyptians studied, compiled, and utilized immense geographical data about the surface of the earth (including water surfaces) with actual measurements. In a country that relies on agriculture, geodesy (the science of earth measurement) is critical for dry-weather farming, because this information is needed for the design, construction and operation of canals and dikes, as required for the distribution of water to the farmlands.

The Ancient Egyptians built numerous channels for irrigation, drainage, as well as for navigating all types of ships that went through Egypt via the River Nile, and many man-made canals. It should be remembered that during the time of the Pharaoh **Mena** (5000 years ago), the course of the Nile was changed by establishing a new waterway course—a major project even in our present times.

The pavilion of **Senwasert** (Sesostris) I (1971–1926 BCE), at Karnak Temple, incorporates geodesic knowledge in its design, and it also provides a wealth of geodesic information. It shows (among many things) a list of all the provinces of Egypt with their respective land surface areas, proving that actual surveys were made. Major towns are listed, the total length of Egypt is given, and the normal height of the Nile flood noted at three principal points along the length of the river. A lot of other useful information is also provided.

Accurate measurement for long distances can only be obtained through astronomical means. A systematic kind of astronomical observation began in Ancient Egypt at a very early time. The most ancient astronomical texts (presently known) are found on the lids of wooden coffins dating from the 9th Dynasty (c. 2150 BCE). These texts are called *diagonal calendars* or *diagonal star clocks*. They give the names of the decans (stars that rise at ten-day intervals at the same time as the sun), of which there are 36. More elaborate star charts were found on the ceilings of numerous tombs from the New Kingdom (1550–1070 BCE).

While Western academia attributes the knowledge of astronomy to the Greeks, early historians reported otherwise. The great Strabo (64 BCE–25 CE) admitted that:

The Egyptian priests are supreme in the science of the sky...

Clement Alexandrinus (200 CE) mentions 42 volumes on various subjects accredited to the Egyptian **neter** (god) of knowledge/wisdom—**Tehuti** (Thoth). Four books were on astronomy, one containing a list of the fixed stars, another on the phenomena of the sun and moon, two others on the rising of the stars. Another contained a cosmography and geography, the course of the sun, moon, and the five planets.

It is abundantly clear that the Ancient Egyptians had the technical knowledge to travel the high seas and the geographic (descriptive and measurement) data of various areas of the earth. It was the Ancient Egyptians who passed some of their knowledge to the Phoenicians who manned their ships. Herodotus (500 BCE) reported that the Ancient Egyptians were masters of the sea (not the Phoenicians), since King Necho (c. 610–595 BCE) commissioned the Phoenicians to sail Egyptian ships around Africa:

. . .the Egyptian king Neco, . . . ***sent out a fleet manned by a Phoenician crew with orders to sail round and return to Egypt and the Mediterranean by way of the Pillars of Heracles****. [Herodotus 4-229]*

Little, if any, credit is given to Ancient Egypt as the source of the detailed descriptions and measurements that are found in Strabo's volumes, *Geography*. Strabo obtained the detailed descriptions of the world geography (that took centuries to compile by the Egyptian geographers) from Egypt—where he studied for several years.

Patrons and Shrines of the Seafarers

The religious beliefs and practices that relate to the seafaring activities were:

1. Deities with special attributes important to the well-being of the sailors;

2. Shoreline sanctuaries and temples with special associations for sailors;

3. The concept of the ship itself possessing a divine spirit; and

4. Religious ceremonies or acts performed by seafarers regarding the safety of the voyage.

The Ancient Egyptians, since time immemorial, had numerous harbor temples and shoreline shrines dedicated to their patron deities, along the shores of their navigable waterways within and outside Egypt proper. Egyptian mariners, like their classical and modern counterparts, were making distinct offerings to their patron deities in port. Having reached their destination, preparations commenced for a general thanksgiving in the principal temple/shrine, and suitable offerings were made to the presiding deity. The seaside shrines gave a link to their divine protectors while away from homeport, as well as serving as landmarks that aided navigation and marked freshwater sources.

The Ancient Egyptians (as per Herodotus' testimony) were the most religious people of all nations of the world. In order to appreciate their religious practices, as it relates to traveling, we should start with their main religious premise. The Ancient Egyptians believed in One God who was self-produced, self-existent, immortal, invisible, eternal, omniscient, almighty, etc. This One God was represented through the functions and attributes of "His" domain. These attributes were called the **neteru** (pronounced ***net-er-u***; masculine singular: **neter**; feminine singular: **netert**). There is an indefinite number of divinities (**neteru**), because the Divine has an endless number of aspects/attributes.

The real names of the deities (gods, goddesses) were kept secret. The real name was/is imbued with magical powers and properties. To know and pronounce the real name of a **neter/netert** (god/goddess) is to exercise power over it. To guard the cosmic power of the deity, the Ancient Egyptians (and later the Phoenicians) often used "*names*" with religious connotations. **Baal** simply means *Lord* or *ruler*, and so we hear of the **Baal** or the **Baalat** (*Lady*) of such-and-such a city. Similarly, a deity will be called **Melek**, meaning *King*. So too **Adon**, which means *Lord* or *Master*. **Melqart** meant *King of the City*. Other "names" meaning *favored by the gods* or *granted by the gods* were translated to Latin as *Fortunatus, Felix, Donatus, Concessus*, and so on.

The following are the most recognized deities who are related to travel in Ancient Egypt, and which were later adopted by the Phoenicians and others. Regarding the "different" pronunciation of "names", read about the phenomenon of sound shifts in chapter 12.

Reshpu (Reshef/Resheph)— represents wilderness and travel. As such, **Reshpu** (Reshef) appears unshaven, as per the Ancient Egyptian custom of not shaving while traveling. The tradition of the unshaven Egyptian traveler was well recognized by classical Greek and Roman writers, such as Diodorus, who wrote in his *Book I,* [2]:

> *And when all his [travel] preparations had been completed Osiris made a vow to the gods that he would let his hair grow until his return to Egypt and then made his way through Ethio-*

pia; and this is the reason why this custom with regard to their hair was observed among the ***Egyptians until recent times, and why those who journeyed abroad let their hair grow until their return home****.*

This is the reason that some male deities are shown in beards and long hair—not because they are "Syrians", but because they are Egyptians during travel. Such unshaven representation of male deities will be naturally found in shrines and temples outside Egypt proper, because that is where the travel occurs.

Anat— represents the motherhood aspect of guardianship. The symbol of a mother protecting her offspring is the most powerful representation. A good guard is always ready to deter any outside threat. Therefore, **Anat** is represented as a woman holding a shield and an axe. **Anat** is associated with **Sekhmet**—the lion-headed goddess—the Fearless One.

Anat is one of the 10,000 aspects/attributes of the Great Mother goddess **Auset** (Isis).

Het-Heru (Hathor)/Astarte— like other Egyptian deities, is also commonly known as **Asera / Serah / Sarah**, which means *a noble lady*. To leave no doubt of her Egyptian origin, **Aserah** is always portrayed in her Egyptian form with a crescent-and-disk on her headdress. **Het-Heru** (Hathor) represents the matrix of the metaphysical spiritual principle, providing spiritual nourishment, healing, joy, lovemaking, music, and cheerfulness.

Het-Heru (Hathor), as the symbol of spiritual nourishment, also plays an important role in the transformational (funerary) texts, furnishing the spiritual nourishment/guidance required by the soul of the deceased, as it travels across the cosmic sea. Consequently, **Het-Heru** (Hathor)/**Aserah** is the Egyptian travel and sailing patroness, and as a result she appears in this role more often outside Egypt. An Egyptian coffin text [coffin text no. 61] from the Middle Kingdom (2040–1783 BCE) describes her as **Het-Heru the Lady who is said to 'hold the steering oars of . . . barks'.** **Het-Heru's** head is therefore always depicted right above the stern of ships, where the twin rudders, which expert pilots used to guide the vessel, were mounted.

In her role as a guardian of travelers, **Het-Heru** is called **Astarte**. Her temples were found at border cities—being a traveler patroness. Her temple at Cádiz was one of the major monuments at this holy city. The role of **Astarte** in Ancient Egypt is well documented. From small fragments of the time of Ramses II (1304–1237 BCE), the role of **Astarte** as patroness of overseas travel is evident. In one fragment, the role of **Astarte** as seafarer patroness is clearly stated:

> .... Behold, **Astarte dwelleth in the region of the sea**. . .

In another fragment, **Renenutet** addresses **Astarte**:

> Behold, if thou bringest him tribute, he will be gracious unto thee. . .Therefore give him his **tribute in silver, gold, lapis lazuli, and. . . wood**.

And she said unto the Ennead of **neteru**(gods/goddesses):

> . . . the **tribute of the sea; may he hearken unto us**. . . .

Our (Holy) Mother of the Sea

During (and subsequent to) the turbulent times of the Reconquest, many people fled from the Iberian Peninsula to North Africa, Egypt, and France. The most prominent festival in southern France is held by the (Egyptian) Romany at the seaside by the Mediterranean Sea, towards the end of spring. The pilgrimage destination is the Church of ***Notre Dame de La Mer***. The name of the church is Ancient Egyptian—**Notre** (means *our holy/goddess*), **Dame** (**Da-me** means *the mother*), ***de la*** **Mer** (means *water body/sea*—same in Spanish). This Romany pilgrimage is the oldest in France.

The "historical" tradition associated with this Romany festival had a solid connection to Egypt. According to tradition, a dark-skinned Egyptian maiden called St. Sarah arrived in a tiny boat without oars or sail, together with two white-skinned maidens, whose names are Mary Salome and Mary Jacobe. Their boat is said to have landed on this part of the Mediterranean coast, having drifted across the Mediterranean Sea, about 42 CE. [More about the "Two Marys" in chapter 2.]

The "name" of the centerstage character of this festival is also significant. Her name—**Sarah**—is an Ancient Egyptian word that is the feminine form of **Sar** = *a person of high/noble status.* Sarah therefore means the *Noble Lady*, in the Ancient Egyptian language. In the Ancient Egyptian traditions, Saint Sarah is **Het-Heru** (Hathor)—*Patroness of Travelers by Water*. Her name, **Sarah**, is consistent with her being—*Our Holy Mother of the Sea*, as stated above.

It is no accident that the theme of a (woman) saint and her two guardian angels (Mary Salome and Mary Jacobe) that we find in southern France is also found at Elche, in the region where the "***Morisco***" culture is dominant. Here we see again the same practices and traditions by Romany/***Gitanos/Moriscos/Mudejars***—the dark/tanned-skin people—the descendants of the Egyptian Pharaohs.

7

Merchants of the Seas

The Phoenicians' Homeland

The Phoenicians are arbitrarily credited with introducing numerous settlements, highly productive farming techniques, crafts, organizational government, arts, etc. into the Iberian Peninsula. Yet the Phoenicians never had a history of such "talents" in their home country.

Present-day Lebanon is the location that answers to the meaning of "Phoenicia" in classical references. The mountains of modern-day Lebanon extend some 110 miles [175 km] from north to south, with many of its western foothills reaching the Mediterranean. The Lebanon range presents a monolithic facade to the Mediterranean coast with no natural passes (other than difficult gorges) to the interior. Travel inland went over—not through: a day's journey in either direction consisted of a long, laborious ascent followed by a lengthy but somewhat less arduous descent. Such topography of the land makes it inaccessible to travel from the Mediterranean shore towards the east. As a consequence, the destiny of the inhabitants of Phoenicia was linked with the sea, because of how cramped they may have felt on land with its formidable mountain barriers and impenetrable torrential rivers. The sea with its wide expanse was their only way to make a living.

As in Greece, a country devoid of great plains and traversed by steep mountain chains and deep gorges of torrential streams, the natural resources of Phoenicia were limited.

Phoenicia's main natural resource was lumber. Byblos became the center of a lumber trade, where vast quantities of cedar and pine trees were felled in the adjacent Lebanon hills, rolled or carted down to Byblos, and from there towed in rafts to Egypt. The destiny of the Phoenicians was thus tied to the demands of lumber by Egypt.

The Egyptian-Phoenician Connection

The tenure of Byblos in a sort of alliance was necessary, because Egypt, which was one of the largest timber-consuming countries of antiquity, lacked timber that was essential for her buildings, her boats, her furniture and fuel, and especially her funerary equipment. Alabaster vases bearing the names of most of the Egyptian kings of the 3rd–6th Dynasties (2649–2152 BCE)—but especially those of Pepi I and Pepi II of the 6th Dynasty—were found in large quantities at Byblos during excavations, or by chance discovery. A large number of these vases are at the National Museum in Beirut and a smaller number may be seen at the Louvre Museum and the Archaeological Museum of the American University of Beirut. Furthermore, the Palermo Stone states that 40 vessels loaded with fir trees arrived in Egypt during the reign of Snefru (2575-2551 BCE), or as early as 2800 BCE, during the reign of Khasekhem, the last king of the 2nd Dynasty. However, the relationship between the two countries may go back beyond that date, as we may see in the allegory of **Auset** (Isis) and **Ausar** (Osiris), where the coffin of the dead **Ausar** flowed to Byblos, where **Auset** went to bring his body back to Egypt. [Read a summary of this allegory in chapter 2.]

The need for timber supplies explains, at least in part, the importance of the permanent settlement—a kind of protectorate—which the Egyptians had at Byblos, in the middle of the Phoenician coast, from the earliest days of the Old Kingdom (c. 2575 BCE). The kings of Byblos were invested with such Egyptian titles as "prince", "count", or "sheikh of sheikhs". Their precise political standing in relation to Egypt is unknown, but they were probably vassal kings or high commissioners controlling a local population subject to Egypt.

Byblos was dependent on the Egyptian economy. During the anarchy that prevailed in Egypt under the 7th–10th Dynasties (2150–2040 BCE), contact with Byblos seems to have been disrupted, and Byblos lay in ruins at the time.

During the Middle Kingdom, whose central period was that of the 12th Dynasty (1991–1783 BCE), Egypt revitalized its relations with the Phoenician coast and principally with Byblos. The relationship with Egypt was especially close. Royal tombs built into the cliffs on the shore of Byblos have been found with their treasures intact, and objects from rifled tombs have found their way to museums in Paris and Beirut. Among the intact tombs are those of Abi-shemu (*Abi-is-my-father*) and his son Ypshemu-abi (*my-father's-name-is-good*), contemporaries of Pharaohs Amenemhet III and IV (1844–1787 BCE). An obsidian ointment jar bearing the cartouche of Amenemhet III was found in Abi-shemu's tomb and a gift box of incense from Amenemhet IV in the tomb of his son; while golden pectorals, other pieces of jewelry and ornamented jars had been sent to unnamed kings.

Phoenicia exported timber to Egypt in exchange for Egyptian-made alabaster vases, pottery, furniture, and many other goods. The Egyptian origin of the Phoenician tomb findings include golden regalia, an Egyptian diadem, a **Heru** (Horus)-hawk collar and a scimitar-shaped scepter, a **Tet**

(Djed) pillar—symbol of renewed kingship; a **waz** scepter bearing the Phoenician ruler's name in inlaid Egyptian hieroglyphs; an **ankh** sign—symbolizing life; and the cobra (uraeus)—symbolizing royalty.

During the early New Kingdom era (c. 1575 BCE), Phoenicia enjoyed a period of prosperity under the Pharaohs who succeeded Tuthomosis III: Amenhotep II, Tuthomosis IV, and the early part of the reign of Amenhotep III (c. 1400 BCE).

Egypt fulfilled its alliance obligations by providing all means to protect its allies in Asia. The letters of Tell el Amarna convey the stress and strain of the times and the anxiety of the various correspondents. When the Hittites invaded the Egyptian allies in Asia, Seti I (1333–1304 BCE) took the field against the Hittites and was able to recover Phoenicia and Palestine. His successor Ramses II (1304–1237 BCE) carried on a long struggle with the Hittites as well, which ended in a treaty whereby Egypt retained Phoenicia and Palestine, and Hatti maintained its sovereignty over the Amorites of the hinterland and Naharin. Shafatbaal and Ahiram were contemporary kings of Byblos and welcomed the return of the Egyptians to their country. Ahiram, a contemporary of Ramses II, was buried in a stone sarcophagus carved with motifs strongly reminiscent of Egyptian art.

The Egyptianized Phoenicians

The livelihood of the Phoenicians was totally dependent on Ancient Egypt, and the Egyptian goods are found prominently in Phoenician tombs. It should not be a surprise to find that the Phoenicians were Egyptianized in all aspects of their existence. Temples, tombs, artifacts, religion, language, system of government, etc., were all Ancient Egyptian.

The Egyptian temple at Byblos, evidently the seat of the Egyptian governor, where the kings of Egypt had offerings made in their name, is a significant indication of this special relationship. According to the finds yielded by excavations in the Egyptian temple at Byblos, the duration of that temple and of the occupation to which it bears witness extended from the Old Kingdom (2575–2150 BCE) throughout the Middle and New Kingdoms (2040–1070 BCE). Many Egyptian scarabs of the Middle Kingdom [i.e. the period of the 12th Dynasty, and the period immediately following] have been found among the deposits in the temple. A remarkable royal monument has also been recovered—a great bas-relief depicting the Prince of Byblos, before the legend of a Pharaoh of the period following the 12th Dynasty, with all these names and particulars in Egyptian hieroglyphics.

In art, sculpture, and architecture, the Phoenicians copied the Egyptian style. However, the execution is far inferior to that of Egypt.

All "names" of deities that are arbitrarily described as *Phoenicians* by uninformed writers, are all Ancient Egyptian deities—as listed and explained in chapter 6.

Earlier settlements in Carthage shares the same Egyptianized objects (faience and jewelry in particular) that are found in the earlier grave material in Phoenicia.

With such a total and complete dependence on Egypt in all aspects of its existence, how can anyone expect Phoenicians but to speak and write the Egyptian language? Egyptian inscriptions are found everywhere and in all periods throughout Phoenicia.

Western academic linguists try to bypass Ancient Egypt

as the most prominent literate (among other things) civilization in the ancient world. In order to ignore Ancient Egypt, they invented the story of "Phoenician" mine workers in the Egyptian Sinai Peninsula as the first inventors of the consonantal alphabet.

In 1906 in Sinai, Egyptologist William Flinders Petrie discovered a stele with hieroglyphic inscriptions, and ten tablets of rock, inscribed with 30 characters that are basically cursive forms of Ancient Egypt hieroglyphs, which were arbitrarily labeled as *proto-Sinaitic* inscriptions. [More about the various forms and styles of writing later in chapter 12.]

Because similar looking inscriptions (to the inscription found in Sinai) were found in Phoenicia at a later date, Western academia made a big and unsubstantiated assumption that these inscriptions found in Sinai (of earlier times) must then be Phoenician! In order to establish a Phoenician presence in the Egyptian Sinai, they fabricated a story based entirely on a "by default" premise, i.e. because Phoenician texts are similar to Sinai texts, the Phoenicians must have been in Sinai working the mines. In other words, western academicians have fabricated history based on pre-conceived notions, with no evidence to support their claims.

It is a total fabrication to assume that Phoenicians worked the mines in the Egyptian Sinai. Then add another assumption to the first baseless assumption—that those miners (who were not literate people), after working the mines all day, were able to "invent" the consonantal alphabet during their "after-hours spare time"! Shamelessly, Western academia reported that proto-Sinaitic inscriptions were found to be derived from the Ancient Egyptian hieroglyphics. In other words, from beginning to end this is the Ancient Egyptian consonantal alphabet, which is based on the acrophonic principle whereby each letter is derived from the initial sound of each pictorial hieroglyph. (As an example, the letter *a* resembles an ox head, which in Ancient Egyptian is *aḥ*.)

All the evidence from fragmented and diverse sources in Sinai, Moab, etc, show the Ancient Egyptian pictorial hieroglyphs as the basis for the consonantal alphabet known later as *abgd*. A complete and accurate list is shown on pages 186-7, which shows the Ancient Egyptian script as the basis for the "proto-Sinaitic", "Moabi", and other scripts throughout the Mediterranean Basin.

The Seafaring Phoenician/Carthaginians

During the first millennium BCE, the Ancient Egyptians began to employ Phoenicians as sailors on the Egyptian ships. This move was probably prompted by the rise of the Assyrians' power in the region. Records in Iberia show that the Phoenician traders made their appearance not before the 7th or 8th century BCE.

When the Phoenicians began overseas sailing (as per Herodotus), they were working for the Egyptians and not independently. Herodotus (500 BCE) reported [4-229] that the Ancient Egyptians during King Necho's rule (c. 610–594 BCE) commissioned the Phoenicians to sail Egyptian ships around Africa:

> *As for Libya [the Greek name for the African continent], we know that it is washed on all sides by the sea except where it joins Asia, as was first demonstrated, so far as our knowledge goes, by the Egyptian king Neco, who, after calling off the construction of the canal between the Nile and the Arabian [presently Suez] gulf, **sent out a fleet manned by a Phoenician crew with orders to sail round and return to Egypt and the Mediterranean by way of the Pillars of Heracles**. The Phoenicians sailed from the Red Sea into the southern ocean, and every autumn put in where they were on the Libyan coast, sowed a patch of ground, and waited for next year's harvest. Then, having got in their grain, they put to sea again, and after*

*two full years **rounded the Pillars of Heracles** in the course of the third, and returned to Egypt.*

The role of the Phoenicians (and Carthaginians) in the history of Iberia has been exaggerated. The Phoenicians were basically sailors who transported goods between the different countries. Their home was the sea, as they traveled between the different harbors. Their presence at Iberian harbors does not mean that they built these harbors. It only means that they transported goods to and from such harbors, and just like any salesperson, did not have anything to do with the manufacturing of the goods that they were selling.

It is assumed by most writers—without any evidence whatsoever—that any ship found off the Iberian coast is "Phoenician", so much so that "Phoenician" is an attached adjective to the word "ship" in history books written about Iberia. Yet there is no archeological evidence or any historical evidence of shipbuilding by the Phoenicians.

During the 1st millennium BCE, there was an increase in trade between Sub-Sahara Africa and the Mediterranean Basin. This led to the flourishing of activity along the North African coast. This is commonly misunderstood by war-minded writers as the rise of the Carthaginian "Empire", "colonies", etc. These so-called "colonies" were nothing more than small coastal stations, which provided the frequent harborage necessary to a coastal carrying trade.

It is advertised that Carthage was founded soon after 814 BCE by fugitives from Tyre and Sidon, at the beginning of the Assyrian expansion. There is no evidence to support this "common theory". Carthage existed long before 814 BCE. There was an increase in activities in Carthage, mostly because of the new markets in sub-Sahara Africa.

Maríe Cruz Fernández Castro, in her book, *Iberia in Pre-*

history [1995, page 239], sums up the careless and arbitrary history writing on this subject,

> *The Carthaginian role in Iberia is probably a good example of the academic obstacles that one faces when bringing together information provided by Greek geographers and Roman historians - which is not always accurately dated or precise, and which is seldom impartial - and the meager and often vague archaeological data. Regrettably, historians - both Ancient and modern - have faced enormous problems in making sense of all the available quotations.*

The (Non-) Phoenician Iberian Colonies

Many writers about the history of Iberia are very careless in using the term "Phoenician" as an adjective to words such as *settlement* and *ship*, in every sentence, without any supporting evidence. The arbitrary basis for attributing a settlement to "Phoenicia/Punic" is only based on the characteristics/style of items of "oriental nature/origin" found in tombs. Their arbitrary accreditation gets worse, when after making the tomb "Phoenician", the whole settlement automatically becomes "Phoenician".

Early writers confused the sailors with the passengers of the ships. Strabo [3.5.8], citing earlier sources from the 1st century BCE, calls the people from Cádiz, *Phoenicians*; the people living along what is today the Costa del Sol were sometimes referred to as *Blastophoenicians* or *Libyophoenicians*. Strabo has never visited Iberia and his account of "Phoenicians" for the new settlers is vague.

Maríe Cruz Fernández Castro, in her book, *Iberia in Prehistory* [1995, page 191], dismisses the Phoenician colonization theory,

> *For a long time scholars were unable to contradict the Ancient written sources, and accepted the Ancient texts as being reliable. To reach, exploit and export silver from the region of Tartessus was said to be the primary objective of the Phoenician colonists. In other words,* ***Phoenician 'colonization' was basically regarded as a matter of trading perfume, textiles, jewelry and small commodities for metal ore, ostensibly for the benefit of both parties - Phoenicians and natives****. . . .* ***The term 'colonies' no longer sounds totally convincing****.*

It was by the provision of markets (rather than in exploitation) that the Phoenicians made their living at these numerous (mostly small) trading places/stations. The Greek word, *emporia* (markets), used in many of the ancient records, gives us the true sense of these small localities. We must envision small settlements of at most a few hundred people, at places to which native tribes brought their goods to trade, which could serve as anchorages and watering places. The most favored sites were those that always appealed to the seafarers—offshore islands, headlands, and estuaries. In no case can any Phoenician penetration of the hinterland for commercial purposes be demonstrated.

The Phoenician seafarers transferred people and goods. They did not, however, transfer themselves or abandon their livelihood as seafarers by building settlements. Phoenicians did not have any experience in building settlements, farming, industry, etc. They never built colonies, and didn't even have the number of people necessary to populate Iberia.

The archeological evidence—as will unfold in the upcoming chapters—shows that the majority of settlers in Iberia during the 1st millennium BCE and CE came from Egypt, to rejoin earlier Egyptian settlers or to build new settlements.

8

Canopus and Cádiz: A Tale of Two Harbors

The Gitano Dancers of Cádiz

Early Roman historians were impressed by the music and dance of the people at Cádiz.

The (Egyptian) Romany have populated the areas of Cádiz, Jerez, and Sevilla (and beyond), since ancient times. Federico Garcia Lorca, in a 1933 interview, stated,

> *From Jerez to Cadiz, ten (Egipciano) Gitana extended families of absolutely pure blood are guarding the glorious tradition of flamenco.*

Ancient Egyptian flamenco dancer

The (Egyptian) Romany have always been connected with music and dance. The Egyptian origin of the Romany of Hispania was noted by Voltaire, who could easily see the figurative relationship between the ancient dancers at Cádiz and the modern (Egyptian) Romany of Hispania. In his *Essai sur les moeurs*, Voltaire maintained that the *Romany (of Hispania) were the descendants of the priests and priestesses of* ***Auset*** *(Isis), whose castanets and tambourines derived directly from antiquity.* [Vaux de Foletier pgs. 25 and 238]. Richard Ford [1845] was totally convinced that the dances of antiquity and those of the (Egyptian) Romany of Hispania were virtually identical.

Ancient Egyptian dancers [15th cent. BCE]

From time immemorial, dance has been considered a religious activity, as numerous Ancient Egyptian works illustrate. Ecstatic dancing formed an integral part of the rites of **Auset** (Isis) and **Ausar** (Osiris). The Ancient Egyptian goddess of song and dance was **Het-Heru** (Hathor), known also as Aphrodite (Venus). [More about the Egyptian-Hispanic musical heritage in chapter 14.]

Egyptian Fishing Techniques at Cádiz

The bluefin tuna fishery off the Atlantic coast of Spain near the Straits of Herakles (Gibraltar) extends far into ancient times. At some undetermined time, early fishermen began to work together to catch the giant fish in an organized fashion. The method for trapping these migrating bluefins as they enter the Mediterranean—known since ancient times as the ***almadraba*** (meaning *clapping*)—has remained virtually identical since that time.

The technique of clap-net fishing, commonly known as ***almadraba***, is arbitrarily credited to the non-fishing Berbers and Arabs, because the word ***almadraba*** has an "Arabic" sound and meaning. Yet there is no history of fishing (or this technique) with said desert dwellers. Once it is recognized that the Arabic language is an offshoot of the Ancient Egyptian language [see chapter 12 re. *Languages*], the real origin of the word ***almadraba*** will be recognized as Ancient Egyptian. Furthermore, this technique was (and continues to be) used in Egypt, since time immemorial.

The ***almadraba*** fishing technique was used to catch the torpedo-shaped bluefins as they swarmed through the Straits of Herakles on their annual spawning run. During the full moon of May, the heaviest concentrations entered the region of the Pillars of Hercules/Herakles.

At Cádiz, the tuna came in closer to shore and were netted by encircling them with the boats. The fishermen clap the net to confuse the fish into a state of frenzy—so as to trap them quickly. ***Almadraba*** refers to the act of clapping the net and gaffing the fighting big fish. The tuna were directed by blocking nets into a series of chambers. Once the fish were in the final chamber, this "death chamber" could be hauled up by the circle of boats above, bringing the "bottom," as it were, to the surface where the tuna could be gaffed in the same old fashion.

These fishing techniques at Cádiz are identical to Ancient Egyptian fishing practices, as depicted on the walls of Egyptian temples and tombs. Large-scale fishing consisted of well-coordinated efforts of several people, who joined forces and used a seine-net (a large net with cork floats along the top edge and weights along the bottom edge). The net was weighted with lead [an example of these lead weights are presently housed at the Berlin Museum].

The Ancient Egyptian fishermen also fished with the bow-net or with the drag-net. We see how the latter is set upright in the water (common in modern times), with corks fastened on the upper edge and lead weights on the lower edge. Seven or eight fishermen then drag it through the water to the land, or onto boats.

Tuna became famous in antiquity because the process of preserving the flesh by curing it with salt allowed the fish to be transported to areas beyond the immediate coastline. The Egyptian salted fish was popular and well known in the ancient world.

The Many (Egyptian) Names of Cádiz

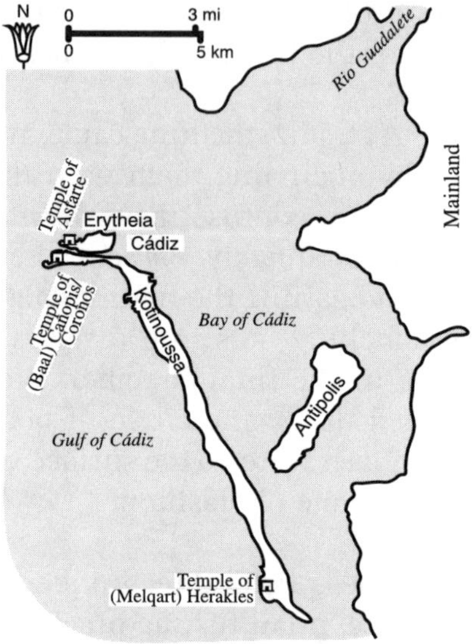

Approximate Locations of Islands and Temples of Ancient Cádiz

The modern city of Cádiz is a long peninsula that faces the Bay of Cádiz on its northern coastline and the ocean on its southern seafront. The chain barrier of three islands of ancient times has become a long strip of terra firma. It is almost possible to reconstruct the outlines of Erytheia and Kotinoussa. The precise location of the third island of the group—Antipolis—remains unexplored, but it is generally identified with the present zone of San Fernando. Even the contemporary isle of San Fernando (or the island of Leon) has gradually merged with the Cádiz peninsula.

The place is known in ancient writings by several "names". There is *Gadir* or *Aggadir*. To the Greeks the place was known as *Gadeira*. The Romans referred to it as *Gades*. The "Arabs" called it *Qadis*. This word in "Arabic" means, *the holy (ground)*, which will reinforce the evidence that *Qadis* is Egyptian-named, as explained below.

All these "names" are basically correct and can only be explained as Egyptian terms.

Gadira (in Egyptian) means an *island*, which because of its long length, acts as a barrier, i.e. an *agadir*—meaning *a fortified place* that acts against the waves of the open sea and thus provides calm water for the enclosed deep water harbor.

The place became *Qadis/Cádiz*, meaning *holy/sacred*, because of the temples present on such island(s). The Ancient Egyptians have called many places *Cádiz*—as holy sites, because of the presence of sacred shrines/temples. Adolf Erman, in *Life in Ancient Egypt* [1971, page 279], explains this Ancient Egyptian concept,

> *We cannot conceive an Egyptian god without his house, the "House of God" in which he lives, in which his festivals are solemnized, and which he never leaves except on processional days.* ***The site on which it is built is generally holy ground****, i.e. a spot on which, since the memory of man, an older sanctuary of the god had stood.*

Linguistically and theologically, the various "names" for Cádiz are tied to Ancient Egypt.

The Immortal Hercules: The Egyptian Lord of Travel

One finds several ways to spell the name, Herakles/Hercules/Horakles, who is considered in some regards as a god/god-like man. In either/both case(s), he is purely Ancient Egyptian (not Greek), as acknowledged by classical Greek writers, such as the testimony of the Greek historian Herodotus, in his *Book 2* [102], where he states emphatically,

> ***It was not the Egyptians who took the name Heracles from the Greeks. The opposite is true: it was the Greeks who took it from the Egyptians*** *– those Greeks, I mean, who gave the name to the son of Amphitryon. There is plenty of evidence to prove the truth of this, in particular the fact that* ***both parents of Heracles – Amphitryon and Alcmene – were of Egyptian origin****.*

Herodotus [in *563, 30*] explains further,

In the Iliad Heracles is referred to as the son of Zues (XIX. 98ff), and the son of Amphitryon (V. 392). Amphitryon and Alcmene were descendants of ***Perseus and thus Egyptian****.*

Herodotus, once again in *Book 2* [102], states,

. . . ***the Egyptians have had a god named Heracles from time immemorial****. They say that 17,000 years before the reign of Amasis the 12 gods were produced from the 8; and of the 12 they hold Heracles to be one.*

Diodorus, *I,* [23-24, 1-8], also confirms how Herakles is Egyptian, and that it was he who set up the pillars [23,8—24,1-8],

The Greeks appropriate to themselves the most renowned of both Egyptian heroes and gods, and so also the colonies sent out by them*. [Diodorus I. 23. 8]*

24. ***Heracles, for instance, was by birth an Egyptian****, who by virtue of his manly vigour* ***visited a large part of the inhabited world and set up his pillars at the end of Libya*** *(meaning the African continent); [The Pillars of Heracles are described in Book 4. 18. 4-7.] . . . . .*

Herakles is recognized as the chief **neter** (god) of the ancient capital of the 20th Upper Egyptian nome (province), and as such this Egyptian region acquired the classical name *Herakleopolis Magna*. He is recognized there in his role as the *initiate god* who achieved immortality—as Harsaphes / **Herishef** /Harsaphis. The temples in Herakleopolis Magna date to the earliest history of Ancient Egypt, and they were continued in use throughout the Pharaonic Era.

As an initiate patron, Herakles serves as a model for the mortal human beings who desire immortality, through hard labor. This transformation from mortality to immortality is well described in Diodorus, I, [2, 3-5]:

> *. . .; and while in the case of those who in their lifetime have done nothing worthy of note, everything which has pertained to them in life also perishes when their bodies die, yet in the ease of those who by their virtue have achieved fame, their deeds are remembered for evermore, since they are heralded abroad by history's voice most divine.*
>
> *Now it is an excellent thing, methinks, as all men of understanding must agree, to **receive in exchange for mortal labours an immortal fame**. In the case of **Heracles**, for instance, it is generally agreed that during the whole time which he spent among men he submitted to great and continuous labours and perils willingly, in order that he might confer benefits upon the race of men and thereby **gain immortality**; and likewise in the ease of other great and good men, some have attained to heroic honours and others to honours equal to the divine, and all have been thought to be worthy of great praise, since history immortalizes their achievements.*

Herakles, through the tales of his adventurous twelve tasks, became the paradigm of the intrepid traveler, and is prominently found at travel stations, promontories, islands, and ports. Pausanias stated clearly that the statue of Herakles, which was found *in the god's temple in Erytheia at Cádiz came from Egypt on a wooden raft.*

In addition to the famed Herakleopolis Magna, there were many other worship centers in Egypt for Herakles. An example is the vast Ancient Egyptian town of Herakleion (east of present-day Alexandria) with its impressive ancient temple of Herakles—as a testament to the role of Herakles as patron of travel.

The town of Herakleion with its temple of Herakles sits at the crossroads between Europe, Africa, and Asia. Likewise, Cádiz with its Herakles temple sits as the western gateway to Europe, Africa, and beyond.

The Greater Canopus Harbor (Alexandria before Alexander) - Maiden of the Seas

The present-day metropolitan city of Alexandria was called Canopus in ancient times, even long after Alexander's death in 323 BCE. The Canopus region is very extensive and old, and extended for about 18 mi [30 km] from the Canopus mouth at its eastern end, to the Pharos harbors at its western end. It was an already established multi-harbor region with several fabulous temples, long before Alexander's arrival. Numerous ancient texts speak of the importance of the region and its constituent quarters/towns, even prior to the Greek historian Herodotus.

The huge site of the Greater Canopus region included several quarters (towns), several deepwater harbors, navigable canals to bypass the rough seas and the Nile siltation at the mouth of the Canopic Delta branch, freshwater supply from the Nile's canals, as well as numerous temples for Herakles and the Ancient Egyptian bull-god (**neter**) **Apis**.

The most westerly Delta branch—the Canopic branch (one of seven branches of the Nile Delta)—was historically the most important branch. Herodotus entered Egypt through this gate in 450 BCE, but when Strabo came to Egypt in 24 BCE, he came to Canopus via the Pharos harbor. Herodotus, the father of history, described the ancient city of Herakleion, with its magnificent temple of Herakles, at the mouth of the Canopus Branch. Strabo noted the geographic location of the towns within the Greater Canopus Harbor region.

The Ancient Egyptian monuments of the Greater Canopus region were ravaged by the early Christians, and the Arab nomads finished the ugly job in the 7th century. A lack of maintenance of the shorelines allowed the sea waves to destroy the ancient sites. The ruins of the great monuments can now be revealed through underwater archeology.

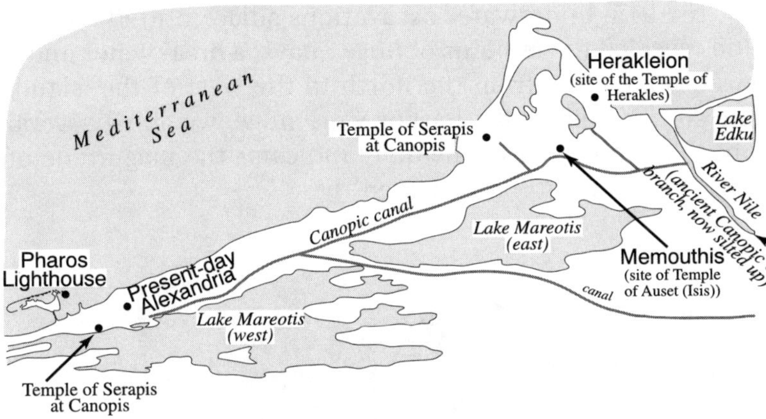

Layout of the Greater Canopus Region During the Pharaonic Era

The city of Herakleion, which got its name from its magnificent temple of Herakles, was a very important economic center. In the water near the Herakleion area, archeologists found huge buildings and heads of Pharaonic statues of kings about 13 ft [4m] high, as well as the remains of hundreds of granite pillars from temples.

The City of Menouthis is located about 2.5 miles [4 km] from Herakleion. It was connected with the worship of the **neter** (god) **Serapis** and the **netert** (goddess) **Auset** (Isis). An area of about 550 x 765 yds [500m x 700m] was found of the city of Menouthis underwater, which shows destroyed pillars, sphinxes and statues, heads of kings and **neteru** (gods). Some of the statues are up to 13ft [4m] high, and the sphinx statues represent kings of several Pharaonic Periods.

At the western end of the Greater Canopus area is the deepwater harbor of Pharos, created by a rocky island, less than a mile [1.6 km] long. The fame of this harbor was mentioned in Homer's *Iliad*, along with its renowned Lighthouse—one of the seven wonders of the ancient world.

In 1915, underwater excavations adjacent to Pharos Island revealed the remains of huge quays, a breakwater and a harbor extending from the north to the west of the island. The stones used in the harbor were huge, weighing several tons. The huge size of the quay indicates the magnitude of maritime trade at Pharos Island.

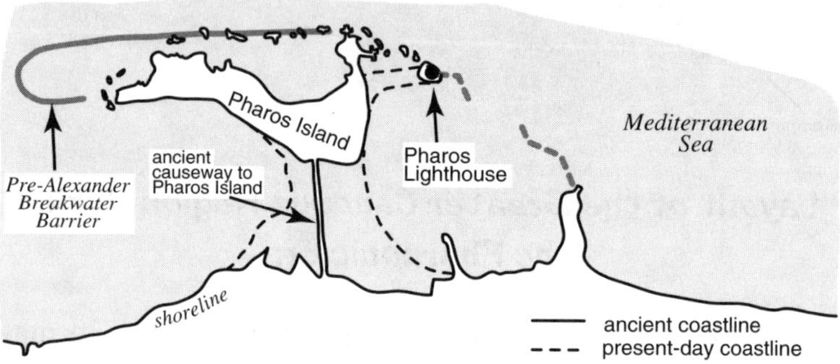

The harbor by the island of Pharos was mentioned in the *Odyssey*. It served as the last port of call before entering Egypt through the Canopic mouth of the Nile about 18 miles [30 km] from Pharos. According to Herodotus, all vessels had to enter Egypt through the Canopic branch, where customs dues were collected.

There is no historical evidence to support the notion that during Alexander's era, a causeway connecting the island of Pharos with the coast near Rhakotis was established. All indications are that the causeway existed *before* the arrival of Alexander, and that it was regularly maintained and widened. This tongue of land divided the water body south of Pharos Island into two capacious water bodies.

To the south of the city, Lake Mareotis, which itself had a harbor on its northern shore, was linked by canals to the Canopic branch of the Nile Delta, giving access to the river valley and beyond.

The Ancient Egyptian city of **Ameria/Almeria** (now called the village of Hawara) lies on the southern shore of Lake Mareotis, about 20 miles [32 km] south of Canopus (ancient Alexandria). The regional governate that includes this ancient city still maintains its Ancient Egyptian name—**Ameria/Almeria**, which means *harbor*. The name of Lake Mareotis (derived from the Ancient Egyptian word, **Mer**, for *water body*) dates to time immemorial in Ancient Egypt.

The magnificent harbors of the Canopus region accommodated an immense volume of maritime trade with the Mediterranean world and also made Canopus an important center of the shipbuilding industry. The resulting influx of wealth (both public and private) into the Greater Canopus region was enormous. Throughout the history of the ancient world, Canopus (ancient Alexandria) remained the most important commercial city of the Mediterranean world. The strategic location of Canopus allowed access, not only to the Mediterranean Basin, but also to the Nile Valley, which was also connected to commerce in the east via the Red Sea. The significance of Canopus is well described in the encomium of Dio of Prusa (Dio Chrysostom),

> *Not only have you a* ***monopoly of the shipping of the entire Mediterranean because of the beauty of your harbours****, the magnitude of your fleet, and the abundance and marketing of the products of every land, but also the outer waters that lie beyond are in your grasp, both the Red Sea and the Indian Ocean... The result is that the trade, not merely of islands, ports, a few straits and isthmuses, but of practically the whole world is yours.* ***For Canopus is situated, as it were, at the crossroads of the whole world****, of even its most remote nations, as if it were a market serving a single city, bringing together all men into one place, displaying them to one another and, as far as possible, making them of the same race.*

Canopus without a doubt has earned the title of *Maiden of the Seas*—at *"the crossroads of the whole world"*.

The Foundation of Cádiz

Ancient Cádiz was similar in many ways to the deepwater multi-harbors of Canopus in Egypt. Cádiz was also located at a major crossroad, providing access to Africa, northern Europe, and beyond. Cádiz carries an Egyptian name(s), and is occupied since time immemorial by the tan-skinned Romany—the descendants of the Ancient Egyptians.

Cádiz was, in the eyes of ancient authors—especially the Romans—one of the most important cities in the western Mediterranean, because of its strategic location in the sea lanes.

The foundation of Cádiz is arbitrarily attributed—contrary to archeological evidence—to the Phoenicians. Maríe Cruz Fernández Castro, in *Iberia in Prehistory* [1995, page 179], shows how "Phoenician" biases are in conflict with archeological evidence,

> ***Traditionally, therefore, the foundation of Gades is considered to have taken place at around 1100 BC***. *This date accords well with the* ***mythical affinity*** *between Gades and Tartessus,* ***but so far it has defied archaeological investigation. . . . "Phoenician" Gades does not make any impact on Spanish archaeology before the eighth century BC***.

The evidence shows an active Cádiz thousands of years before the Phoenicians sailed the Mediterranean Sea in the 8th century BCE. People of Cádiz have traded up the Atlantic coast as far as islands off the coast of Brittany, or at any rate Galicia; and they knew Britain and Ireland. The maritime communities were linked in a complex of exchange networks probably stretching back in time at least to the Neolithic period, along the "tin route", which provided the tin needed to make bronze [as discussed in chapter 4 of this book]. In other words, Cádiz was built before the Phoenicians became seafarers for hire, in the 8th century BCE.

Strabo, who never visited Iberia, reported in *Geography* [3,5,5], that Cádiz was "founded" after three trials. The first attempt was without success—to found the city in Sexi (Almunecar), and then subsequently in Onuba (Huelva). It was only on the third expedition that the site of Cádiz was eventually established. Strabo tells us of how the Phoenicians were ordered to carry out this investigation near the Pillars of Herakles.

Since the accounts in *Geography* [3,5,5] contradict the archeological evidence, it is possible that Strabo may have tangled historical account of two different expeditions to Cádiz, from two different eras—the first expedition when the three trials occurred (which happened in much earlier times—but not involving Phoenicians), and a second one that occurred in the 8th century by the Phoenician sailors on another assignment.

That the Ancient Egyptians went as far as the Pillars of Herakles/Hercules, in the very early pre-historic times, has been documented and shown in previous chapters. The Egyptian influence reached far beyond the Mediterranean Basin. Herodotus (500 BCE) reported that the Ancient Egyptian King Necho (c. 610–594 BCE) commissioned the Phoenicians to sail Egyptian ships around Africa:

> *. . .the Egyptian king Neco. . .* ***sent out a fleet manned by a Phoenician crew with orders to sail round and return to Egypt and the Mediterranean by way of the Pillars of Heracles****. [Histories, 4-229]*

The account of Herodotus shows that the Ancient Egyptians knew the geography of Africa and its surrounding waters, and they planned the expedition and their fleet accordingly. In other words, it was not an adventure into the unknown. There was specific work for the Phoenician sailors to do. It is in this context that we should recognize the role of the Phoenicians as sailors for hire. The mission of their investigation was directed by someone else—the Egyptians.

Even if Cádiz was "founded" or more possibly expanded—during the 8th century BCE or later, we should recognize their role along the same theme—that the Phoenicians were sent to investigate a specific operation at Cádiz, on behalf of someone else. Strabo never stated that the Phoenicians made this journey to Cádiz on their own will. It is therefore a wrong assumption to call Cádiz a "Phoenician" city, and by extension to assume that its temples must have been "Phoenician".

Additionally, after all the dust settles, regarding the assertive and repetitive statements of "Phoenician this", "Carthaginians that", the archeological facts don't support such arbitrary assertions. The facts actually point to Ancient Egypt. The design and layout of these two deepwater harbors at Cádiz and Pharos (Alexandria before Alexander) are very much alike—each has a protective island barrier, is near a freshwater supply, has several significant temples, and has a famed lighthouse. Strabo, in his *Geography* [3. I. 9-2, I], tells us about the look-alike Egyptian and Spanish lighthouses,

> *Then immediately comes **the outlet of the Baetis, which has a twofold division**; and the island that is enclosed by the two mouths has a coastal boundary of one hundred stadia, or, as some say, still more than that. **Hereabouts is the oracle of Menestheus**; and also **the tower of Caepio, which is situated upon a rock that is washed on all sides by the waves, and, like the Pharos tower*** [see 1. 2. 23 and 17. 1. 9], ***is a marvelous structure**. . . . .*

The Lost Temples of Cádiz

The Egyptian naming of Cádiz recognizes the holiness of its location because of its famed ancient temples. Just like the Greater Canopus area that included Pharos (Alexandria before Alexander), Cádiz also had several renowned temples that were lost due to neglect, water erosion, and human destruction.

Some academicians overcompensate—for absence of evidence—by making and repeating assertive statements using the words, *Phoenician*, *Tyrian*, or *Punic* as adjectives when referring to temples/gods. Academic writers use what appears to be "Phoenician"-sounding names of gods/goddesses—to change the identity of an Egyptian temple to a "Phoenician" one. The temples of Cádiz, contrary to archeological evidence, are described as "Phoenician"! Yet as we reviewed the evidence in chapters 6 and 7 of this book, temples in Phoenicia are Ancient Egyptian, and all names of deities that are described as "Phoenician" are all Ancient Egyptian deities. We have also shown how the real names of deities were kept secret and each deity was called with words bearing religious connotation, such as *Melqart* meaning *king/lord*, *Baal* meaning *lord/ruler*, etc. As such, Herakles-Milqart simply means *Herakles, the Lord of the City*. The word *Milqart/Melqart* does not make Herakles a "Phoenician" or "Tyrian" deity, no matter how Herakles or Milqart are spelled.

The recovered archeological artifacts from the seabed, near the headland of Sancti Petri, give a strong indication of the actual location of the temple of Heracles/Herakles/Hercules, at the southeast corner of the main (and largest) island of Kotinoussa. The found artifacts, close to the presumed locations of the temples do not corroborate the dates given by the Roman authors. On the other hand, we have direct evidence regarding the Egyptian origin of Cádiz' Herakles temple from Pausanias, who recorded the Egyptian origin of the statue of Herakles, which came on a wooden raft (from Egypt) and was found in the temple in Erytheia.

Additional evidence points to Ancient Egypt as the builder and keeper of Cádiz' holy sites. One cannot perceive a temple as just a "monument", but as a living shrine that must be maintained by specific rituals. All the evidence points to Ancient Egyptian priests in charge of temple rituals. It

has been reported that Hannibal visited the famous temple of Hercules/ Herakles to consult with the *"bald, linen-clad priests"* just before his famous elephant-march on Italy. Only Egyptian priests were body and head-shaven, and wore linen clothes. Hannibal's account also concurs with the description of the temple priests by Silius Italicus, as being *"dressed in long linen robes, had shaven heads, and went barefoot".* [*Silius Italicus, 3.24-8*] He added that the priesthood was hierarchical, with a high priest at its head, which is the case in the Ancient Egyptian temples. According to Strabo [*Geography, 3.5.7*], there was a spring that allowed ritual ablutions to be performed in the court of the temple. Pliny gives a slightly different account, saying that the spring was near the temple rather than located within its grounds. In any event, this water basin constitutes the sacred lake (which was always a constituent element in the Ancient Egyptian temple complex), which was used for the purification of the priests performing the temple rituals.

The other famed temple in Cádiz is dedicated to **Het-Heru** (Hathor) in her aspect as the seafarer **netert** (goddess) **Astarte** [the Egyptian origin of **Astarte** is referred to in chapter 6]. Terracotta offerings—an incense burner, lamps and other items—have been recovered from the ocean floor near the sea cliffs of Punta del Nao, on which the Temple of **Astarte** is thought to have stood. These are possibly the surviving ex-voti dedicated to this ***Notre Dame de La Mer***—*Our (Holy) Mother of the Sea*—the **netert** (goddess) to whom sailors were particularly devoted.

9

The Assyrian Devastation and Aftershocks

The Assyrian Assaults

The archeological evidence in the Iberian Peninsula testifies to sudden and major demographic changes in the peninsula, which began in the 8th century BCE. Such a major immigration wave coincides with the rise of the Assyrian's power and their devastation of the most populated country in the region—Egypt.

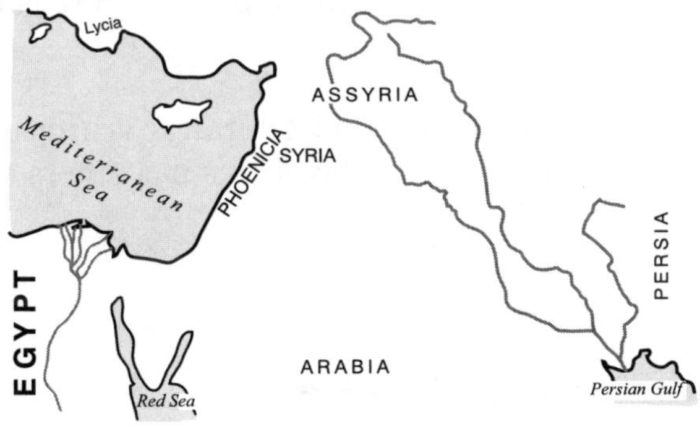

The Assyrian conflict with Egypt began when Phoenicia was invaded by the Assyrians, during the early centuries of the 1st millenium BCE. To counter the Assyrian aggression against Phoenicia and neighboring territories, King Shabaka (716–

701 BCE) led an army (made mostly of African mercenaries) and marched toward Palestine and Syria. The campaigns were at first fought with varying success in Syria, but eventually the Assyrians overcame Shabaka's army and regained their dominance in Asia Minor. This victory inspired the Assyrians to march into Egypt and conquer the country as far as **Ta-Apet** (Thebes). Twice the Assyrians were forced to retreat, but they again succeeded in re-entering the country, and in the year 662 BCE, Egypt became an Assyrian province. In 654 BCE, the Egyptian Psammatichus, from Sais, with the help of Greek mercenaries, succeeded in driving the Assyrians out of Egypt.

With their land being the major battleground between these foreign forces, massive Egyptian depopulation occurred during this period—the 8th and 7th centuries, which coincided with sudden demographic changes in Iberia. Turdetanian culture, like that of Etruria, experienced a rapid phase of "orientalization", most readily apparent in the high quality of goods found in the graves of the 8th and 7th centuries. The increase in people and wealth in the new places changed the dynamics of commerce in the Mediterranean Basin. The 8th century saw a consolidation of the sea routes, via Tunisia (Carthage), western Sicily, and Sardinia—to southern Andalusia and Cádiz, and a dramatic intensification of trade with the west.

The haphazard and arbitrary writings about Carthage were discussed in the last two subchapters of chapter 7.

The Egyptian Exodus

The early settlements in Iberia during the 3rd and 2nd millennium BCE were discussed in chapter 5 of this book. A second major wave of immigration to Iberia occurred during the 8th and 7th centuries BCE—with new societies created in Carthage and in the Iberian Peninsula. These new settlements were reported to be self-sufficient. There was an abundance of agricultural and maritime resources. These newer immigrants were able to settle peacefully among (and close to) the existing population, i.e. in all probability, they knew the existing population and shared with them the same roots, beliefs, and traditions.

The sudden demographic increases in population that began as a result of the Assyrian assaults were accompanied by an increase in the general wealth, peace and prosperity in Iberia, with a similar arrival and prominence of the "mysterious" Etruscans to Italy. The sudden increase in number of settlements throughout the western Mediterranean during the 8th and 7th centuries could never have taken place, without the newcomers having knowledge and experience in agriculture (dry-weather farming), mining, metalworking, city planning, governmental infrastructure, . . . etc, as well as the wealth and capital needed to start projects and sustain them until they become fruitful for the society.

The descriptions of these new settlers, their system, lifestyle, social structure, etc, points to the Ancient Egyptians as the main source of this sudden demographic increase. Naturally, new immigrants settle in areas where they know existing residents, i.e. both the existing population and newcomers came from the same country. Also, newcomers choose areas with similar geographic and weather conditions as their homelands. Once again, these qualifications can only fit with immigrants from Ancient Egypt, who met with earlier settlers in the same environment—dry weather, plains for farming, close to mining sites, etc.

The newer settlement sites established good communication links with the fertile upper Guadalquivir valley from the end of the 8th century BCE to the 6th century BCE, and most settlements had their own necropolis. During the 7th–

6th centuries BCE, there were major improvements in building, housing, and defense techniques. The newcomers carried on Ancient Egyptian funerary burial practices, ceremonies, symbols, and rituals. There is evidence of the typical Egyptian orderly social stratification in these communities.

In other words, the newcomers were experienced in all aspects of civilization and implemented their knowledge promptly. The Egyptians, and nobody else, meet all these important factors required to establish the new societies. Egypt was the most populous, civilized, and wealthiest country in the area.

The claim that it was a Phoenician/Carthaginian immigration/settlement is totally discredited [as explained in chapter 7, under *The (Non-) Phoenician Iberian Colonies*].

Turdetania Urbanization

The geographical boundaries of Turdetania are approximately defined by the course of the river Guadiana (Anas) in the north and by the stretch of coastline between the mouth of this river and the Pillars of Hercules in the southwest.

The urbanization in Turdetania, which we read about extensively in the ancient sources, is a long and discontinuous process that began to be noticeable at the end of the 7th century BCE or early in the 6th century BCE. The available data (geographical, archeological and historical) from the southern region and the upper Guadalquivir Valley (the campinas of Córdoba and Jaén) point to an increase in civic and domestic building programs after the end of the 6th century BCE, which continued for two centuries. In the southwest, it took longer for towns—that is, settlements that are distinct from the countryside, with a considerable number of dwellings and inhabitants—to develop.

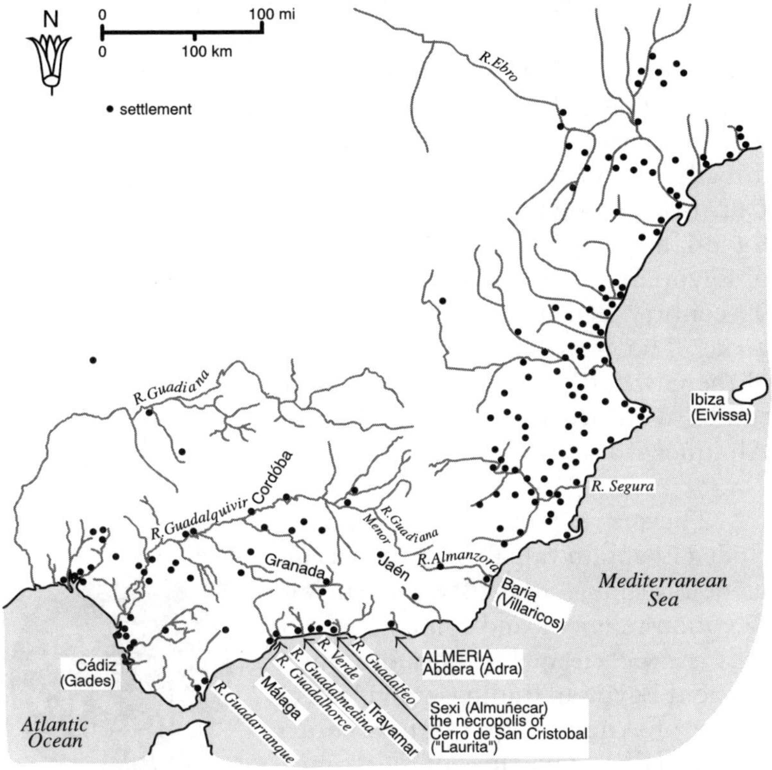

Map showing the sites discussed in this text

The southeastern coastline of Spain, from eastern Cádiz to Almeria, has a series of settlements located on headlands, bays, peninsulas or islands, which spread from the river Guadarranque to the river Almanzora. Settlements in the plain were clearly agricultural. The early settlements were established on the coast of Málaga and Granada (from the river Guadalhorce to the river Verde in Almuñécar). Occasionally, the abandonment of a site was followed by the foundation of a new, neighboring settlement. In renowned cities, such as Málaga, Abdera, Baria and the island of Ibiza (*Eivissa*), the population seems to have settled at the end of the 7th century BCE or very early in the 6th century BCE.

It is most unfortunate that the academicians who reviewed and have possession of the archeological findings don't provide illustrations of such findings—and instead describe them as "eastern", "oriental", and other vague terms. The little evidence that is shown in their publications points directly to Ancient Egypt. As an example, the tombs of the Laurita necropolis (700–625 BCE) were found to contain rich Egyptian gravegoods. The Laurita tombs held alabaster urns of Egyptian provenance—three of them with inscriptions of 9th century BCE kings—jewelry, and other less significant goods. The graves leave us in no doubt about the character of the new settlers, or about their wealth. Twenty well-type tombs were uncovered in El Cerro de San Cristobal in Almunecar (Sexi).

The gravegoods at Trayamar included Egyptian valuables such as a gold medallion [from tomb 4], with Ancient Egyptian religious and symbolic meanings [shown herein]. Furthermore, these Ancient Egyptian findings provided evidence of Ancient Egyptian funerary rituals (libations, use of perfumes, wakes, and so on) which, from this point forward, would become an integral aspect of the Iberian culture. The tombs of Trayamar required competent architects, who built the same types of Ancient Egyptian tombs.

In addition to specific Ancient Egyptian findings, the conclusion from the sum of all the findings points to highly civilized, organized, peaceful, and wealthy immigrants, who were able to implement immediate improvements in agricultural techniques, the establishment of a commercial network, the building of houses and streets on a much grander scale, and the introduction of civic ceremonies and religious rituals. All the evidence points to Egypt as the only source of these sudden changes.

The Persian Rampage of Egypt

Archeological evidence in Iberia indicates another wave of immigration, which coincided with another destructive foreign force—the Persians—on the land of Egypt. The Persians invaded Egypt several times:

- The Persians, under Cambyses (525–522 BCE), invaded and occupied Egypt in 525 BCE. They rampaged through Egypt, pillaging and destroying everything destructible, even killing the **Apis** bull. In Egyptian eyes this was the most heinous crime of all. Egypt became a Persian province; several rebellions were cruelly suppressed; and the country was entirely ruined. The Persians were eventually expelled from Egypt in 404 BCE.

- The Persians came back to Egypt in 343 BCE. The Egyptians sought outside help and in 323 BCE, Alexander and his Macedonian soldiers expelled the Persians again out of Egypt.

- The Persians came back during the Byzantines rule in 616 CE and withdrew out of Egypt in 628 CE.

The Persian rampage of Egypt and subsequent depopulation coincides with the rise of activities in Iberian sites such as the settlement of Baria, in close proximity to the Malaga coast. Louis Siret and his foreman Pedro Flores worked in the necropolis of Villaricos for about 40 years (c. 1893–1931), with the result that they unearthed more than 2000 graves, across several hills in the vicinity. The discovered graves show that the new settlers share general characteristics with Ancient Egyptian funerary beliefs and rituals. They uncovered Ancient Egyptian altars dedicated to the **netert** (goddess) **Het-Heru** (Hathor/**Astarte**), stelae, figurines depicting the Egyptian **neter** (god) **Bes**, painted eggshells, amulets and jewels.

Baria was a very productive place, and in this sense it was an authentic colony. Apart from the metal ores in the Sierra Almagrera and the Sierra de Herrerias (copper, silver, lead, gold and large quantifies of iron), the region was provided with salt and fish to produce *garum*, murex mollusks to use in *purpura* dyeing, esparto grass needed to make ropes, wood required to build vessels, and so on. Baria was also well situated to export the minerals and other goods, and it enjoyed fairly easy access to the grain resources of the upper Guadalquivir valley.

The community in Baria can be traced back as far as the 6th century BCE [zone Q of the necropolis]. However, as is the case in Cádiz and in Eivissa, it was during the 4th century BCE that Baria reached its highest level of activity. There is an upper mound in Villaricos, a citadel that Siret called an 'acropolis', in which two defensive ditches were apparently unearthed on the most exposed sides. Cisterns and industrial premises have also been recorded in the city of Baria, There is no indication of friction between the pre-existing population and the newcomers. The community at Baria survived up to the Roman conquest in 209 CE.

Once again, we find the unique aspects of the Ancient Egyptian civilization being duplicated in the new and expanded societies in the Iberian Peninsula. As soon as more illustrations and descriptions of the found goods are released by academicians and museum keepers, the Ancient Egyptian origin of most of these goods will become even clearer.

10

Romanticizing the Romans

Romanticizing the Romans

It is the "sacred duty" of Western writers to elevate the status of the Romans in the history of the world. The Western pride is dependent on the prominence of the Romans. The role of the Romans has been totally exaggerated in the history of Iberia. Yet a closer look at the Romans' accreditation in Iberia (and elsewhere) will prove that the (Roman)—as in Hans Christian Anderson's Fairy Tales—Emperor has no clothes. All the claims about Roman temples and Roman goods are totally false and contrary to the evidence, as will unfold in this chapter.

Western academia portrays the invaders of Iberia (and other places) such as the Romans and Moors, as the bringers of light and a new civilization to the people they conquer. Since the "victorious" invaders had/have the *might*, they granted themselves the *right* to write historical events in their favor. The fact remains that the invaders actually came to profit and to dominate, not to "civilize". The writings of Ibn Khaldun—himself a proud warrior—testifies to the nature of the warrior and how it is contrary to the nature of civilization. [More about Ibn Khaldun's writings in the next chapter.]

The Romans had only one interest, which was to enrich

themselves by enslaving other people to exact tribute (taxes). Iberia (or parts of it) was already prosperous before the Romans went there (to profit not to civilize). Classical writers from this era confirm the civilized pre-Roman Iberia, as follows:

Strabo, in *Geography,* [3, 2, 3], stated:
The Baetis ***has a large population along its shores****, and is navigable for approximately one thousand two hundred stadia from the sea up to Corduba and the regions a little higher up. Furthermore, the land along the river, and the little islands in the river, are* ***exceedingly well cultivated****.*

Strabo, in *Geography,* [3, 2, 4], stated:
The whole country is navigable and convenient both for exporting and importing merchandise.

Strabo, in *Geography,* [3, 1, 6], wrote,
The Turdetanians are ranked as the wisest of the Iberians; and they make use of an alphabet, and ***possess records of their ancient history, poems, and laws written in verse that are six thousand years old, as they assert.***

Strabo, in *Geography* [3, 2, 8], wrote,
. . . . . as for Turdetania and the territory adjoining it, there is no worthy word of praise left to him who wishes to praise their excellence in this respect. Up to the present moment, in fact, neither gold, nor silver, nor yet copper, nor iron, has been / found anywhere in the world, in a natural state, either in such quantity or of such good quality.

The Fictional Romanization of Iberia

It has been said and repeated that Iberia was totally Romanized under the Roman rule. Yet, the archeological and historical evidence shows that the so-called "Iberian Romanization" is total fiction. Iberia was already developed and cultured, before the arrival of the Roman soldiers. The relationship of rulers to the people, the division of the land, mining, fishing, farming, class structure, religion, law, trading and commerce, art—practically every facet of Iberian life, was already in existence and well developed—before the Romans arrived.

William E. Mierse, in his book, *Temples and Towns in Roman Iberia: The Social and Architectural Dynamics of Sanctuary Designs from the Third Century B.C. to the Third Century A.D.* [1999, page 1], stated,

> *There was no specific Republican policy toward the newly acquired territory. The land and its people were open to exploitation by those with power. At the same time, **there was little attempt to force or even encourage a particular type of Romanization, at least one that can be recognized in the archaeological record**. **As long as the local communities remained passive, they were free to continue in their traditional manner and build as they saw fit**.*

The absence of Roman "influence" on the Iberian societies is best described by A.T. Fear, in his book *Rome and Baetica: Urbanization in Southern Spain c.50 BC—AD 150* [1996, page 267], as follows:

> *Practically all forms of native organization have survived during and after the Roman Era. This phenomenon has existed in many modern colonial societies where the **upper classes, while adopting the customs of the colonial power to try to gain access to the ruling group**, are still linked by traditional ties to the rest of their society. This hypothesis of an Iberian 'countryside' in Baetica is strengthened by the fact that Iberian-style grain silos were used throughout the Roman period, and **various measurements of land were known by Iberian terms**. Varro records that land-measurement in the area was recorded by the iugum, rather than the Roman iugerum, in his day, and writing at the end of antiquity Isidore tells us that the non-Roman terms 'arapennis' and 'porea' were given to areas 120 x 120 feet and 830 × 830 feet respectively. The fact that Isidore is familiar with such vocabulary suggests that it was in*

use throughout the Roman period.

Regarding the absence of any Roman cultural influence on Iberian societies, Fear states [on page 249 in the same book],

> *From the above survey a variety of conclusions can be drawn. The first is that there appears to have been no strategy to enforce changes in cultural behavior towards a standard norm by the governing power. A converse conclusion can also be drawn—namely that* ***provincial groups perceived no reason to abandon wholesale their own cultural practices in favor of those of Rome****.* ***Roman titles were perceived by the local population as simply seen as the continuation of older offices under new Latin titles****.*

Fear states [on page 256 of the same book],

> *Settlements retained many native features. Although the town magistrates were* ***referred to in Roman terms, native nomenclature also persisted****. There seems to have been no pressure by Rome to change this style of life.*

Fear comments on Strabo's claim of Romanization, [on page 250 of the same book],

> *Strabo stated that the Iberians of Turdetania, especially those living by the Baetis, had become completely Romanized and had forgotten their own language.* ***Strabo never visited Spain, and is drawing on earlier sources*** *(although some of these, as has been seen above on his discussion of the population of Gades, appear to be contemporary, adding yet another problem to the equation). If he is correct, native culture should already have almost vanished by the beginning of the imperial period.* ***The passage contrasts oddly, however, with Strabo's comment of only two chapters previously****, that the majority of towns in Turdetania were* ***inhabited by Phoenicians****. [Strabo 3.2.13]*

The last sentence above, regarding *"Phoenician inhabitants"*, is also without foundation or logic, just like his claim about *"Romanization"*.

Fear sums up his findings [on page 269], regarding the fictional Romanization of Iberia,

> ***<u>Therefore, the view that there was a conscious attempt to change native cultural practices by Rome appears to be incorrect</u>.***

From the above, it is shown that a detailed study of the facts show that there was no influence of the Romans on the Iberian Peninsula. There is no evidence of Roman mass migration to Iberia in the Roman Empire history. A logical conclusion should follow that the Romans did not influence the language(s)/dialects in Iberia. Yet some make assertions contrary to logic and facts. Their unfounded claims are guided by sacred duty to elevate the status of the Romans by assertion and not by evidence, logic, or rationale.

Retracing the origin of the "Latin" language—if there was such a thing—is beyond the scope of this book. However, it will suffice to follow the table on pages 186-7, to find the Ancient Egyptian origin of "Classical Latin alphabets".

The (Non-) Roman Temples and Tombs

As shown in chapter 3, the Ancient Egyptian religion, deities, and practices spread into Italy. During Roman times, the religious practices in the Iberian Peninsula were quite evident. The Roman Avienus, writing around 400 CE, tells of still seeing the yearly rites of Hercules performed there—an allusion to the famous temple near Cádiz. All over Baetica, there existed shrines and temples to Ancient Egyptian divinities (advertised as "eastern deities"), including among many others the Egyptian **Auset** (Isis).

A.T. Fear, in his book, *Rome and Baetica: Urbanization in Southern Spain c.50 BC—AD 150* [1996, pgs 188-9], stated,

> ***There is not any epigraphic evidence or otherwise to support the notion that any temple in Iberia was built by the Romans****, or that any is, we cannot be sure that the temples were of a "Roman form". The motivation for their erection is totally unknown in a Roman setting.*

Regarding the capricious and arbitrary accreditation of temples to the Romans, William E. Mierse, in his book *Temples and Towns in Roman Iberia: The Social and Architectural Dynamics of Sanctuary Designs from the Third Century B.C. to the Third Century A.D.* [1999, page 70], exposes an example of such an intentional falsehood:

> *The name "Temple of Diana" (at Augusta Emerita) was first applied to the ruins in the second forum in the 17th century, without any justification.*

Mierse further gives a more general statement [page 121] about the intentional attempt to "Romanize" temples in the Iberian Peninsula,

> *None of the peninsular temples discussed in this section has a dedication, and so none has a known cult.* ***Attempts have been made to assign an Imperial Cult dedication*** *to the temples at Barcino, Ebora, and Augusta Emerita.*

Lacking any archeological or historical evidence, academicians start making straws, so that they can grasp them. They give a Latin/Roman name to a certain artistic design/style of a temple, column, glassware, mosaic, ...etc., even though that same design was used in Ancient Egypt thousands of years earlier. Any item that appears to resemble this particular design is then automatically credited to the Romans, and as a result we keep reading of "Roman" temples, "Roman" mosaics, etc, with no supporting archeological/historical evidence whatsoever. To compound the wrong assertion that something is Roman, based on a style, we find the authors have given arbitrary dates (Roman Era) based on their arbitrary premise of the origin of such a finding.

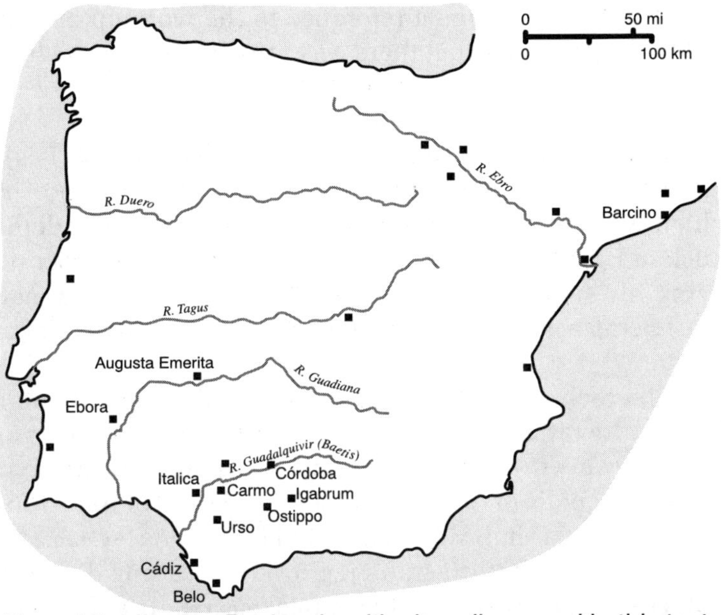

Map of the Iberian Peninsula with sites discussed in this text

The facts remain: that these temples in the Iberian Peninsula existed before the Romans; and that the Phoenicians never built temples in their homeland; and that the deities worshipped/depicted at these temples are all Ancient Egyptian, disguised in apparent non-Egyptian "names".

Whenever there is a reference in the ancient writings to temple priests, they are always described as head-shaven and wearing a linen outfit—which is only applicable to Ancient Egyptian priests. [More details about testimonials of early historians of the practices, rituals, and traditions of the Egyptian priesthood at temples outside Egypt proper are described in chapter 8.]

In the midst of this arbitrary Roman attribution, we find evidence that the temples are Ancient Egyptian. At Belo, we find a definite Egyptian temple, identified by inscriptions found *in situ* as a temple of **Auset** (Isis). Another small shrine to **Auset** (Isis) has recently been uncovered in Italica, built into a porticoed square behind the theater. An inscription from Igabrum contains a reference to the worship of **Auset** (Isis). This indicates that there was a further temple or shrine, in some form, to the Egyptian **Auset** (Isis) here.

The reverence of the Ancient Egyptian **Auset** (Isis) is distinctly visible in the Ostippo stones. The Ostippo *stele*, which was found in a group along with six others, depicts Ancient Egyptian deities, such as **Heru-p-khart** (Harpocrates) giving his sign of silence, another Ancient Egyptian **neter** (god) **Serapis**, and a third showing the hawk of **Heru** (Horus).

The rock-cut tombs in Spain are reminiscent of similar Ancient Egyptian tombs. Examples are found at Cádiz and Urso. However, the best Egyptian-like examples are found in the necropolis of Carmo. The standard form of tomb found here is that of a shaft with hand- and foot-holds [e.g. tomb 363], or a sloping shaft with stairs [e.g. tomb 50] leading down to a rock-cut chamber. Another example [tomb Q], is entered by a flight of steps, which then opens out into a courtyard. Off this courtyard opens a standard burial chamber. These forms of tombs are typically Ancient Egyptian in conception, having many parallels in Ancient Egypt. Many of the tombs at Carmo have classical-style Ancient Egyptian wall paintings in the funerary chamber, reminiscent of Ancient Egyptian religious and motif context.

It is curious to note that practically all temples and Ancient Egyptian-style tombs in the Iberian Peninsula are found near mining areas—which was a common practice in Ancient Egyptian mining sites. Furthermore, the areas at/near these temples and tombs in the Iberian Peninsula, we find populated by the (Egyptian) Romanys / ***Gitanos / Moriscos / Mudejars / Mozarabs***—the Ancient Egyptian descendants.

11

The Moors and the Egyptians

The Identification of the "Moors" (The Moabi Brothers)

Much is made of the "Arab-Islamic influence" in the Iberian Peninsula through the people described as the "Moors". Unfortunately, most writers did not distinguish between a minority ruthless ruling class and the peaceful civilized majority.

The combined forces of Arab Bedouins and mercenary Berbers were able to invade Hispania, without a great resistance. This relatively small force was extremely lucky. However, these Arab-Berber gangsters were a small minority in a culture that had already been substantially orientalized for over three millennia. Additionally, the vast majority of the non-ruling class of the newcomers to Iberia (under the Moorish rule) were from Egypt, by all historical accounts.

The relatively small number of the ruling class was only interested in subordinating the working people of Hispania, so as to exact tributes. For that, they needed mercenaries and tax collectors. This ruling minority of Arab-Berbers have never done anything but collect money, live lavishly, and fight each other.

This combined alliance of rulers, mercenaries, and tax collectors had a common origin—the Moabi desert region. Diodorus, *Book I,* [28, 1-4], tells of an Egyptian colony at present-day Moab, which is the origin of the Arab and Jews who collaborated to govern Iberia,

> *. . . that the nation of the Colchi in Pontus and* ***that of the Jews, which lies between Arabia and Syria, were founded as colonies by certain emigrants from their country [Egypt]; and this is the reason why it is a long-established institution among these two peoples to circumcise their male children, the custom having been brought over from Egypt****.*

The location mentioned by Diodorus is the vicinity of the Moab. This location of Moab is very important in understanding the identification of the Moorish alliance, and thus the dynamics and history in Iberia. Moab is the origin of the three groups—Arabs (Syrians), Berbers, and Jews—that joined forces to control Moorish Spain.

The Moabi region was also the source of the Arabic, Hebrew, and Aramaic/Syriac dialects, which were offshoots of the Ancient Egypt language. Ibn Hazm (died 1064), the medieval Arabic scholar of Córdoba, recognized that Aramaic/Syriac, Hebrew, and Arabic were kindred dialects, derived from the **Mudar**, the dialect in which the Koran had been disclosed. Later in chapter 12, we will show that **Mudar** is an Ancient Egyptian term meaning *language*, and that all three languages/dialects are offshoots of the Ancient Egyptian language.

The Moorish alliance never forgot their Moabi origin. Christian chronicles sometimes referred to the Almoravids as "Moabites". There are numerous references to "Moabites" in the *Chronica Adephonsi* [e.g. [35], [42], [53], [96], [127]; the references are to paragraphs], and the reference to "Ali" and "Texufinus" (Tashufin) as *kings of the Moabite*s would seem to support the theory that this term refers to Almoravids.

Two of the most powerful Berber tribes during the Moorish rule were the Zanata and Sinhaja. The Jewish background of the Zanata, and possibly also parts of the Sinhaja, was evident when the Sinhaja rulers of Granada installed a Jewish prime minister and commander-in-chief (Ibn Naghrillah), whom they staunchly supported against the armed opposition of their enemies.

The Moabi origin of the Moorish alliance can explain the reason why the name of the last prince of the Banu Marwan family was Abd al-Rahman b. Mucawiya, but "al-Razi" (i.e., his Portuguese translator) gives his name as "Abderrahemen ***filho de Moabia.***"

The conquest of Spain in 711 was entirely by Berber troops of North Africa, led by Berber and Syrian commanders. The Moslem invasion in 711 brought Visigothic rule on the peninsula to an end.

The Nomadic Moorish Rulers

The Arabs and Berbers who served in the ranks of the invading army were nomads (*Arab* means "*nomad*"). Ibn Khaldun—himself a proud nomad—testifies in his writings to the nature of the nomad and how it is contrary to the nature of civilization. Ibn Khaldun was born in 1332, of Spanish Arab descent, in Tunisia. He moved around between Tunis, Spain, Morocco, Algeria, and in 1382 he settled in Egypt where he remained until his death in 1406.

Ibn Khaldun is renowned for his monumental *Universal History* (*Kitab al-Ibar*) in seven volumes, the first volume of which constitutes the famous *Introduction to History* (*Muqaddimah* or *Prolegomena*), and on his *Introduction/Foreword*, translated as *Autobiography* (Ta'rif).

Ibn Khaldun admitted in his *Muqaddimah* that the Arab-Berbers alliance had nothing to do with the civilization aspects in Iberia. The following points were made by Ibn Khaldun, with each point of reference in his book:

1. Nomads are superior to civilized (sedentary) people. In other words, as far as a nomadic concern, being civilized (sedentary) and peaceful is inferior to being an un-sedentary nomad. [chapter 2, section 15]

2. Learning and perfecting all types of crafts requires a long time that takes several generations and requires teaching. [chapter 5, section 15]

3. The crafts are firmly rooted in a city only when sedentary culture is firmly rooted and of long duration. [chapter 5, section 17]

4. The Arabs are not good in crafts, because they are not sedentary people and because they are more firmly rooted in desert life. [chapter 5, section 20]

5. The Berbers—like the Arabs—are not good in crafts for the same reasons given above. [chapter 5, section 20]

6. The necessary crafts of a civilization include agriculture, architecture, arts, manufacturing and industries, medicine, the art of writing, book production, music, ...etc. [chapter 5, section 22]

Both the Arabs and the Berbers were made up of a number of hostile tribes or clans, many of whom had been engaged in deadly blood-feuds for several generations, and all of whom were moved by a spirit of tribal jealousy which was never entirely extinguished. The Arabs and Berbers in Iberia were totally preoccupied with their own self preservation. Their history in Iberia is a series of fights and conflicts—mostly among each other.

During the first 50 years of Moorish rule, governors were appointed, deposed, or murdered, in deference to the mandates of some faction, which resented the government being entrusted to a man of the Medina faction, or would not have a clansman of Kays, or objected to the nomination of a member of the Yemen party, and on and on.

The years between the departure of Musa b. Nusayr in 714 and the installation of Balj b. Bishr al-Qushayri as governor in 741 was a period of infighting within the Arab rulers. It is a period of great confusion: governors succeeded each other with bewildering speed and only one ('Anbasa b. Su .haym al-Kalbi, 721–26) lasted for more than a year or two.

In the autumn of 741 the Berbers overcame the Arab rulers and drove them out of vast areas. The Berbers marched south towards Córdoba, and Ibn Qatan found himself unable to resist them effectively.

In the spring of 742, the Syrians were helped to cross into Andalusia. The battle-hardened Syrians defeated the Berbers in Spain and regained Arab control. After their victory, the two Arab factions turned against each other. The Syrians had the upper hand. The Syrians remained in possession of Córdoba, and chose a new governor from their own ranks, who defeated the opposition (composed of both Arabs and Berbers). Many Arabs of distinguished lineage were sold cheaply as slaves.

The Arab-dominated Umayyad dynasty at Damascus was overthrown in 756 by the Abbasids, who moved the caliphate to Baghdad. One Umayyad prince fled to Spain and, under the name of Abd al Rahman (r. 756–88), founded a politically independent amirate, which was then the farthest extremity of the Islamic world. His dynasty lasted for 250 years. Spain became the haven for those escaping the Abbasids—such as the Egyptians.

In 929, Abd al Rahman III (r. 912–61), elevated the amirate to the status of a caliphate (the Caliphate of Córdoba). This action cut Spain's ties with Baghdad and established that thereafter Andalusia's rulers would enjoy complete religious and political sovereignty.

Soon thereafter, they began fighting each other again. Rival claimants to the throne—local aristocrats, and army commanders who staked out taifas, or independent regional city-states—tore the caliphate apart. Some taifas, such as Seville, Granada, Valencia, and Zaragoza, became strong amirates, but all faced frequent political upheavals, war among themselves, and long-term accommodations to emerging Christian states.

These truly "petty" Moslem kingdoms engaged in constant warfare with each other, frequently employing Christian mercenaries against their Moslem neighbors, preaching jihads against each other. However, "religious purity" was not their aim. Their only intention was to increase their influence and collect more exactions (taxes).

Weakened by their disunity, the 11th century taifas fell piecemeal to the Castilians. When Toledo was lost in 1085, the alarmed amirs appealed for aid to the Almoravids, a militant Berber party, who in a few years had won control of the Maghreb (northwest Africa). The Almoravids conquered all of Andalusia, except Zaragoza. Officially their mission was jihad, but in reality it was plunder.

The Almoravid state fell apart by the mid-12th century under pressure from another Islamic group—the Almohads—who extended their control from Morocco to Spain and made Seville their capital. Their expansion was stopped decisively in the epic battle of Las Navas de Tolosa (1212), a watershed in the history of the Reconquest. Moslem strength ebbed thereafter, and the Reconquest proceeded in earnest towards total victory, in a few centuries.

The Civilized Populace

While the loud war-like minority rulers get credit for the civilization, the true builders were the immigrants who settled, built quietly, and paid off exactions to the Moorish rulers to keep them at bay.

The people far away from the Middle East (such as in the Iberian Peninsula) may describe everybody coming from North Africa as "Arabs". The people from the Middle East who "converted" to Islam were arbitrarily called "Arabs". The Egyptians are not Arabs. The official language in Egypt now is "Arabic". But that doesn't make the Egyptians "Arabs". In other words, the "official spoken" language does not change the ethnicity of the people.

The records of Arab historians, such as Ibn 'Idhari, reported a "considerable influx" of immigrants to Iberia, the majority of which came from Egypt. This is confirmed by the evidence of the suddenness in the appearance of excellent works in all areas of society, such as art, literature, science, mathematics, astronomy, botany, philosophy and jurisprudence. The practical work of the field, the scientific methods of irrigation, the arts of fortification and shipbuilding, the highest and most elaborate products of the loom, the graver and the hammer, the potter's wheel and the mason's trowel, were brought to perfection by the newcomers. Such suddenness in performance excellence can only be caused by qualified, knowledgeable and experienced people—the Egyptians.

The historical records show that the vast majority of the newcomers to Iberia during the Moorish rule came from Egypt. The Egyptians saw their country collapsing under Islamic rule—the Umayyads of Damascus (661–749 CE) and the Abbasids of Baghdad (749–868 CE). Most of Egypt's great agricultural wealth was channeled into the coffers of the central treasury of Damascus and Baghdad.

The records of Arab historians refer to the new immigrants to Iberia by the Arabic term, *Jund*—which comes from the verb *Janad/Ganad*, which means *to draft/assign for duty*, which could be civilian or military. The careful review of the Arab records reveals that the term, *Jund*, applied to both military and civilians. The account we have, in a report from Ahmad al-Razi (d. 955), explains that the Syrian *jundis*, whose names were recorded in the public records (*diwan*), were divided into two groups—one that went on campaign and the other that stayed at home. Furthermore, the *diwan* indicates that only Yemeni and Syrian (and no Egyptian) commanders were in charge of the fighting forces. The Egyptians throughout their history have never been war-like, and have always employed foreign mercenaries to defend themselves. Egypt is one of the last places on earth to seek fighting soldiers.

The 11th century geography of al-'Udhri included a document describing the taxes paid by villages in the Córdoba area in the early 9th century, which shows that 49.68 % of the revenue came from payment in place of military service. Such a very high percentage shows that non-military *Jund* were required to pay the Syrian rulers of Iberia substantial amounts.

Naturally, people from the same tribal and ethnic backgrounds tend to settle in the same areas where relatives and friends are known, and/or in areas they considered appropriate for their lifestyle (farming, fishing, industries, etc). As such, the new Egyptian immigrants (the largest contingent) went to big cities and cultivatable lands. The newcomers from Egypt settled in areas extending from the Algarve in the west to Tudmir in the east—the lands originally governed by the treaty with the Visigoth Theodemir, as well as Zaragoza and the middle Ebro valley.

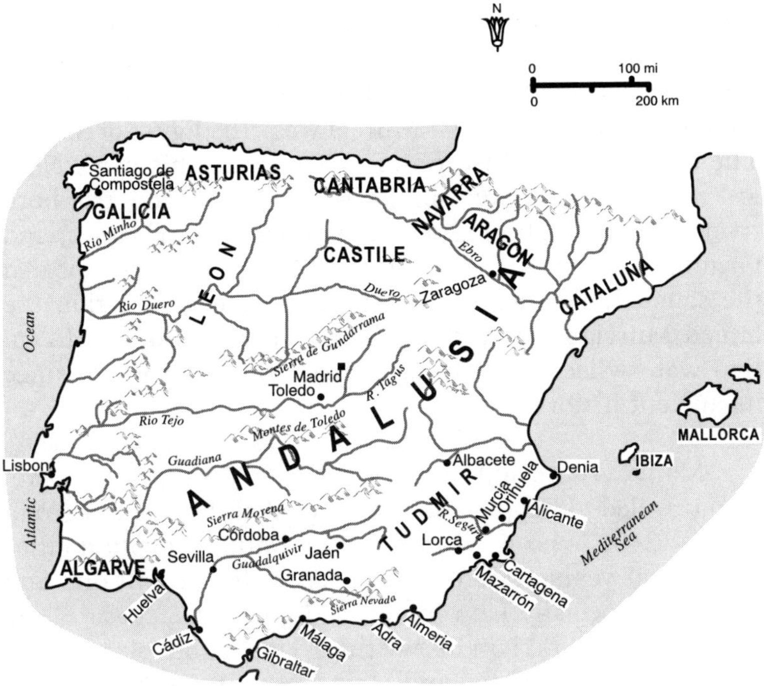

Map showing the sites discussed in this text

The arrival of the Egyptians, in the 9th century, began a period of intense economic height. A detailed description of the Egyptian impacts, as a result of this largest contingent of immigrants, is beyond the scope of this book. An example of such impact on Tudmir will be mentioned here briefly. The relationship between Egypt and the region of Tudmir (present-day Murcia, Alicante, and southern Valencia) is deep and very old. The name of the Murcian city ***Mazarrón***

(Massarrun) means *Little Egypt*, which was an important mining site in ancient times. The newest Egyptian immigrants in the 9th century controlled the course of the Segura River, to create a complex irrigation network of drains, pipes, waterwheels, and aqueducts. During the Middle Ages, some Arab writers declared that Murcia was "the Egypt of Spain". The great Algerian historian Al-Maqqari, in his work *Nafh al-Tib*, listed numerous similarities in the behavior of both rivers of Egypt (Nile) and Murcia (Segura), irrigation, and farming techniques. Other authors, like Al-Himyari, repeated the same similarities with Al-Maqqari and added that the famed Murcian waterwheels were duplicates of the Egyptian waterwheels, which have been utilized in Egypt since its ancient history.

Many writers and intellectuals from the old Tudmir region traveled to Egypt. The most famed of these is Ibn Arabi (1165–1240), who lived in Cairo and other Egyptian cities for several years, where he learned of Sufi traditions and teachers, especially Dhu-'I-Nun El Massri. [More about him in chapter 13.] Ibn Arabi, in his writings, lauded the role of Egypt as the source of Sufism, and Dhu-'I-Nun, the Egyptian. Ibn Arabi brought back the typical Egyptian strophic poetry to Iberia. [More about poetry in chapter 14.]

The vocabulary in the Tudmir region has more "Arabic-sounding" words than any other region in Iberia. In the next chapter, we will show the Egyptian origin of the "Arabic" language and words.

The excellent farmers in the dry weather farming regions of Iberia, and the superior artisans described as ***Moriscos*** and ***Mudejars***—all came from Egypt. In chapter 1 of this book, we have shown the affinity between the ***Egipcianos***, being called Romany, ***Moriscos***, ***Mudejars***, and ***Mozarabs***. In all these (and other) well-farmed areas throughout the Iberian Peninsula, we always meet these tan/brown-skinned people.

The Egyptian Green Revolution

It has been claimed without any evidence or rationale that the Moorish ruling caste of Berbers-Arabs—whose homes were the deserts—were the harbingers of the so-called *green revolution* in Iberia. Such credit must go to the people responsible for farming, irrigation, and drainage techniques and practices. The ruling class of Berber-Arabs was only interested in collecting money from the working classes. These rulers collected money for their own pleasure and never for the construction of infrastructure for public benefit.

The present-day area of Murcia, Alicante, and southern Valencia is called *Europe's Orchard*. This green haven is the product of Egyptian working hands. The Egyptian immigrant farmers grew every conceivable kind of vegetable and fruit known today, such as rice, olives, guavas, vines (grapes), cauliflower, sugarcane, sugar beets, citrus fruits, corn, cucumbers, cotton, hard wheat (from which pasta is made), all types of fruit orchard crops such as apples, bananas, pears, peaches, plums, apricots, cherries, figs, nuts, etc.

The variety and abundance of agricultural crops were the result of their efficient and extensive use of irrigation techniques, which were duplicates of the Ancient Egyptian techniques—dry-weather irrigation and farming. Egypt was/is one of the most arid areas in the world. The River Nile in Egypt received 90 % of its water during a 100-day flood period every year, as noted by Herodotus, in *The Histories,* [2, 92], where he states:

> . . . . ***the water begins to rise at the summer solstice, continues to do so for a hundred days, and then falls again at the end of that period, so that it remains low throughout the winter until the summer solstice comes round again in the following year***.

The Ancient Egyptians managed their limited water resources efficiently, and became the best dry-weather agrarians in the world. Diodorus spoke of the efficient Egyptian farming system,

> *. . .being from their infancy brought up to agricultural pursuits, they far excelled the husband-men of other countries, and had become acquainted with the capabilities of the land, the mode of irrigation, the exact season for sowing and reaping, as well as all the most useful secrets connected with the harvest, which they had derived from their ancestors, and had improved by their own experience.*

The available limited water resources in Ancient Egypt were utilized and managed most efficiently. According to Strabo, the Egyptian communal irrigation system was so admirably managed,

> *. . .that art contrived sometimes to supply what nature denied, and, by means of canals and embankments, there was little difference in the quantity of land irrigated, whether the flood was deficient or abundant.*

The Ancient Egyptians made precise observations of the increase of the Nile elevation during the inundation season. Nilometers, for measuring the gradual rise and fall of the Nile, were constructed in various parts of Egypt, and water surface fluctuations were recorded and reported. The elevations at the Nilometers throughout Egypt were all tied to a single common datum. Regulating the flow amounts and duration was controlled by well-learned officials, using sluice gate(s) to control the flow of water to a determined height and duration. Diodorus, in *I.* [19. 5-6], affirms:

> *. . .at flood-time it might not form stagnant pools over the land to its detriment, but that the* ***flood-water might be let upon the countryside****, in a gentle flow as it might be needed,* ***through gates which they [Egyptians] had built****.*

The Ancient Egyptians were not content with providing water only to lowlands, but were able to irrigate those lands that were too far from the river to be directly flooded by it. They were able to reach all the way to the sands of the desert. It was possible to supply these channels with water using ingenious and highly efficient devices. Water was elevated to higher canals in Ancient Egypt by using:

1. The *shadoof*—the common mode of raising water from the Nile or feeding channels for a small quantity of water. It consists basically of a pole and a bucket.

2. The *foot machine* (pump)—mentioned by Philo, which is echoed in Deuteronomy [xi. 40],
   Egypt where thou sowedst thy seed, and wateredst it with thy foot as a garden of herbs.

3. The *hydraulic screw*—Egyptian water pumps were famed worldwide, and were used in the mining activities in Iberia, as per the following testimony of Strabo, *Geography*, [3.2.9]:

   So Poseidonius implies that the energy and industry of the Turdetanian miners is similar, since they cut their shafts aslant and deep, and, as regards ***the streams that meet them in the shafts, oftentimes draw them off with the Egyptian screw****.*

4. The *waterwheel*—known in Egypt and the Iberian Peninsula as *noria*, with its scoops for taking up water from the rivers and feeding it into irrigation canals. The **noria** was introduced to Murcia and other regions of the Iberian Peninsula by the Egyptians. **Noria** is actually an Egyptian (not Arabic) word, which means *water* (**No/Nu**) *wheel* (**Re**/circle), with *ia* as a suffix.

The excellent and productive farming of the Egyptian immigrants both allowed and benefited the development of numerous cities, such as Córdoba. These centers attracted industries, such as textiles, ceramics, glass, metal, leather, etc. There again, they hired qualified craftsmen from Egypt.

The Egyptian Hispanic Arts and Crafts

We repeatedly read of Moorish/Islamic/Arabic artistic designs and crafts. Yet there is no prior history of such achievements in Arabia, North Africa, or elsewhere, except in Egypt. The contention that there is "Islamic art" is an oxymoron. Islam is against art and never called for special buildings of worship (mosques) or specific religious design patterns.

The Moorish rulers in Córdoba and Granada, typical of invaders, usurped existing temples to build vain and lavish palaces. Even the so-called "Great Mosque" in Córdoba is basically a lavish monument. It is too large to be a functional mosque, which requires that the worshippers be able to hear the sermon. With no microphones during the Moorish era, the sound of the sermon cannot be heard in this huge spacious lavish monument.

The so-called "Moorish design patterns", which can generally be categorized as floral, geometric, figurative, or a combination of two or all three, were known in Ancient Egypt. [See such variations in chapter 6, under *Egyptian Goods*.] The simple beauty and harmony of the decorative motifs found in Iberia bear a strong resemblance to motifs in Ancient Egyptian art, and this is understandable if we remember that the caliphs sent to Egypt for sculptors and mosaicists, known later as ***Moriscos*** and ***Mudejars***.

In addition to the examples shown in chapter 6 of this book, here are a few examples of Ancient Egyptian artistic designs as found in their tombs, which should

Plants from the sculptures, from the tomb of Ramses III.

leave no doubt about the Egyptian origin of the artistic design patterns during the Iberian Moorish era.

The numerous findings in the Ancient Egyptian temples and tombs attest to their experience in manufacturing all types of materials, such as stone vessels, ceramic/tile/mosaic, terracotta, faience glazed stones, glass, wood, ivory, metal, etc. It was the Egyptians who were the masons and artisans who were hired by other countries to build similar works in such countries.

As artisans and craftsmen, ***Mudejars*** (the dark/tanned-skinned ***Egipcianos***) were unrivalled, especially in such skilled techniques as decorative plasterwork, marquetry, wood carving and the construction of ornate ceilings and doors from jointed pieces of wood (the so-called '***artesanado***' work), the making of delicate fabrics and above all the manufacture of tiles and ceramics.

In chapter 4 [under subchapter, *The Glazing Alloys*], we have shown the chemical and metallurgical knowledge of the Ancient Egyptians and how their works manifested such knowledge. We find similar talents appearing during the Moorish era. In Hispania, abruptly and all of a sudden, we find extensive and excellent works, such as ceramics, from the 9th and 10th centuries onwards. The sudden change is caused by the arrival of the largest immigrant contingent from Egypt—as detailed earlier.

The experienced Egyptian artisans and craftsmen duplicated their talented achievements in building techniques. The basic structure of the building was to erect bare walls and then to cover them with decoration in the form of glazed tiles. Ancient Egyptians used the same technique. The sudden appearance of blue tiles, with their high glaze and designs in an intense blue on a white ground, which were found during the Moorish era in Valencia and Catalonia, are reminiscent of Sakkara's Southern Chamber's blue tiles, which date to the Egyptian Pharaoh Zoser, more than 4500 years ago. [See chapter 4 for more details.]

The Egyptian Housing and Gardens of Iberia

Housing and gardening are accredited (incredibly!) to the nomadic Berber-Arabs, who have no prior history or knowledge of such, before arriving to Iberia. Once again, all the so-called Moorish/Arabic/Islamic buildings, gardens, styles were only found in Ancient Egypt.

Because of the warm climate, the Egyptians, like the Iberians, lived much in the open air; and the houses were constructed to be cool throughout the summer; currents of refreshing air being made to circulate freely through them by the judicious arrangement of the passages and courts. Corridors, supported on columns, gave access to the different apartments through a succession of shady avenues and areas, with one side open to the air.

It is/was also common for several Egyptian houses to share a common courtyard. The open court located in the center of the Ancient Egyptian house was planted as a garden with palms and other trees, sometimes paved with stone, or containing a few trees, a small tank, or a fountain in its center.

Some roofs were vaulted, especially in the warmer areas of southern Egypt, and built like the rest of the house of crude brick. The Ancient Egyptians utilized arches and vaulted roofs in their buildings, since their earliest history.

The early invention of the brick, by the Ancient Egyptians, led to the invention of the arch; and we find arches in Egypt as far back as the 27th century BCE, in Sakkara.

The ceilings of the Ancient Egyptian buildings were of stucco, richly painted with various devices, tasteful both in their form and the arrangement of the colors; among the oldest of which is the Guilloche, often miss-called the "Tuscan" or "Greek" border.

The Egyptians, like Iberians, love(d) their gardens, which were always found in private, public, and semi-public places. Several papyri are found showing how the Ancient Egyptians prepared landscaping plans around all the types of buildings—from temples to small houses.

In the oldest periods, there were parks and gardens, and Egyptians talked of their shady trees, sweet-smelling plants, and cool tanks. In a document from Pharaoh **Snefru's** time (2575–2551 BCE), we read about the design of a beautiful park and how the landscaper

> **dug a great tank and planted fig-trees and vines. . .In the middle of the garden he made a vineyard, which yielded much wine.**

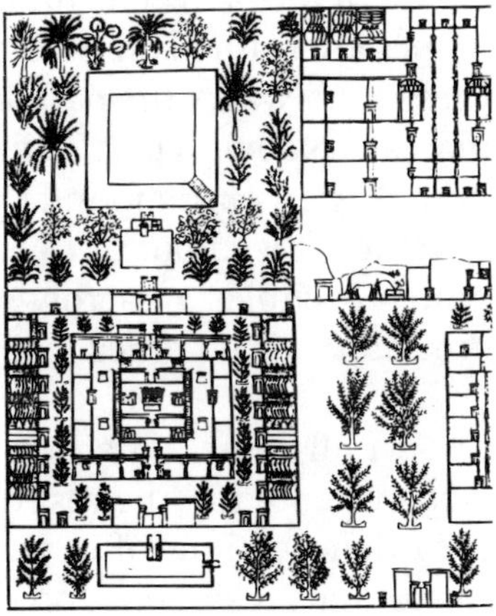

Partial plan of an Ancient Egyptian temple showing the landscaping on the temple proper (Middle Egypt)

Landscaping public places was essential in Ancient Egypt. For example, Ramses III (1194–1163 BCE) planted trees and papyrus plants in **Ta-Apet** (Thebes) [as stated in the Harris Papyrus, i. 7,11], and in the new town which he founded in the Delta he made "**great vineyards; walks shaded by all kinds of sweet fruit trees laden with their fruit; a sacred way, splendid with flowers from all countries, with lotus and papyrus, countless as**

the sand." [as stated in the Harris Papyrus, i. 8,3-4.] It is not a mere saying that flowers from all countries were planted there; for the enjoyment of gardening and of raising flowers had really led to the importation of exotic plants.

Several remarkable pictures from **Ta-Apet** (Theban) tombs of the time of the New Kingdom (1550-1070 BCE) give us further details as to the arrangement of the gardens and country houses, which look practically the same as the ones found in the Iberian Peninsula during the Moorish rule.

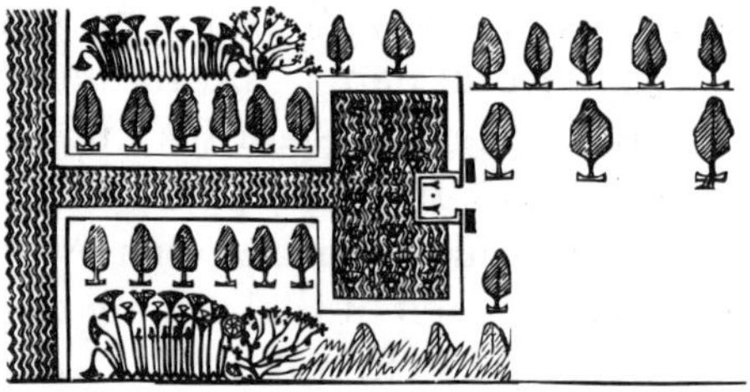

A garden in a villa. (Thebes)

A typical Ancient Egyptian house (as depicted on a found papyrus) had a high castellated wall surrounding the piece of ground. The house is located at the back of the property, surrounded by a double row of palms and high trees. The vineyard is located in the center of the plan. The luxuriant vines with their large purple grapes are trained on trelliswork built up with stone; through these vine-walks the path leads straight up to the house. The plan also shows a part of the garden resembling a small park; here there is a fishpond surrounded by palms and shrubs. Two doors lead out of this garden; one into the palm garden which occupies a narrow strip on either side of the piece of ground, and the other leads to a "cool tank".

In all cases, whether the orchard stood apart from, or was united with, the rest of the garden, it was supplied, like the other portions of it, with abundance of water, preserved in spacious reservoirs, on either side of which stood a row of palms, or an avenue of shady sycamores.

12

The Origin of the Hispanic Languages/Dialects

The Egyptian Source of the Arabic Language

It is generally accepted that the Castilian (Spanish) language contains at least 4000 "Arabic-sounding" words. Other Hispanic languages/dialects, such as in Murcia (the language/dialect of its mostly ***Morisco*** citizens) have many more "Arabic-sounding" words. When the history of the "Arabic" language is studied, it becomes clear that "Arabic" is an offshoot of the Ancient Egyptian language, and that these thousands of apparently "Arabic-sounding" words found in Hispanic languages are of Egyptian and not Arabic or North African Berber origin. The "Arabic" language is an offshoot of the Egyptian language, and not the other way around.

These 4,000 "Arabic-sounding" words are the tip of the iceberg. Upon further examination of many words, taking into account the phenomenon of sound shifts and reversal of letters in words [to be explained later in this chapter], as well as the impact of imposing the "Latin" alphabet to write existing spoken language/dialect after the Reconquest, there will be many more words that can find their origin in Egypt. We have shown throughout this book numerous words in Iberia that are of Ancient Egyptian origin.

It is commonly acknowledged that the spoken language(s)/dialect(s) of the Iberian Peninsula, in the pre-Moorish era, sounded "like Arabic", but not really "Arabic". Egyptian is the only language that sounds "like Arabic", which leads us to the conclusion (on a linguistic basis) that Ancient Egypt is the source of language(s) in the Iberian Peninsula. Instead of facing the fact that the Egyptian language is the source of the "Arabic language", western academia termed the Hispanic dialects erroneously by numerous and vague terms such as "vulgar Arabic", "colloquial Arabic", "Mossarabic", "Hispano-Arabic", "Romance", "pre-Romance", etc.

That the Moorish rule of Iberia resulted in "Arabic" vocabulary, saturating the Iberian languages/dialects is contrary to evidence, logic, and rationale.

Firstly, the Berber-Arab rulers were a minority that was interested only in collecting money and living lavishly. They did not intend to convert people to Islam, so as not to deprive themselves from charging a non-Moslem poll-tax.

Secondly, "Arabic" was never declared as an official language in Iberia. The populace never surrendered their tongue, and the rulers relied on translators to communicate with the populace.

Thirdly, the religious zealotry that followed the Reconquest included linguistic "purification," as Arabic books were burned in Granada, and the use of Arabic (and even Arabic borrowings) was increasingly condemned throughout the 16th century.

Fourthly, the vast working-class majority of immigrants during the Moorish rule came from Egypt, who (one may say) spoke an "Arabic-sounding language", namely the Egyptian—the mother language of Arabic and many other languages.

Tracing the history of the Arabic language will lead us to Ancient Egypt. Ibn Hazm, the medieval Arabic scholar of Córdoba (d. 1064), recognized that Aramaic/Syriac, Hebrew, and Arabic were kindred dialects, derived from the **Mudar**, the dialect in which the Koran had been disclosed. The original home of Arabic—the Arabic of the Koran—came from the northwestern region of the Arabian Peninsula. These three kindred dialects (Aramaic/Syriac, Hebrew, and Arabic) originated from the Moab region, which was under the control of Ancient Egypt [discussed in chapter 11]. It is therefore a logical step to consider the role of the Ancient Egypt language, as it relates to the later formulated Arabic language.

To decipher the Ancient Egyptian language and its grammar and syntax, modern-day Egyptologists studied the Arabic language. They assumed that Arabic, being an offshoot of the Ancient Egyptian language, would share much of the same grammar/syntax and vocabulary. It was generally the right assumption and thus Egyptologists were able to address the subject of the Ancient Egyptian grammar and syntax.

The Ancient Egyptian-controlled Moabi region is regarded as the home of the **Mudar** language, the forerunner of Arabic. The name **Mudar** is an abbreviated form of the Ancient Egyptian term, **Medu-Neter**, meaning the *words/language of angels/gods*. It is no accident that Moslems say that Arabic is the "*language of angels*", in imitation of the Ancient Egyptian **Medu Neter**. The people of this Ancient Egyptian colony (Moabi) spoke and wrote the Egyptian language. Scripts found in the Moabi region look exactly like the Ancient Egyptian demotic style of writing [as shown on pages 186-7].

The Egyptians were the only people in the Moabi region who had an available writing surface (papyri), and its associated writing tools of pens and inks. When Ancient Egypt lost power in Asia, there was no one to maintain a literate **Mudar** language, and as a result no more than a handful of written texts were found, because writing was/is not part of the nomadic life—a fact that was also affirmed by Ibn Khaldun in his *Muqaddimah*, as shown in the last chapter of this book.

The rise and unexpected sweeping success of the Islamic forces, in the 7th century CE, prompted the need to write the Koran. The new Moslem Arabs came up with a haphazard system of writing, which was/is very cumbersome. It took a few centuries to keep on fixing its flaws, and in the process, made it even more difficult. It took a couple of centuries after Mohammed's disclosure of the Koran for an "Arabic script" to have some form. The end result was an Arabic script that looks basically like the Ancient Egyptian non-pictorial style of writing, some variation in sound of vocabulary (because of the phenomena of sound shift), as well as the incorporation of some local Arabic vocabulary.

The Ancient Egyptian demotic writing, such as depicted on the Rosetta stone, resembles very much the **Mudar**—the forerunner of present-day Arabic writing. The Arabic script survived and continues to survive only because it is the only permitted language of the Koran and prayers for the Moslems. The fate of Arabic is connected to the fate of Islam.

The (Koranic) Arabic language tried to look different from its Ancient Egyptian (Semitic) source, by re-arranging the order of the *abgd* alphabet to *a, b, t, th, dj, ḥ, kh, d,*...etc, which caused them more problems. Other Semitic languages like Hebrew maintained the same order of the *abgd* alphabet.

Despite the Islamization of Egypt and making Arabic its official and only language, the spoken Ancient Egyptian language didn't die. The so-called "colloquial Arabic" in Egypt is practically the Ancient Egyptian language with some intrusive (Koranic) Arabic dialect vocabulary. The spoken language in Egypt has its own peculiar ancient vocabulary, grammar, and syntax. To call the spoken Egyptian language "colloquial" or "vulgar" Arabic is a misrepresentation of the history and content of the languages of the region where Egypt was a prominent literate country that has fallen prey to the illiterate nomadic Islamic Arabs since 639 CE.

Sound Shifts and Linguistic Studies

The categorization and history writing of languages in the world is generally biased and flawed. Academic linguists follow the process described by them as lexicostatistics, by comparing 20-50 words of the most basic vocabulary in a language, in order to categorize the language and its speakers' origin. This is a flawed process that does not take into account the phenomena of sound shifts.

From the earliest days of comparative philology, it was noticed that the sounds of related languages corresponded in apparently systematic ways. The most famous of these "sound shifts" were worked out by Jacob Grimm in 1822, and have become known as "Grimm's Law".

The circular relationship between these correspondences is a major feature:

g → k → x → gh → g
kh → k → kh
t → th → dh → d → t
p → f (ph) → bh → b → p

The following are examples of correspondences that are noted in the Levant regions:

- *m* is often exchanged for *n*.
- *m* often becomes *b*.
- *r* and *l* are often confused.
- *gi* is often exchanged with *di*.
- *k* or *c* may be pronounced *g*.
- *z* may be pronounced *ts* (emphatic *s* like the English word, *false*).
- *h* may be added or dropped at the end of a word.
- *d* may be dropped at the end of a word.

- *s* may be used instead of *sh*.
- *w* may be *v*.
- *th* may be *f*.
- Span. *j* / Egyptian *ḥ* may be pronounced *kh*, *k*, or *h*.

As an example of the phenomenon of sound shift, a person's name can still be recognized in vastly different sounds, such as *Santiago* / *San Diego* / *San Jacob* and *Saint James*. *Jacob* / *Jack* / *Jaques* / *James*, are one and the same name, which exemplifies the phenomenon of sound shift. Another simple example is: *Mi**ch**ael*, *Mi**kh**ael*, *Mi**g**uel*, *Mi**q**ael*, etc, which despite being the same name, varies only in one sound in the middle of the name. One can imagine that variation in two and even more sounds in the same word/ name, will make the changed name/word sound like a totally different name/word.

In addition to the numerous variations of soundshifts, many people have tendencies to reverse letters (consonants and/or vowels) of a word. As a result, we end up with what appear to be totally different words. An example of such reversal is the Egyptian (not Arabic) word **bose** (meaning a *kiss*), which is ***beso*** in Spanish—reversing the vowels *o* and *e*.

The Distinction of a Language

The categorization of languages in the world by academic linguists, based on the lexicostatistic process, is also insufficient in distinguishing or proving the grouping of language families. Other aspects that an analyst must consider in linguistic studies are: grammar, syntax, and mode of expression (style and literature). These four pillars (lexicography, grammar, syntax, and mode of expression) differ in emphasis (as to their importance) according to the different degrees (of usefulness) they possess for conveying the intended meaning of speech.

The first and most important of the four pillars of a language is *grammar*, since it gives a clear indication of the basic principles used in expressing the various intended meanings. Grammar is more important than lexicography, since ignorance of grammar is very harmful to mutual understanding. This is not the case with lexicography.

Syntax is the orderly or systematic arrangement. **a)** the arrangement of words as elements in a sentence to show their relationship to one another; **b)** the organization and relationship of word groups, phrases, clauses, sentences, and sentence structure; **c)** the branch of grammar dealing with this.

Word order in a sentence indicates the intended emphasis. The following sentences [followed by their English sentence structure] show the word order in Ancient Egypt, which matches the word order in Hispanic languages/dialects.

1. now found person-his stone this in shape hawk divine

His Person found this stone in the shape of a divine hawk.

2. was-he as youth now commanded to-him Amun to-do kingship two-lands as

When he was a youth, Amun commanded him to perform the kingship of the Two Lands as:

3. Horus bull mighty perfect appearances lord manifestations-enduring-Re giver/given life like Re

Horus "Mighty Bull, perfect of appearances," Lord of Appearances, Menkheprure, giver of/given life like Re.

It should be noted that the Arabic language has a slight to moderate variation in its word order, than shown above.

It is therefore that the spoken language in Hispania was called "vulgar Arabic", "colloquial Arabic", "Hispano-Arabic", etc.

Lastly, it should be emphasized that the written form of a language does not necessarily concur with the origin and/or the categorization/classification of language families, such as the example given later in this chapter about the change of form in the Turkish language. In other words, seeing a text written in the "Latin" alphabet does not necessarily mean that the language of the text is Latin. [More about this subject later in this chapter.]

The Intimate Egyptian-Iberian Tongue

The four pillars of a language are found to be compatible between the Ancient Egyptian language and the Hispanic languages/dialects. Such compatibility is most evident among the (Egyptian) Romany, who constitute the link between Ancient Egypt and the Iberian Peninsula. The Romany of Hispania are known to speak a language or jargon amongst themselves, which other modern natives of Spain do not understand. The Romany spoken language "sounds" like Spanish (Castilian). This antiquated "Castilianized" language includes several thousand words (or parts of words) of the original Ancient Egyptian tongue, preserved by memory among the (Egyptian) Romany.

As for the second and third pillars—*grammar* and *syntax*—they are consistent with both Castilian and Ancient Egyptian in areas such as in the conjugation of verbs, the declension of its nouns, etc. Anybody who is familiar with the Ancient Egyptian grammar and syntax, etc, will find that the Hispanic dialects/languages follow the same exact Ancient Egyptian patterns. Additional information about grammar and syntax are provided in the next subchapter.

In regard to the fourth pillar, namely mode of expression (*style and literature*), we find an exact match [as shown in chapter 14], regarding the forms, themes, and style of poetry.

Western academia repeats, without supporting evidence, that the Hispanic languages are of "Latin" origin. The idea of a "Latin language", as associated with the militaristic Roman Empire, was created in post-Roman era in order to enhance the image of the Romans. Such a "Latin language" was conveniently created from an existing language—similar to the history of the "Arabic" language, which was also created after the success of the militaristic Islamic Arabian forces. It is beyond the scope of this book to show the differences and similarities between Latin/Hispanic/Egyptian except for one important distinction, which is that regarding the gender. In Latin, there are three genders: masculine, feminine, and neuter. Languages such as German and English follow these three categories (he, she, it). The Hispanic languages do not follow the three gender classifications.

The Hispanic and Ancient Egyptian languages distinguish two genders only: masculine and feminine, for all words. This dual distinction is also consistent with the Ancient Egyptian and Iberian cosmological and Animistic beliefs. The two-gender division expresses the true nature of the created universe in animated expression, namely the duality between the male and female aspects of the universe.

The fact that in Hispanic languages/dialects, nouns and pronouns are either 'masculine' or 'feminine', and that the gender for all words is exactly the same in Iberian/Egyptian languages, is by itself sufficient to prove that Ancient Egypt is the origin of these twin-gendered languages.

Regarding the intimate relationship between writing styles in Ancient Egypt and the Iberian Peninsula, see later in this chapter.

The Divine Mother Language

It is an historical fact that Ancient Egypt was the most (if not the only) literate and civilized country in the ancient world. Additionally, Egypt was the most powerful (economically) and most populated country. The fact is that the Ancient Egyptian language was the language of the powerful during ancient times, and therefore it was the most important international language of communication. Therefore, her language dominated all. Ignoring the significance of the Egyptian prevalent powers leads to flawed linguistic studies in the Mediterranean Basin and elsewhere.

Because of Egypt's unique geographic location and her prominence as the most populous, literate, and richest country in the ancient world, the (Ancient) Egyptian language is considered to be the source (and a member) of several language families, such as the Afro-Asiatic and Semitic language families. The Ancient Egyptian language is also most influential in the Indo-European language family. The "progression" of the written alphabets in the Mediterranean Basin, as shown in the table on pages 186-7, proves/discloses that the Ancient Egyptian hieroglyphic and demotic script is the source of the European languages family. Further detailed discussion of such Ancient Egypt linguistic influence is beyond the scope of this book. The point is that the Ancient Egyptian language was the basis for at least these three language families—Afro-Asiatic, Semitic, and Indo-European. We will focus here on the "Semitic family", since it provides the original and purest form of all languages.

Western and religious biases cause linguists to ignore Ancient Egypt as the mother of the Semitic language family, in its purest and original form. It is contemptuously admitted that the Ancient Egyptian language "shares most features with Semitic languages". Such an admission means that the Ancient Egyptian language—being older than other Semitic languages—is the mother of all these languages—in its original purest form. The Phoenicians, the Hebrews, and the other peoples of the lands at the eastern end of the Mediterranean, all spoke dialects of the same Semitic language, and used the same consonantal alphabet in their script. In word formation and phonetics, the Ancient Egyptian and present Semitic offshoot languages have much in common, including tri-consonantal roots and the consonants (*'ayin*, *ḳ*, and *ḥ*).

The Ancient Egyptians called their language **Medu Neter**, meaning *words of* ***neter*** *(god)*. The Egyptian term is indicative of the unity of speech and script, i.e. sound and form. Plato's *Collected Dialogues* affirms the Ancient Egyptian intent of their language, in *Philebus* [18-d]:

> *...he [the Ancient Egyptian Tehuti/Thoth] conceived of 'letter' as a kind of bond of unity, uniting as it were all these sounds into one, and so he gave utterance to the expression 'art of letters,' implying that there was one art that dealt with the sounds.*

The Ancient Egyptian consonantal alphabet consists of 22 letters [see pages 186-7]. The slight sound variation in pronouncing three letters (*b,k,p*) results in 25 sounds of the alphabet—which Plutarch referred to in *Moralia Vol V*, [56A],

> *Five makes a square of itself, as many as the letters of the Egyptian alphabet.*

By stating that the Ancient Egyptian consonantal alphabet consists of 25 letters, Plutarch is referring to the three additional consonantal sounds/letters *v, kh,* and *ph*, which are the loose pronounciation of the consonantal letters *b, k,* and *p*, which are pronounced emphatically.

The Ancient Egyptian alphabet consists only of consonant letters—no written vowels. By definition and method, the script is purely consonantal at base. It is from this Ancient Egyptian system (that denotes only consonants) that the *abgd* (*abjad* for Arabic) type of writing system is now recognized.

The Ancient Egyptian consonantal letters were/are based on the acrophonic principle, whereby a letter stands for the initial sound in the word for the object of which it is a picture. Such a relationship/principle is found in the two main Ancient Egyptian forms of writing, whereby the (pictorial) hieroglyphic script is the basis for the (cursive) demotic script. An example of such a relationship/principle is the letter *m*, which is derived from the Ancient Egyptian word **mar/mer** (meaning *water body/sea*). Therefore, the letter *M/m* is always represented by the figure of the wavy surface of water [see table on pages 186-7].

As in all Semitic styles of writings, Ancient Egyptian writing was limited to the consonants of the words. In all these languages, the meaning of the word is generally contained in the consonants, while unwritten/implicit vowels indicate the grammatical forms. For people (even at the present time) who are brought up in Semitic language speaking countries, it is very easy to figure out the pronunciation of any word (without notating vowels and other phonetic marks), based on the context or a syntactical feature. As an example, the name Mohammed is spelled in four Arabic letters, and is written (even in our present time) as such—MHMD. Any Arabic-speaking person has no problem vocalizing MHMD—without vowels and/or phonetic marks.

Ancient Egyptian (and Semitic) grammar distinguishes three parts of speech: nouns, verbs, and particles. What would be called adjectives, adverbs, and pronouns in other languages are considered nouns in the Egyptian-Semitic language family. In its purest Ancient Egyptian form, all nouns can be easily derived from simple tri-consonantal verbs—in the past tense. The root verb (*verb-stem*) consists of three consonants, which are called radicals. It should be noted also that all Ancient Egyptian verb-stems consist of only 3 radicals. The number 3 represents the building block in all aspects of the created universe and the Ancient Egyptian language represents such a fundamental principle. Verb-stems in offshoot Semitic languages are mostly of three, but some of two, four, or (rarely) even more consonants.

The Ancient Egyptian language is a dynamic form of expression, since because words are derived from the verb-stem—in the past tense, i.e. the point of beginning, everything is a forward (positive) derivation with suffixes and prefixes. Words are formed from roots by the addition of (unwritten) vowels, prefixes, infixes, or suffixes according to certain fixed patterns. For example, using the radicals *ḥ-s-b* (both an Ancient Egyptian and an Arabic word) it is theoretically possible to derive as many as 14 new verbs and scores of nouns. The root *ḥ-s-b* refers to the basic concept of "calculation". The verb, of course, is analyzable as a derivation from a typically tri-consonantal root.

In Semitic languages (following the Egyptian system), two genders, masculine and feminine, are distinguished for nouns, adjectives, and also verbs. The feminine forms are regularly derived from the masculine by adding the suffix *at/et* at the end of the word, for singular form. In the spoken language, the letter *t* is usually silent.

The Ancient Egyptian main negative particle usually stood at the beginning of a sentence, and that place was also reserved for their mark of interrogation. The above two features are also peculiar to Hispanic languages.

There are two basic sentence types traditionally referred to as the nominal and the verbal sentences in the Egyptian (and other Semitic) languages. A highly generalized representation of these two sentence types follows:

- nominal sentence = noun phrase + predicate
- verbal sentence = intransitive verb + noun phrase or transitive verb + noun phrase + noun phrase.

More complex sentences, and sentences that appear to deviate from these patterns, can easily be explained as transforms of them. There were rules regarding word order to indicate the intended emphasis [as shown earlier in this chapter].

Both the tri-consonantal root verb (and its rich derivatives) and the varied sounds of vowels that change the grammatical character of the word make this language very poetic, powerful, expressive, energetic, and easy for everyone to compose poetry, puns, word plays, etc.

Romancing the Mother Tongue

During the later stages of the Moors' grip on Iberia, Castille became a dominant power in the north, and was the center from which the Reconquest of the peninsula was launched. The religious zealotry that followed the Reconquest included linguistic "purification". We are told that as the Reconquest was succeeding in moving south, Romance languages "emerged"—how "poetic"!

The so-called "emergence of Romance languages" in Iberia was similar to what happened in Turkey, about a century ago, where their leader, Mustafa Kemal Atatürk, after losing the Ottoman Empire in WWI, wanted to sever ties with the East, by abandoning the "Arabic" alphabet for a "Latin" alphabet. His action did not change the Turkish language. He merely wrote the same spoken language in a different alphabet and a different direction (left to right), which incidentally complicated their writing system. The same thing could be said of the "emergence of the Romance languages", i.e.

there was no change in the spoken languages, but merely a change in the specific form of writing. Such changes resulted in a wide gap between official "Latinized" languages and folk-spoken language. Likewise, in Islamic-ruled Egypt, adopting Arabic as the only official language never affected the spoken language of every and all Egyptians for 13 centuries, and the gap between the two languages never closed.

The language used by the common people of Iberia, which was evident in their many styles of poetry, is called by many different names—depending on the personal/religious/ethnic/cultural prejudices of the writer on the subject. Such a language is called: "**Mozarabic**", "vulgar Arabic", "colloquial Arabic", "Hispano-Arabic", etc. The use of these undefined and ambiguous terms indicates that the utilized language does not belong to any "officially accepted language". The reason is that the populace spoke the Egyptian language, which is older than all "politically/religiously recognized languages".

Let us begin with **Mozarabic** as a point of reference. The term **Mozarabic** is often applied to the Hispanic liturgy and chant as a whole, both before and after the period of Moslem domination. Actually, this term refers to Egyptians since *Mozarabic* is pronounced *Mossarabic/Moss-arabic*, meaning Egyptian Arab / Egyptian dialect of Arabic, and hence it is referred to as "vulgar Arabic". *Mossr/Massr* is the name of Egypt known to Arabs and other countries ever since Pharaonic times. All records show that most of the working-class immigrants during the Moorish rule were from Egypt. As such, we hear of a language described as "**Mozarabic**", "vulgar Arabic", "colloquial Arabic", etc. The dialect, which is designated as "**Mozarabic**", has many points of resemblance to Navarro-Aragonese and to Leonese; like them it differs from Castilian in retaining a number of "archaizing" features.

Analysis of history and structure of the languages: (Ancient) Egyptian, Hispanic, Latin, Etruscan, Arabic, Berber, Basque, and Celtic, will show the great affinities between the languages/dialects (old and new) in Iberia and the Egyptian language. By taking a closer look at the subject without the usual biases, we will find Ancient Egypt as the source of a wide range of languages in Iberia, the Mediterranean Basin, and elsewhere.

The present-day Iberian "official" and "co-official" languages have a high common measure of agreement between them. One may be characterized by a regular alternation of vowels and consonants, another appears as predominantly vocalic, and yet another as predominantly consonantal. Fundamentally, the same material is subjected to variants of differing rhythms.

In this book, we will give some attention to what is considered the most ancient language in the Iberian Peninsula, namely the Basque, which is recognized as the most "fossilized" language in the Iberian Peninsula. The Basque tongue cannot be classed with any Indo-European or Semitic tongue, and appears to be of earlier origin. This must bring to mind the very old Ancient Egyptian language, which is also older than (and the source of many of) present-day language families. It is also interesting that one legend in Basque calls their language the **language of the angels**, which is exactly what the Ancient Egyptians called their language—**Medu Neter**, which means *words/language of the gods/angels*. The grammar and syntax of Basque is basically the same as the Ancient Egyptian language. The Egyptian origin of countless numbers of words in Basque and other Iberian languages/dialects becomes more evident once the phenomena of sound shift [explained earlier in this chapter] are accounted for. Lastly, it should be noted that the Vascones or Basques are thought to have been Iberians who strayed up from the south, which makes their relationship with Ancient Egypt even more logical. As stated in chapter 1 of this book, the Egyptian origin of the Romany (Gypsies, ***Gitanos***, etc) of Hispania is recognized in the Basque provinces, where they are called ***Egipcioac***, or Egyptians.

Writing Variations and Linguistic Studies

The writing variations in the Ancient Egyptian language's offshoot language families—Afro-Asiatic, Semitic, and Indo-European, are categorized as "different alphabets". The source of the apparent "different alphabet" is Ancient Egyptian, as shown on pages 186-7 and explained below.

The Ancient Egyptians were very organized and as a result, government was invented thousands of years ago. In their daily existence, people often communicated with one another by letter. All government business was put into writing. The Egyptians kept economic and labor records on papyri. These written communications followed a particular form, models of which have survived until today.

All early Greek and Roman writers affirmed that there were basically two forms of Ancient Egyptian writings: hieroglyphs (sacred script) and the abbreviated form of the hieroglyphic symbols, characterized as a script without pictorial forms. Western academia arbitrarily splits the non-pictorial type into two forms—hieratic and demotic. However, there are no distinct three styles of writing, but a wide range of styles from the perfectly executed pictorial forms (of hieroglyphs) to non-pictorial form.

The objective of writing determines the style and care used by the scribe. Some were extremely stylized/ornate/ornamented, others were simple and plain. Sometimes, letters/symbols were printed individually; in certain cases, two or more signs were joined to form a ligature (stylized or simple).

Egyptians were able to utilize writings in all aspects of their lives, by inventing excellent writing materials and books. They used writing materials of leather, stone, wood, and papyrus, as opposed to the Minoan-Mycenean, Babylonians, and others, who had to imprint their signs on clay, a procedure that has produced the unpleasant shapes of cuneiform.

The Ancient Egyptians manufactured books by gumming separate sheets of papyrus together; and there are magnificent manuscripts measuring 65 and 130 ft [20 and 40 m]. The Egyptians utilized pens and ink of indestructible permanence, which they ground on a wooden palette. The availability of these writing surfaces and tools allowed the scribes to write manuscripts drawn in clear, elegant, round, firm signs. Using a pen (instead of a pointed tool) results in a more rounded shape of letters.

The purpose of scripts determines the style of writing: "formal," ""cursive," "semi-formal" or "semi-cursive." The terms *cursive* and *formal* refer neither to the material used for writing, nor to the content of inscriptions. Rather they refer fundamentally to script types, that is, to the manner in which letters are written, and to the resultant forms. A cursive script is one that is written in a fluid or rounded manner, with an economy of movement on the part of the scribe's hand. A formal script tends to be square or segmented, and apparently required a more frequent lifting of the writing instrument from the writing material. These ways of writing produced different forms of the letters at various times.

In Ancient Egypt, since there was no authority to standardize the non-pictorial forms, it was natural that local scripts at different centers had widely divergent characteristics. These different styles (like our present-day variety of fonts) appear to the untrained foreign eyes as different alphabets. But for people of the same culture, they can all read these different handwritings—as of one language.

Free handwriting varies from neat to poor and may seem like different alphabets. An example in "Latin" is a poorly written letter *g* can appear to be the letter *q*. A poorly written letter *q* may appear to be the letter *a*. Therefore, the same letter transcribed a few times will appear distinctly different. Additionally, people may reverse the direction of some letters such as *pq*, *bd*, especially in earlier times when many languages allowed writing in both directions between right and left.

The orientation of the hieroglyphic characters and their derivative alphabets could be affected by a multitude of factors: such as the type of material written on, the position of the text in relation to figures or other texts, or the nature of the inscription, or limitation of space that results in changing direction from horizontal to vertical, or vice-versa. They may be written in columns (mostly from top to bottom) or in horizontal lines, which are sometimes to be read from left to right and sometimes from right to left. In some cases, they used a combination of horizontal and vertical for the same word, and/or for the same sentence. This is/was in conjunction with their artistic variety in calligraphic writings, which were usually highly ornate.

It should be noted that several variants of the Greek alphabet continued to exist for more than three centuries until 403/402 BCE, when the Ionic alphabet of Miletus was officially adopted as a standard in Athens, and this is what we know as the *classical Greek alphabet*. By that time, the left-to-right direction had prevailed, i.e. before 402 BCE, the Greeks used to write in both directions, just as the Ancient Egyptians did.

In conclusion, we should consider that different handwritings (with different orientation) may appear to represent different alphabets. By taking these points into account, we can trace numerous scripts throughout the Mediterranean Basin and beyond, to its origin—namely the Ancient Egyptian non-pictorial style of demotic [shown on the following two pages in the plainest style used by the Egyptians]. The table provides a visual examination, showing that the depicted "alphabets" in the Mediterranean Basin were really never different alphabets, but a single alphabet, namely Egyptian.

Ancient Egyptian Hieroglyphs	Description of Sign	Phonetic Value	AE Demotic Script ("Phoenician") in varied directions	Moabite Script	East Greek			Classical Greek				West Greek	Etruscan	Archaic Latin	Classic Latin	
𓃾	ox head	a	𐤀	𐤀	Δ Δ	ΔA	a	A	α	Alpha	a	ΔA	A	ΔA	A	a
𓄀	lion's head & mane	b	𐤁	𐤁	B B	B	b	B	β	Beta	b	BB		BB	B	b
𓂧	forearm with palm of hand downward	g	𐤂	𐤂	Γ Λ	Γ	g	Γ	γ	Gamma	g	/((	) [k]	) [k,g]	([k]	g
𓆛	fish tail	d	◁ △	◁	Δ D	Δ	d	Δ	δ	Delta	d	ΔD		D	D	d
𓀠	man praying	h	ш Ǝ	Ǝ	E E	E E	e	E	ε	Epsilon	ĕ	E	Ǝ	Ǝ	E	e
𓎛	horns of ox	w	Y	Y			v					F [		ꟻ [f]	F [f]	v
𓇛	plant	z	I	I	I	I	z	Z	ζ	Zeta	z,dz	I	≠	I [z]	G [g]	z
𓉗	wall	ḥ	H B	目	B	BH	h(ē)	H	η	Eta	ē	BH	B	B	H	h
⊗	mark of authority	ṭ	⊗	⊗	⊕	⊗⊕	th	Θ	θ	Theta	th	⊕ ⊙	⊗			th
𓂝	hand	y	𐤉	𐤉	I	I	i	I	ι	Iota	i					i
𓎡	claw	k	𐤊	𐤊	K	K K	k	K	κ	Kappa	k	K	ꓘ	ꓘK	K	k
𓍇	ox goad	l	(L	𐤋	L L	Λ Λ	l	Λ	λ	Lambda	l	L	J	J	L	l
𓈖	water	m	𐤌	𐤌	M	M	m	M	μ	Mu	m	M	𐤌	𐤌	M	m
𓅐	vulture	n	𐤍	𐤍	N	N N	n	N	ν	Nu	n	N	𐤍	𐤍	N	n

Ancient Egyptian Hieroglyphs	Description of Sign	Phonetic Value	AE Demotic Script ("Phoenician") in varied directions	Moabite Script
𓊽	backbone & ribs	s	ǂ	ǂ
𓁹	eye	ʿ	O	O
𓉐	house/shrine	p	ʔ	J
𓆓	serpent	ṣ	ɼ	h
[illegible]	back of head	q	Φ	Φ
[illegible]	human head	r	4	9
[illegible]	row of teeth	ś	w ξ	w
X	mark of cross	t	x +	x

East Greek			Classical Greek				West Greek	Etruscan	Archaic Latin	Classic Latin	
	ǂ Ŧ	ks	Ξ	ξ	Xi	ks					x
O	O	o	O	o	Omikron	ŏ	⊙		O	O	o
Γ	Γ Π	p	Π	π	Pi	p	Γ	⅂	⅂ Γ	P	p
		s						M			ś
Ϙ	Ϙ	q					Ϙ	Ϙ	Ϙ	Q	q
P R	P P D	r	P	ρ	Rho	r	P P P	D	9	R	r
ϟ <	≷	s	Σ	σ ς	Sigma	s	≷	<	ς	S	s
T	T	t	T	τ	Tau	t	T	↑	T T	T	t
V	V	u,ü	Υ	υ	Upsilon	ü	Y V	V	V	V	u
Φ Φ	⊘	ph	Φ	φ	Phi	ph	X +		X	X	ks
X +	X	kh	Χ	χ	Chi	kh	Φ Φ	Φ	O		ph
	Ψ Υ	ps	Ψ	ψ	Psi	ps	Ψ ⊥	↓			kh
	Ω	ō	Ω	ω	Omega	ō		8 8			f

Sources
AE Hieroglyphs and "Sinaitic" - Gardiner and Culican pg 125
AE Demotic - U. Chicago and Baldi Table 4.1 (The Foundations of Latin, 1999)
Moabite Script - Daniels pg. 95 (Garbini 1979, fig 5)
Scripts in Europe - Baldi Table 4.1

The Origin and "Progression" of Alphabets in the Mediterranean Basin Regions

Many unearthed artifacts (such as coins, lead tablets, ceramic pieces, tombstones and bronze objects) have been turning up throughout most of the Iberian Peninsula. These artifacts have inscriptions that are described by many as "of an unknown alphabet", or as "Iberian-Tartesian".

The number of the old inscriptions in Iberia counted to date is over 500, although many are in bad condition. They come from the regions of Andalusia, Extremadura, Castilla-La Mancha, Valencia, Murcia, Aragón, Cataluña, Navarra, etc. But they have also been found in some areas of France, Portugal, Italy, and North Africa. Engraved on lead, bronze, ceramic and stone, Iberian texts are found in tombs, cemeteries, lintels of doorways to houses, ancient corrals, wells, etc. Because of the different (and difficult to write) surfaces used, there appears to be certain differences in "spelling". The disadvantages that they must have faced, such as transcribing them onto physical supports—lead, bronze, stone, etc—become evident.

These inscriptions date from the 4th-5th centuries BCE until CE. This time span coincides with the major immigration from Ancient Egypt and subsequent demographic changes in Iberia [see chapter 9 for details]. Without a doubt, this style of script remained in use until well after the Romans had conquered most of the Iberian Peninsula.

By comparing the Ancient Egyptian demotic form of writing with Tartesian, Iberian writings [as shown on the opposite page], the affinity between Ancient Egypt and Iberia becomes obvious. The table shows the Ancient Iberian-Tartesian writing, and its comparison with the Ancient Egyptian writing, according to M. Gomez-Moreno. [Source: *Prehistoric Iberia*, ed. By Antonio Arnaiz-Villena, (2000), page 167.] We have not changed the organization or order of the signs according to Gomez-Moreno. However it is easy to see that these symbols/letters are exactly shown on pages 186-7—from which the phonetic value of each letter could be found.

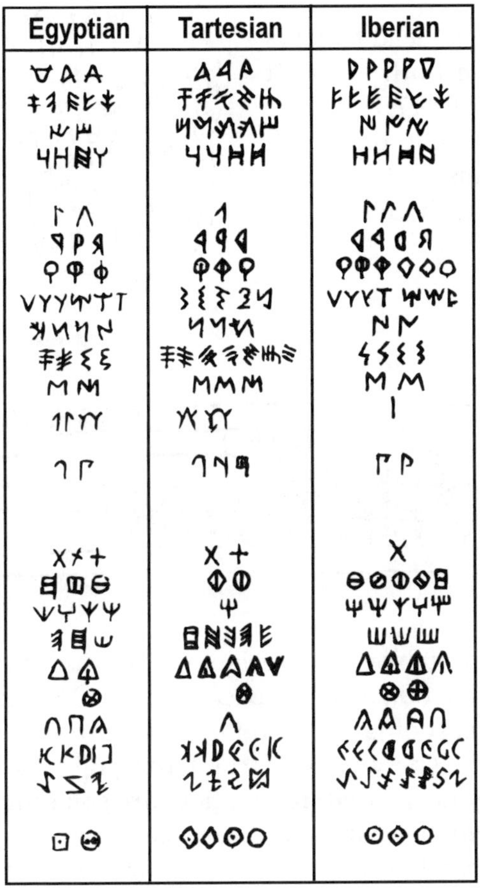

Some individual examples include:

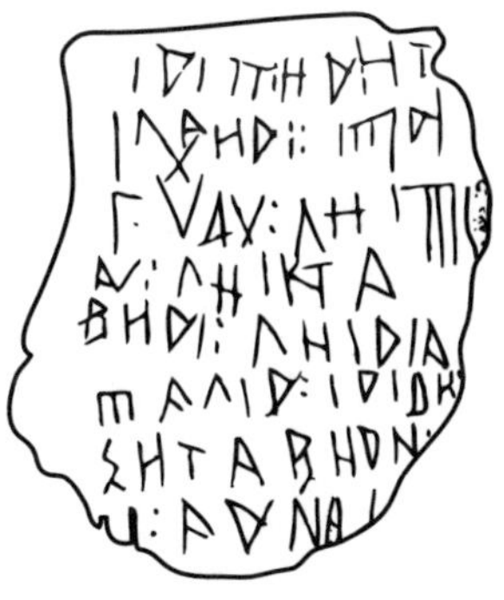

This alcoy tablet shows an inscription in the Ancient Egyptian demotic alphabet. It is one of several found in the ruins of the Iberian sanctuary of La Serreta.

This small lead tablet is inscribed on both sides. It has a total of 117 letters or signs on the side on which the text begins, and 59 on the side on which it ends.

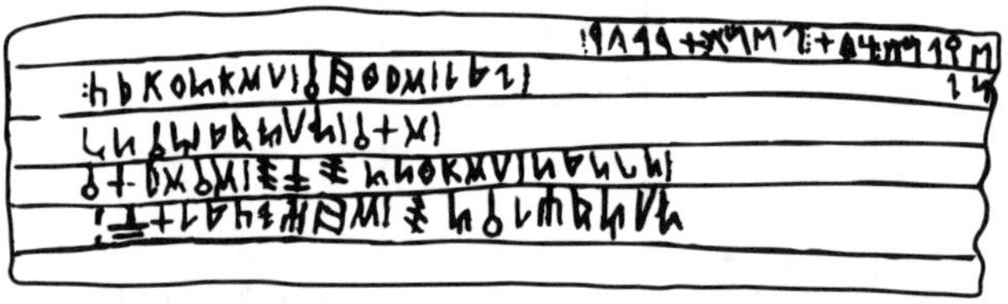

This lead tablet [shown above] was found in 1928 in the ruins of La Bastida de los Alcuses (Pais de Valencia, Spain), to the southeast of Jativa, a settlement destroyed circa the 4th century BCE. The **writing runs from right to left,** and is separated by horizontal lines. There are sometimes barriers of points, which separate different paragraphs. This is identical to the Ancient Egypt style and form of writing.

13

The Animated Religious Traditions

The Animated Cosmic Order

The Romany people of Hispania are intensely spiritual—as Animists and not by attending church services. For the untrained eyes, it appears that the Romany traditions are a blend of "Christianity" and "paganism". As explained in chapters 1 and 2, both the Ancient Egyptians of Egypt and the Romany of Hispania are Animists who concur with the spiritual (not historical) message of the Gospel. This chapter will elaborate on the Animistic traditions of the (Egyptian) Romany and how their traditions spread to the furthest corners of the Iberian Peninsula.

The Ancient (and Baladi) Egyptians and Iberians share a similar belief in Animism—the concept that all things in the universe are animated (energized) by life forces. This concept concurs, scientifically, with the kinetic theory, which states that each minute particle of any matter is in constant motion, i.e. energized with life forces.

The universe is basically a hierarchy of energies, at different orders of density. Our senses are most familiar with *matter*—the densest form of energy. Since Einstein's relativity theory, it has been known and accepted that *matter* is a form of *energy*, a coagulation or condensation of energy. This matrix of energies came as a result of the initial act of creation and the subsequent effects of the *Big Bang* that created the universe. The hierarchy of energies is interrelated, and each level is sustained by the level below it. This hierarchy of energies is set neatly into a vast matrix of deeply interfaced natural laws. It is both physical and metaphysical.

The faster form of energies—these invisible energies in the universe—are called *spirits* by many. Spirits/energies are organized at different orders of densities, which relates to the different speeds of molecules. These faster (invisible) energies inhabit certain areas, or are associated with particular natural phenomena.

The spirit/energy matrix that animates the human flesh/matter at birth, and leaves the body (matter) at death, can likewise reside in any other matter, for as long as it wants to. In order to communicate with a departed (free) spirit, a dwelling place—a condensed form of energy, possibly matter—is needed, in order for the free spirit to manifest and communicate its will and influence to the living beings on earth. Therefore, the Ancient and *Baladi* Egyptians provide dwelling places for spirits of all kinds, in the form of statues and amulets. The Ancient Egyptians maintained strict specifications for the design, proportions, colors, materials, etc, of their statues, relics, effigies.

With proper rituals, at specific times, supernatural powers may occupy an object for certain durations. The same exact concept and practices are held in the Iberian Peninsula where it is believed that folk saints manifest their holiness most conspicuously in material objects. It was in their bodily remains or in their waxen images that their spiritual graces resided for the community to tap. Consequently, the miraculous properties of relics are appreciated, once they are empowered/selected by supernatural powers.

The Role of Saints

The folk saints are those few individuals who succeeded in traveling the spiritual Path, and as a result have attained union with the Divine. He/she becomes the Perfected Person or the Universal Succor, to whom all resort for aid. They are capable of performing supernatural acts, influence and predict future events, etc. As a result, they become the intermediaries between the earthly living beings and the supernatural in the heavenly realms. They are called upon to intercede on behalf of the community and individuals.

After his/her death, the folk saint often becomes the patron and protector of the locality or social group in which he/she lived. In both Egypt and Iberia, each patron saint has/had at least two shrines in each locality. Academic Egyptologists describe these folk saints as *local* or *minor gods*.

Saints, shrines, and pilgrimages have strong similarities in both Ancient (and present-day) Egypt and Iberia. Since such practices are contrary to Islam and Christianity, the peoples of both Egypt and Iberia had to work around the wrath of Islamists and Catholics. In their distinctive clever ways (in both Egypt and Iberia), the populace made the idea of veneration of folk saints a Moslem/Christian idea.

In the 7th century, the Church conceded and accepted the veneration of holy people into the ecclesiastical administrative order of the kingdom. The Church pretended that saint veneration was no longer to be a matter of personal, private worship, because that would leave the way open for private veneration of a local holy person.

To appease Islamists and Christians, the locals (in both Egypt and Iberia) came up with a narrative of the history of the saint as being a good Moslem/Christian, and how he/she died (not necessarily *killed*) for the *cause*—and became a *martyr*. The Church/Islamists could then "accept" that the veneration of the saint encouraged the faithful in orthodox belief. In spite of this move to bring the folk saints into the circle of orthodoxy, the saints were never completely separated from the popular images that had surrounded them long before their "narratives" were written down.

Ethnologists and theologians alike agree that the veneration of patron saints in both Egypt and Iberia has been the most potent and decisive vehicle in their existence. In the darkest ages of Iberian/Egyptian history, the people never stopped trusting in their saints. People continue to communicate with them at each's meeting place—shrines, hermitages and chapels, which were/are administered by the mystical confraternities, who also helped to organize the celebration of local votive feast days, processions and pilgrimages.

The Cyclical Renewal Festivals

The main theme of the Ancient Egyptian texts is the cyclical nature of the universe and the constant need for the renewal of such cycles, through well-designated festivals. The Egyptians, like their cousins—the Romany of Hispania—viewed/view these festivals as part of human existence, which constitutes the rhythm of the life of the community and the individual. This rhythm results from the order of cosmic life. All the elements and rules governing the Ancient Egyptian festivals are exactly applicable to present-day festivals with organized and detailed schemes.

The renewal and rejuvenation of the life of the cosmos, of the community, and of the individual are affected by rites. These rites had/have the power to bring about the rejuvenation and rebirth of divine life. Failure to hold the fiesta as usual might very well produce individual or collective sentiments of culpability. As such, the visitation of shrines is considered an essential practice of folk religion among Ancient (and *Baladi*) Egyptians, their cousins—the Romany of Hispania, and by extension the majority of Iberians. Most of the Egyptians and Iberians not only expect a blessing to follow their visiting the shrine of the folk saint, but they also dread that some misfortune will befall them if they neglect this act.

The important role of the public participation in the festival is manifested most vividly in the ***romería*** (derived from the Ancient Egyptian term, **Rom**, meaning *man/person*), which can be defined as a small-scale pilgrimage in which the inhabitants of a given locality journey in a body to a sanctuary to celebrate the festivity of the supernatural protector housed therein. Sometimes the local community (in both Egypt and Iberia) will converge at the shrine with other nearby towns that share the devotion. During processions, confraternities bring out their most cherished relics to solicit spiritual assistance. Promenaded under the skies in public streets and squares, these physical remains communicate with the supernatural, exerting a force on the heavens set off by believers' passions. Sometimes the sacred image is brought home to visit the local shrine; other images "travel" to spend a few days in each of the towns under their protection.

The ritual sacrifice of the bull in the festival represents the renewal of the cosmic forces through the death and resurrection of the bull-god. [See chapter 2 for more information.]

The central religious act at the festival is the visit to the shrine by the public, of all ages and classes. In addition to visitations, people may ask these folk saints for personal favors. Vows are made by individuals that if the folk saint resolves a personal concern, the vower will donate certain items for charity. As a result, offerings have always been made during festival days.

Religious chanting and other pious rites, dancing, singing, and food-sharing are common denominators of such festivals. The (Egyptian) Romany of Hispania, just like their cousins of Ancient and *Baladi* Egyptians, do not categorize the activities at the festivals as sacred or mundane. As such, the gay and secular side of religious ceremonies is an essential part of the festivals. Pilgrimage devotion, the market, and the fair are all connected. Fifty yards/meters from the shrine, a full-blown fair takes place, with ferris wheels, shooting galleries, and bumper cars, beside peddlers selling a wide range of goods.

The pilgrimage to the shrine and all other festival rituals are the same in Iberia and Egypt—the former in Christian garment and the latter in Moslem garment. The religious festivals in Iberia were observed in Ancient Egypt thousands of years ago, before Christianity.

The dates and purpose of countless festivals in Iberia are the same as in Ancient Egypt. Reviewing in detail the similarities between the numerous festivals in Ancient Egypt and Iberia is beyond the scope of this book. We gave a few examples earlier, regarding Assumption Day and Pentecost. [For more information and examples—such as the Holy Week, Christmas, etc—read *Egyptian Mystics: Seekers of the Way*, by Moustafa Gadalla.]

Egyptian Mysticism in Galicia (Priscillianism)

Galicia, in the furthest region of Iberia, was the main source of tin for the Ancient Egyptians. Regular contact along the famed "Tin Route"—between Cádiz and Galicia—was common, as early as the 4th millenium BCE [as explained previously].

The Ancient Egyptian concept of cosmology and mysticism made its way to Iberia a long time ago, and left its mark in Galicia. Not only that Galicia was important as the site of the famous shrine of Santiago de Compostela, named after the patron saint of Spain, St. James the Elder, but this northern part of Iberia is also well known for two Gnostic movements—which are basically one concept that was reported as two separate events—Arianism and Priscillianism. The historical records and the traditions of Arianism, Priscillianism, and Santiago de Compostela point to Egypt as their source.

Arianism was reported and condemned by the Catholic Church as a "heresy" that was taught by **Arius of Alexandria**. It basically deals with the nature of God—as the Supreme Being—as it related to the nature of the biblical Jesus. All the "apparent" conflicting theories about these natures can be explained in the Ancient Egyptian context of the relationship between Ausar (Osiris)—the Father—and his Divine Son—namely Heru (Horus). Discussing the validity of Arius' message is beyond the scope of this book. However, the point to be made here is that the leader, Arius, was reported to have come from Egypt.

Priscillianism had been defined by the Catholic Church as a Gnostic theology that was introduced by **Marcus of Egypt** to Priscillian of Galicia. According to Sulpicius Severus (420 CE), a traveler named Marcus, from the Egyptian city of Men-Nefer (Memphis), brought Gnostic "heresy" to Galicia, where *"his pupils were a certain Agape, a woman of no mean origin, and a rhetorician named Helpidius."* By these *"...Priscillian was instructed, a man of noble birth, of great riches, bold, restless eloquent, learned through much reading, very ready at debate and discussion..."* Sulpicius Severus also wrote, *"[Priscillian] drew into its [the heresy's] acceptance many persons of noble rank and multitudes of the common people by the arts of persuasion."*

Bishops wrote of Priscillianism as a cosmology based on monotheism and that the created universe is based on the dualistic principle, which agrees with the Ancient Egyptian religion. The nature of duality is best expressed in the Ancient Egyptian text, known as the *Bremner-Rhind Papyrus*,

> **I was anterior to the Two Anteriors that I made, for I had priority over the Two Anteriors that I made, for my name was anterior to theirs, for I made them anterior to the Two Anteriors...**

The dual principle in the creation state was expressed in Ancient Egyptian texts, in the pair of **Shu** and **Tefnut.** The pair of husband and wife is the characteristic Egyptian way of expressing duality and polarity. This dual nature was manifested in Ancient Egyptian texts and traditions, since its recovered archeological findings.

The Galician people (like Ancient Egyptians and other Iberian communities), tend to perceive time as a cyclical alternation of paired opposites in accordance with the regular passing and return of the seasons, of occasions for commemoration, of life and death. This confirms exactly to the Ancient Egyptian premise of the role of the "paired opposites" of **Auset** (Isis) and **Ausar** (Osiris), which is best described by Diodorus of Sicily, *Book I*, [11, 5-6], as follows,

> *These two gods [Isis and Osiris], they hold, regulate the entire universe, giving both nourishment and increase to all things by means of a system of three seasons which complete the full cycle through an unobservable movement. . . .*

In the 7th century, the practices of these seasonal cycles in Galicia were given orthodox "legitimacy" by being incorporated into the Church's calendar. "Christian" feast days thus were generated from existing traditional festivities, which were tied to cycles of scarcity and abundance, planting and harvesting.

Priscillianism stressed how the holy books (as taught by Marcus the Egyptian) emphasized the individualism inherent in seeking the divine truth, i.e. an individual could find salvation outside the established ecclesiastical hierarchy. He stressed the role of the laity as individuals but added a strong responsibility for study on the part of each individual seeker. A follower of the mystical path could gain "knowledge" and thus salvation by diligent study combined with ascetic rejection of the flesh. Likewise, the Egyptian model of mysticism (Sufism) is not a matter of creed and dogma, but rather of a personal charter. The Egyptian model of mysticism is a natural expression of personal religion in relation to the expression of religion as a communal matter. It is an assertion of a person's right to seek contact with the source of being and reality, as opposed to institutionalized religion, which is based on authority, a one-way master-slave relationship.

The official Church was always fearful of the individualism and power of holy men and women existing on the periphery of established hierarchy, a fear exacerbated in the late 4th century CE when asceticism in all its forms was associated with Priscillianism, i.e. it was not a localized phenomenon in Galicia, but was widespread and was given a single name—Priscillianism.

The Egyptian mystic utilizes both intellect and intuition to gain knowledge of the nature, attributes and works of God. Likewise, for Priscillian and his followers, asceticism was a means to a very particular end, learning of the Divine through trained intuitive faculties. The progress of the spiritual life is described as a journey or a pilgrimage consisting of slow progressions toward the goal of union with Reality. Such progressive stages are clearly described in the countless Ancient Egyptian texts—detailing the journey of the successful soul from its earthly living—towards the Divine, in order to achieve immortality, as symbolized by the hard work of Herakles—the initiate god.

Galicians, like Ancient (and present-day Baladi) Egyptians, follow the old custom of burying goods along with the deceased. Once the deceased had been buried, the involvement of the living with the dead did not end. Priscillian also advocated the Egyptian belief in the transmigration of souls, and that the dead could be summoned from the other world by suitable ceremonies, which included music. As in Ancient (and Baladi) Egypt, women in Hispania kept a vigil in the cemetery at night, lighting candles for the dead. These contacts with the dead were reaffirmed periodically by bringing offerings to the deceased and by taking meals at the cemetery, to eat in the presence of the dead.

Priscillianism was popular enough to cause a serious Gallegan regional schism in the Iberian Church for almost 200 years. The First Council of Brags attacked and largely forbade the "heresy" of Marcus of Egypt, but the "heresy" of the Gallegan countryside remained, despite the church's execution of Priscillian. But where was this brave man buried? Joyce E. Salisbury, in her book, *Iberian Popular Religion 600BC to 700 AD: Celts, Romans and Visigoths* [1985, page 215], comes to this powerful conclusion,

> ***It is very likely that the official Church never really succeeded in secularizing the site of Priscillian's burial. I concur with Chadwick's speculation that the powerful holy man buried at Santiago de Compostella identified as St. James was Priscillian. If this were the case, the official Church only eradicated the final Priscillianist practice identified***

in the countryside by co-opting the heretical martyr's shrine and making of it a great center of orthodoxy.

The legacy and teachings of Priscillian live on, camouflaged in a Christian garment.

Santiago de Compostela

Santiago de Compostela is located in Galicia, in the northwest corner of Spain. This location was the main center of pilgrimage (and probably still is) in Europe. During the 9th century, when the Catholic Church was getting really powerful, and imposed its will on the inhabitants of Iberia, it was conveniently declared that the body of St. James the Elder made its way to Galicia. At that time, it was announced that St. James died on 25 July. The date, 25 July, at that time, was equal to the Ancient Egyptian 30th of **Abib** (Epiphi). It should be noted that this date was mentioned by Plutarch [*Moralia Vol V*] for the Egyptian festival celebration of **Heru** (Horus) *the Elder* (note how in Galicia it's called St. James *the Elder* as well). Plutarch in his *Moralia*, Vol. V [372,52B]:

> *. . . . . on the* ***thirtieth of the month Epiphi*** *they [the Egyptians] celebrate the annual festival of. .* ***Horus****,*

This particular Ancient Egyptian festival is still being celebrated until this very day in Egypt, camouflaged in an Islamic garment. This festival is held at the town of Desouk, in the Nile Delta, and is called the *Mouled of el-Desouki*. It is incredible, even geographically, how the town of Desouk in Egypt is located about the same distance from the sea as Santiago de Compostela is located from the sea. Miracles and magical (divination) acts are associated with this festival, more than any other festival throughout the year, in both Egypt and Galicia.

The traditions of Santiago de Compostela can easily be explained as Ancient Egyptian traditions. Comparing the traditions and practices of Santiago de Compostela with identical practices in Ancient (and present-day Baladi) Egypt is beyond the scope of this book. Some of these traditions were reported in J.B. Trend's book, *The Music of Spanish History to 1600* [1926, pages 70-72]. We have underlined major points of interest, and have shown some Ancient Egyptian imagery, which corresponds to parts of Trend's text:

Heka—representing the Ancient Egyptian magical powers

Every one has heard of the pilgrimage to Compostela, the shrine of shrines to which the Milky Way pointed and which seemed, from the perils of the way and the mystery which surrounded it, to be already more than half in that Other World to which the whole of life was only a pilgrimage. ***Something of the magic rites of Priscillian lingered, and still lingers****, about the country; and music, as is well known,* ***has always been closely connected with magic****. The pilgrims sang the praises of St. James, and bowed themselves before his sepulchre.* ***Yet it was hinted, and the suspicion never died, that the relics were not those of the son of Zebedee, but of one who had played*** *a far greater part in the history of Galician music. And as to Santiago himself, who was he? He is often to be seen perched upon the top of a stone pillar, like Our Lady of the Pillar of Saragossa. His body was laid on a stone, which was afterwards sunk in a pool of clear water to prevent the wanton hands of pilgrims from reducing it to fragments. In this condition it was shown to the pilgrims in 1581. There was a stone ' bed ' of St. James and also his ' boat ', and* ***there was a petrified boat in which the Virgin Mary had landed on the shores of Galicia****. Folksongs are known, addressed to the* Virxe d'a Barca, *which make it clear that the boat was also rocking stone. A pilgrim who saw it in 1484 stated definitely that the Virxe d'a Barca was herself a rocking stone; he could move it with one hand. Santiago landed from his stone vessel at Padron. He was also a great horseman. Being one of the 'sons of thunder', it was believed (and children in Spain still told it) that thunder was the galloping of St. James.* ***He was*** *__the national and tribal hero; he rose from the dead to fight for his country__, and appeared on a white horse at the battle of Clavijo, like the angels at Mons and the Heavenly Twins at the battle of Lake Regillus. He ruled the storm, the sky, and the sun; his mate was the Lady of the Doves, the 'Saint Proserpine' of an inscription, St. Eulalia and St. Columba, whose birds are still set free at Santiago on Candlemas Day. He took care of the fruits of the earth. Before he came the land was covered with briars and nettles, but when he was buried it brought forth abundance of corn and fruit. __He was also a bull-god__; he gave the Spaniards their totem-animal, to be petted and adored, ritually killed and afterwards eaten—as happens to this day. He had a curious adventure (recorded in an ancient relief at Caldas de los Reyes), in which he appears, like Lohengrin, in a boat drawn by a figure half maiden and __half swan__, with a holy friar seated in the stern, to observe the proprieties and __play to him upon the harp__.*

Apis—the Ancient Egyptian bull-god

Heru (Horus) the Elder, listening to the harpist [now at the Louvre]

Lastly, he was the psychopompos, the shepherd of souls, __the patron of wayfarers__; and wayfarers came from all parts to do honor to their patron.

The famed ***Mozarabic*** rites, which are related to the traditions of Santiago de Compostela, follow the same exact patterns of poetry, music and chanting, which can only be found in Ancient Egypt. [More details in the next chapter.]

The Egyptian/Iberian Mystical Societies

The history and practices of confraternities in Iberia (and southern Italy) coincide exactly with "Sufi" Orders, and all of them are of Ancient Egyptian origin. The mystical torch of the Ancient Egyptians has continued, through the practices and traditions of the silent majority—*Baladi* Egyptians. Some of the *Baladi* Egyptians dedicate themselves to further spiritual enlightenment. These mystics of Egypt are called *"Sufis"* by others. The Egyptian mystical seekers prefer to call themselves *Seekers of the Way*.

Egyptian mysticism (Sufism) is not an offshoot of Islam; it is the old "religion" camouflaged into Arabized/Islamized terms. The term and practices of *"Sufism"* and confraternities surfaced as a result of Islamic conquests and the subsequent terrorization of the populace. In order for the Islamic-terrorized masses to maintain their ancient traditions, they had to camouflage old traditions under an Islamic garment. Such was led by the Egyptian Dhu-'I-Nun (d. 860 CE), who is recognized in all Islamized Sufi references worldwide as the spiritual source of *"Sufism"*, who prepared the way for the presently known form of *"Islamized Sufism"*. Sufis claim him for their own, as a leader and originator of important concepts, such as the mystic's direct knowledge (gnosis) of God and the stations and states of the spiritual Path. Dhu-'I-Nun was knowledgeable of the Ancient Egyptian hieroglyphs. A number of short treatises are attributed to him, which deal with alchemy, magic, and medicine.

Theosophy was and continues to be a dangerous game to play in both Islamized and Christianized countries. Since the preaching of Union with God is open to the charge of blasphemy (and subsequent death), it was necessary to disguise the mystical principles and practices, to keep Islamists and the Church at bay. Islam, like Christianity, sees itself as the final and full revelation of God. The mystics (Sufis), under the ironclad Islamic and Christian rule, have been suffering and killed by Islamists and the Church. In order to survive under the ironclad rule of Islam and Christianity both, the Egyptian mystics (Sufis) and the Iberian confraternities learned to survive by:

1. building mosques (or churches) next to the shrines of the folk saints. In other words, they are hiding in the shadow of Islam/Christianity,

2. dressing up mystical (Sufi) concepts in an Islamic/Christian garment and *generously* giving the credit to Islam/Christianity and Mohammed/Jesus. As a result, they pay an exaggerated deference to "Mohammed/Jesus", in order to keep on good terms with Islamists/Christians,

3. continuing all Ancient Egyptian/Iberian festivals under "Islamized/Christianized" names.

The mystical seekers in Egypt and the Iberian Peninsula generate their own kinds of collective life. Like-minded seekers form networks of masters and disciples called the *Ways*. The diversity of humankind is reflected in the diversity of fellowships/confraternities. All fellowships/confraternities must contain the following elements:

1. A (historic/spiritual chain) link to a particular folk saint.
2. A systematic organization consisting of members at various stages of development/progression.
3. A code of ethics.
4. Modes and programs to attain goals.
5. An active role in society by practicing what they learn. Serving others constitutes an integral aspect of self-development. The individual performance in the society is the true test of his/her success.

6. Maintaining the folk saint shrines, festivals, etc.

Since their inceptions in Egypt and Iberia, these mystical societies continually struggled with the Moslem/Catholic authorities disguised in state laws and regulations. Their trade guilds were periodically condemned and prohibited by royal and ecclesiastical authorities. The same authorities invented laws to penetrate and to minutely control every action they made. As such, all confraternities were theoretically required to draw up official documents, so as to follow them closely.

In Spain, particularly in (Egyptian) Romany areas, such as in Cádiz, Jerez, Seville and the surrounding province of Andalusia, confraternities were (and continue to be) an integral and highly visible part of community life.

14

The Egyptian-Hispanic Musical Heritage

The Egyptian Romany Muses

The wealth of the (Egyptian) Romany of Hispania's musical heritage is well known in poetry, singing, musical performance, and dancing. Their excellence is recognized worldwide, as their ancestors were in Cádiz, during Roman times and before that. The musical heritage in Iberia pre-dates Islam and Christianity, as testified by Strabo and Silius Italicus.

Melodies that are the originals of practically all of the types now considered indigenous to the different regions of Hispania may be found in the *Cantigas*, in the Toledo manuscript of the National Library; hence it is clear that popular tradition has been uninterrupted for many centuries. The music now held to be regional all came from a common origin. Whenever we trace back the origin, we find the (Egyptian) Romany (Gypsies, *Gitanos*, *Moriscos*, and Mossarabs) to be the bearers of ancient musical heritage.

It is generally agreed that the Iberian music has always been "oriental". Accreditation was given to every place in the "Orient" except the true source—Egypt.

The Music of Civilization

Introduction of musical forms, as well as musical instruments, in Iberia was arbitrary and generously accredited to the minority Moorish ruling caste. Yet, in their homeland, they never had such instruments and/or practiced such tones, prior to the Islamic rule of Iberia. This is confirmed in the post-Moorish era, whereby many folk songs of Morocco, Algeria, and Tunisia are still referred to their origin being from Iberia, i.e. these songs did not go from North Africa to Iberia, but rather in the opposite direction.

We repeatedly hear assertions regarding an origin of music being Arabic, Byzantine, etc, with no supporting evidence whatsoever. When invaders (Byzantines, Arabs, etc) adopt/accept the music of their conquered people (such as the Egyptians), the credit for the music cannot be reversed to the invaders. Ibn Khaldun—a Spaniard of Arab descent—summarily dismissed the Arabic origin of music and other aspects of sedentary civilization. The following excerpts from his *Muqaddimah* affirm that music (along with other civilized features/skills/crafts) doesn't come out of thin air and that music is contrary to the nature of nomads such as the Berbers and Arabs.

In chapter 5, Section 15, Ibn Khaldun writes:

> *The mind does not cease transforming all kinds of (arts and crafts), including the composite ones, from potentiality into actuality through the gradual discovery of one thing after the other, until they are perfect.* ***This is achieved in the course of time and of generations. Things are not transformed from potentiality into actuality in one stroke, especially technical matters****. Consequently, a certain amount of time is unavoidable. . . .*

In chapter 5, Section 20, entitled *"The Arabs, of all people, are least familiar with arts and crafts"*, Ibn Khaldun writes:

> *The reason for this is that* ***the Arabs are more firmly rooted in desert life and more remote from sedentary civilization****, the crafts, and the other things that sedentary civilization calls for. . . .*
>
> ***The non-Arabs in the West, the Berbers, are like the Arabs in this respect****, because for a very long period they remained firmly rooted in desert life.*

Western academia tells us that in the post-Islamic era, a peculiar type of music that is associated with a religion (such as Islam), or language (such as Arabic), came into existence. Western academia tells us that out of thin air the Arabized people possessed a musical system of rhythm and mensural values, as early as the 7th century CE. This system did not come out of thin air, but it was an actual existing system. The content and style of such musical treatises, written in the language of the invaders—Arabic—leads us to one source—Ancient Egypt. As stated earlier, the majority of the working-class immigrants under the Moorish rule came from Egypt—to join their earlier immigrants in major cities, cultivated areas, and near mining sites.

The evidence from historical records, archeological findings, and Greek and Roman testimonies shows that the Ancient Egyptians possessed the knowledge of musical theory and practices. Reviewing the dates and manner of appearance of instruments and musical practices leads us to one source only—Egypt.

Tight-stepped musical scales were attributed to post-Islam Persia and some Arabized areas. The evidence in Ancient Egypt shows that Egypt was the source of such scales. Based on evidence from the Old and Middle Kingdoms (4,500 years ago), the Ancient Egyptian instruments and the exhibited playing techniques reveal several types of tight-stepped scales. In other words, such scales were exported from Egypt to the "Arabs", Persians, and Byzantines, who conquered and occupied Egypt.

The Heavenly Musical Forms

The (Egyptian) Romany are intimately related to the oldest and most characteristic and traditionalist type of Andalusian folk music, which is known by the generic name of ***cante jondo*** (or *cante hondo*). *Hondo* (or in its aspirated, provincial form, ***jondo***) signifies *deep* or *profound*. The most genuine representative of this type is the ***seguiriya gitana***, which follows forms of melody that have preserved most marks of antiquity that are distinguished by several peculiar musical elements found, such as:

1. tight-stepped musical scales with enharmonic quality. That is to say, certain functional notes are divided and subdivided into intervals smaller than a semitone,

2. the use of enharmonism as a means of expressive modulation,

3. the alteration by less than a semitone of four out of seven notes of the scale, and

4. the free rhythm of the melodic line and the richness of the modulating inflexions. Such free rhythm does not conform to regular measurement.

These peculiar features belong to Ancient Egyptian musical heritage, where the evidence is clear archeologically and historically. The wall reliefs of the Ancient Egyptian temples and tombs depict numerous types and forms of musical instruments. These musical scenes visibly show the hands of the harp player striking certain strings, and the wind instrument players playing certain chords. The distances of the lute frets clearly show that the corresponding intervals and scales can be measured and calculated. The positions of the harpists' hands on the strings clearly indicate ratios such as the Fourth, the Fifth, and the Octave—revealing an unquestionable knowledge of the laws governing musical harmony. The playing of musical instruments is controlled by the conductors' hand movements, which also help us identify certain tones, intervals and functions of sound.

In addition to the numerous representations of musical scenes pictured in temples and tombs from all periods throughout Egypt's dynastic history (5,000 years ago), we also have access to hundreds of various Ancient Egyptian musical instruments that have been recovered from their tombs.

The depicted musical scenes in Ancient Egyptian tombs, as well as instruments found from the Old and Middle Kingdoms, indicate ratios between the open strings of the harp, the densely ordered frets on the long necks of string instruments, as well as the measurements between the fingerholes in wind instruments that reveal/confirm:

1. Several types of musical scales.
2. Narrow-stepped scales were common from the earliest known Egyptian history (more than 5,000 years ago).

Enharmonism was thus a prominent feature of Ancient Egyptian music modulation. We also have historical confirmation from Flavius Josephus, who in his volumes *History of the Jews*, stated that the Ancient Egyptian temple musicians played an ***enharmonic*** *triangular instrument (órganon trígonon* ***enarmónion****)*.

The Ancient Egyptian tone system was based on the integrity of the Perfect Fifth, which yields the division of the octave into 53 equal intervals (namely the Egyptian comma)—each interval can be further divided into three **buk-nunu** (means *mouth of a baby*, in both Ancient Egyptian and Spanish). Since the octave is commonly divided into 1200 cents (a cent is a standard unit for measuring musical intervals), the Egyptian musical comma equals 22.64 cents. A **buk-nunu** is equal to 7.55 cents. The comma is not an interval by itself, but a discreet increment in the whole spectrum of available tones. Out of this 53-tone compass came a variety of frameworks. Each framework constituted the raw material out of which various seven-natural-tone scales are formed for melody.

Analysis of the holes in found Ancient Egyptian wind instruments, and frets on found string instruments, as well as the ratio of string lengths in the harps, proves with consistency the use of these "unique" discreet increments of the Egyptian comma and **buk-nunu**.

In conclusion, the evidence supports the fact that the peculiarities of the Hispanic tonal system are of Ancient Egyptian origin, and that this peculiar system continued to be practiced by the Romany of Hispania—the dark/tan-skinned people—the descendants of the Pharaohs.

One of the most distinctive features in the musical forms of both Egypt and Iberia (ancient and present) is the alternating style in music, poetry, and dancing.

We hear that in Spain, in the 9th century, poems began to be written in "vulgar Arabic" (meaning *Egyptian*), which were accentual and divided into stanzas. The genre of these poems was the refrain, which came at the beginning, or was repeated after every stanza throughout the poem. This arrangement is found in Spanish poetry of all ages, above all in poetry intended for music, for it is essentially a musical form. It is also the regular pattern of the ***Cantigas*** of Alfonso the Sage; and with slight modification it is the principle adopted by the Provencal Troubadors.

The word, *ador*, is found in Spain, and means *turn* or *time*, which was later replaced in some references with the same significance as *nuba*. **Ador** is an Ancient Egyptian word (with the same meaning), which was also replaced in Arabic references with the word *nuba*. In both Egypt and the Iberian Peninsula, it is said of various singers that each sang when his turn (ador) came. The same term *ador/dor* has, since the earliest times, also become the technical term for stanzas of lyrical poetry.

The concept of this musical form is represented in a typical Ancient Egyptian musical scene since the Old Kingdom [4,500 years ago]. An example can be found 4,300 years ago, on the walls of Mereruka's tomb [6th Dynasty, Sakkara], which shows two men squatting inside an egg-shaped oval, beating two percussion sticks together. The scene represents the typical Egyptian **dor/ador**, a piece of music with a refrain. Other similar graphical representations are depicted in Ancient Egyptian tombs, in harvest scenes of grapes and of grain being taken to the granary.

Alternate singing, the archetype of responsorial and antiphonal practice of singing, was the specialty of the Egyptians since ancient times. Present-day *Baladi* Egyptians of rural population continue the very same tradition—where their singing form, structure, and pattern are rendered by a choir leader (a leading voice). The lead singer provides the melismatic solo parts, and was/is usually accompanied by 4-6 singers who perform the rhythmically formal, strongly bound refrain-like sections.

The application of balanced polarity—alternating sounds—applies to all types of musical performances in Ancient and present-day Egypt. Alternating singing may also occur between male and female individuals or male and female groups. This type of performance applies also to instruments (between different instruments), alternating between a singer and instrument(s), as well as in dancing performances.

The Egyptian (as well as the Iberian) poetry shows this antithetical style, which will be discussed later in this chapter.

This musical form of antiphons, responsories and other chants of the ***Mozarabic*** rite have existed in the Iberian Peninsula long before Moorish rule, and are a unique feature in the poetry and music of the (Egyptian) Romany ***(Gitanos, Moriscos,*** and ***Mozarabs).***

Love Conquers All

Though the themes in the flamenco and ***cante jondo*** songbooks are vast, the majority of the ***coplas*** deal with some form of love. The love of a man for a woman. Entangled in the love poems are the motifs of pain and sorrow. The deeper the feeling of pain and sorrow, the higher the spiritual experience. Joy and sorrow, at their extremes, are very intimate feelings.

While the un-spiritualized people consider love and wine themes to be "secular", spiritual people, like Federico Garcia Lorca, find the art of the (Egyptian) Romany ***cantaor*** (or singer) to be a solemn rite, to be approached with profound religious respect.

The theme of man's love for a woman is the earthly image of the ultimate goal of the mystical seeker of uniting with the Divine. We are separated from the Divine—in our earthly realm. Man's love towards the Divine is a quality that manifests itself in the heart of the Divine seeker, in the form of veneration and magnification, so that he seeks to satisfy his Beloved and becomes impatient and restless in his desire for visions of Him, and cannot rest with anyone except Him.

The whole of Egyptian mysticism rests on the belief that when the individual self is lost, the Universal Self is found. This ecstatic trance of absence from one's self is called "*intoxication*" and the ecstatics are called "*spiritual drunkards*". The drunkenness of the mystics describes the ecstatic frame of mind in which the spirit is intoxicated with the contemplation of God—just as the body is intoxicated with wine. It is therefore that the mystic lives within a perpetual dialogue with the surrounding nature. Wine, love, and nature themes meld to form some of the most delightful lyrics in the anthology, which, by the way, are totally forbidden in Islam.

The theme of divine love manifested itself in the works of Ibn 'Arabi, who spent a few years in Egypt, and thereafter "introduced" the strophic-type poetry—muwashshah—in Iberia. Ancient Egypt is the origin of this strophic-type religious poetry. The type that most closely resembles the muwashshah, however, is the **musammat**, which is derived from **Samaa**—which in the Ancient Egyptian language means *to unite*—through sound/music. Post-Islam mysticism (Sufism) traditions acknowledge that appropriate music is the means of transmission and intermediation between human and Divine. The godfather of post-Islam mysticism (Sufism), namely the Egyptian Dhu-'I-Nun el-Massri, said of **samaa**, *"Those who listen with their souls can hear the heavenly music/call."*

The famed Sufi Al-Ghazali (who spent years in Egypt) introduced music into the Sufi rites, based on Ancient Egyptian practices, which were introduced by Dhu-'I-Nun, the Egyptian. He makes the following statement:

> *The Sufis, most venerated for their sanctity and doctrine, like* ***Dhu-'I-Nun the Egyptian****, had no scruples about the use of*

music as an important element in religious practices of ascetic life.

The Egyptian Dhu-'I-Nun (d. 860 CE) is recognized in all Islamized Sufi references worldwide as the spiritual source of *"Sufism"*, who prepared the way for the presently known form of Islamized Sufism. Sufis claim him for their own, as a leader and originator of important concepts, such as the mystic's direct knowledge (gnosis) of God and the stations and states of the spiritual Path. Dhu-'I-Nun advocated the learning of appropriate music—as the means of transmission and intermediation between human and divine. As such, recitation, singing, and chanting of ***rosarios***, together with ecstatic dancing, were introduced (based on prior Ancient Egyptian traditions) into Sufi practices.

Singing and Poetry

Ancient Egyptian texts show that Egyptians spoke and sang in musical patterns on all occasions and for all purposes—from the most sacred to the most mundane. Present-day Egyptians are like their ancestors—they love to sing about anything and everything. There is nothing that is too insignificant or too large to sing a song to (or about). Likewise, the Spanish folk music is very rich, with all types of songs and poetry. It is no coincidence that the richest and best compositions of songs, poetry, and music are abundant in Extremadura, New Castille, Valencia, and Andalusia—the four provinces where the (Egyptian) Romany most abound.

The Egyptians perceived language and music as two sides of the same coin. Both poetry and singing followed similar rules for musical composition. Poetry is written not only with a rhyme scheme, but also with a recurring pattern of accented and unaccented syllables. Each syllable alternates between accented and unaccented, making a double/quadruple meter and several other varieties. Patterns of set rhythms or lengths of phrases of Ancient Egyptian poems, praises, hymns, and songs of all kinds, which are known to have been chanted or performed with some musical accompaniment, were rhythmic with uniform meters and a structured rhyme.

The themes and metrics of lyrical poetry is the same in both Ancient Egypt and Iberia. Lyrical poetry was made famous in Spain via the Egyptian descendants—the Romany ***(Gitanos/Moriscos/Mudejare/Mozarabs).***

The most common ***copla*** of the (Egyptian) Romany is an octosyllabic quartet with loose alternate rhyme. Many are composed of three, five, and six lines of varying syllabic length. The singer often repeats and lengthens lines, depending on the traditional vocal ornaments of a given style. Likewise, the Ancient (and present-day Baladi) Egyptian poetry has had the same exact structural form and artistic features.

All that the Egyptian writes (whatever the subject is) falls into short lines of approximately equal length. These lines have a verse, i.e. some sort of metrical structure. This is, in many cases, a fixed number of lines—generally there are three or four—that belong together. Four or double-fours are most common. There was/is also the stanza, of a freer structure, the sections in which are of varying length, and display no regularity with regard to the number of lines.

Artistic rhythms, naturalness, brilliancy, and charm of Egyptian and Hispanic poetry strive on wordplay, alliterations, tropes, and puns.

The following is a summary of the various forms/styles of poetry that are found in both the Iberian Peninsula and Ancient (and present-day Baladi) Egypt:

1. The parallelism of the phrases—where two short sentences follow each other, and correspond in arrangement and also as a rule in purport.

2. The parallel phrases may group themselves in strophes, as is shown in numerous poems. These parallel phrases are, moreover, frequently arranged in different order.

3. The antithetical style of poetry.

4. Alliterative style was used as a definite poetic form.

5. Poetry of a metrical nature—poetry divided into short lines, which were distinguished in the manuscripts by red dots. These little verses are punctuated, not merely so as to denote the sense, but also the divisions that are to be observed in recitation. Each verse contains a certain number of primary accents—usually two. The peculiar law of accentuation in the Egyptian language—that several words closely allied in syntax should be invested with one primary accent—lies at the root of this verse construction.

In Hispania, in the 9th century, poems began to be written in what some historians describe as "vulgar Arabic", which were accentual and divided into stanzas. This Ancient Egyptian type of strophic poetry can only be found in Iberia and Egypt. It is claimed that two forms of strophic Hispanic poetry, the *muwashshah* and the *zagal*, were invented in Andalusia. The two are basically two colors of the same strophic poetic form. The characteristic form of the Spanish ***Villancico*** is to all intents and purposes the same as that of the two forms of this (non-Arabic) strophic poetry.

The muwashshah is a group of rhyming phrases molded into a pattern that consists of strophes. The outstanding feature of the genre, the one to which it owes its name of muwashshah, is the regular alternation between two elements: lines with separate rhymes and others with common rhymes. Meter is not an essential feature.

Muwashshahs were not considered a legitimate form of poetic art by the Arabs. Most contemporary scholars would not even include examples of them in literary anthologies, because the meters of these muwashshahat are not in the metrical schemes (a'arid) of the poems of the Arabs. Classical Arabic verse was quantitative and continuous. It is therefore incorrect to call this form of strophic poetry as being "Arabic" or "Hispano-Arabic" or "vulgar Arabic". The strophic form and the language used were Egyptian. It must be remembered that Egypt provided most of the immigrants during the Moorish rule, who settled in areas previously occupied by their ancestors. The language of these Egyptians does not sound exactly like Arabic—so it was arbitrarily called: "vulgar Arabic", "Hispano-Arabic", etc.

Wherever we turn—to the books or the copious biographical dictionaries of the Andalusians, or the historical literature of the period—we find that the muwashshah is completely absent, because it is known as **musmaat**, and dates back to the pre-Islamic period.

The antecedents of the muwashshah were to be sought in the same strophic poetry known in Ancient Egypt as **musammat**, which is a poem of very simple metrical structure: several lines—usually three or four—with a common rhyme are followed by one with a separate rhyme. The scheme of a poem having strophes of four verses (murabba') will thus be: aaaB cccB, that of one with strophes of five verses (mukhammas): aaaaB ccccB.

The first country where the muwashshah appears is Egypt—and the date for the first evidence of its presence there is much earlier than has been generally assumed. The first and most prominent writing about the muwashshah was not by an Andalusian but by an Egyptian, Ibn Sana' al-Mulk, who lived in Egypt from 1155 to 1211. He wrote about the format for writing muwashshahat. Ibn Sana' al-Mulk's text of Dar al-Tiraz is an un-voweled text, which created problems for the unaccustomed people (scholars!), and therefore their work on this subject is full of inaccuracies.

The Ancient Egyptian texts provide an extensive number and variety of **musammat**/muwashshahat in the forms of litanies, rosaries, eulogies, psalms, hymns, etc. Likewise, present-day Egyptian mystics (Sufis) utilize the same ancient poetic and recitative compositions. Egyptian mystics have a countless number of these poetic and musical compositions that they know by heart. The mystical rosaries (*awrad*) are usually a long well composed series, in the form of poetic stanzas of recitations. Each rosary consists of well-designed components/sections, with each's own particular climaxes. These rosaries are replete with wise proverbial sayings, pious reflections, and moral precepts. These hundreds of Egyptian compositions are too old to be accredited to specific authors.

Many of the strophe-poems were known in Spain before the Moors arrived. After all, the ***Pervigilium Veneris*** is a poem with a refrain, and some scholars believe that, too, to be of Spanish origin. Early Spanish, Provencal, and Galician-Portuguese poetry share much and must be linked to the muwashshah's origins—Egypt.

The Musical Instruments

Introduction of musical forms, as well as musical instruments, in Iberia, was arbitrary and generously accredited to the "Arabs", who had no prior history in such areas prior to their arrival to Iberia! Yet only in Ancient Egypt do we have long and documented musical traditions that were admired by Greek and Roman writers. Plato acknowledged these facts and adopted the Egyptian musical theory and practices in his Ideal Laws of the Ideal Republic. [For detailed info, see *Egyptian Rhythm: The Heavenly Melodies*, by Moustafa Gadalla.]

The archeological and traditional Egyptian history of music is much more abundant than in any other country. The wall reliefs of the Ancient Egyptian temples and tombs depict numerous types and forms of musical instruments, the technique in which these instruments were to be played and tuned, the ensemble playing, and much, much more.

The depicted musical scenes in Ancient Egyptian tombs, as well as instruments found from more than 4,500 years ago, reveal/confirm:

a. playing and tuning techniques of string instruments to provide solo and chordal playing of instruments, and
b. playing techniques of wind instruments that provide small increments and organ effect.

The Ancient Egyptians were/are famed worldwide for their mastery of the playing techniques of their musical instruments. The skill of the Egyptians, in the use of these instruments, was affirmed by Athenaeus, who stated (in his texts [iv, 25]) that both the Greeks and "barbarians" were taught music by Egyptian natives.

The Egyptian instruments fall under four major instrument groups:

1. String instruments with open strings, like tri-gonon (zither), lyre, harp, ...etc.

2. String instruments with stopped strings on a neck, like the tanboura, guitar, oud/lute, etc.

3. Wind instruments like the flute, pipe, double pipe, trumpet, etc.

4. Percussion instruments like drums of different shapes, sizes, and functions—cylindrical, small hand drums, and single skin drums, tambourines. The Ancient Egyptian non-membrano-phone instruments included percussion sticks, clappers, sistrums/sistra, cymbals, castanets, bells, xylophones, etc.

Some of the unique Egyptian instruments that have found their way to Iberia are:

1. Short-Neck Lute (present-day *oud*)

Ancient Egyptians were familiar with this type of short-neck lute, which has a sturdy pear-shaped body and a broad fingerboard. The number of strings ranged from two to six strings. In Ancient Egypt, the short-necked lute (l'aud) led the religious processions, validating its present nickname as *king of instruments.*

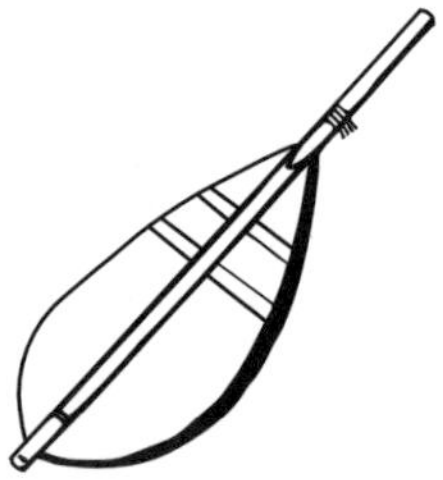

Two lutes of this type came from Ancient Egyptian tombs in Ta-Apet (Thebes) [dated ca. 16th century BCE, now in the Berlin Museum], and are 14" [35cm] and 19" [48.5cm] long. The small one [shown herein] had 2, or possibly 3, strings. The larger one had 4 strings.

The most popular of this type had/have **four strings. Along with the frets**, the instrument was/is able to **provide the most popular 17-interval framework**. This instrument is known today in the Arabized/Islamized countries as *oud/l'aud.*

In addition to the above Egyptian instruments [now at the Berlin Museum], some other examples of this Ancient Egyptian instrument include:

- A short neck type lute is shown in a statuette of a lute player [New Kingdom, ca. 3500 years ago, now at the Cairo Museum, cat. #773].

- A statuette made of burnt clay shows a musician playing a short-neck lute. [19-20th Dynasty, Cairo Museum, cat. #38797.]

2. The Egyptian Guitars

The guitar is essentially a stringed instrument, having an incurred body or sound chest shaped like a figure eight, with flat top and bottom, and a long neck or finger board with frets. The type, in fact, goes back to remote antiquity, as witnessed by Egyptian bas-reliefs dating from the 11th and 12th Dynasties (3762-3703 BCE). The flamenco guitar was brought into Spain by the (Egyptian) Romany, who continued to be the masters of this Egyptian instrument.

The Ancient Egyptian guitar consisted of two parts: a long flat neck, or handle, and a hollow oval body. Guitars are found depicted in numerous Ancient Egyptian tombs from all eras. Several kinds of guitar were used in Egypt.

Four Ancient Egyptian strongly notched guitar-like instruments were found in the Qarara region, which dated to the Middle Kingdom (2040-1783 BCE). In addition to one at Heidelberg, a complete instrument of that kind is found in the Cairo Museum, another in the Metropolitan Museum of Art in New York, and a smaller one in the collection of Moeck, Celle. They are designed for three to six strings.

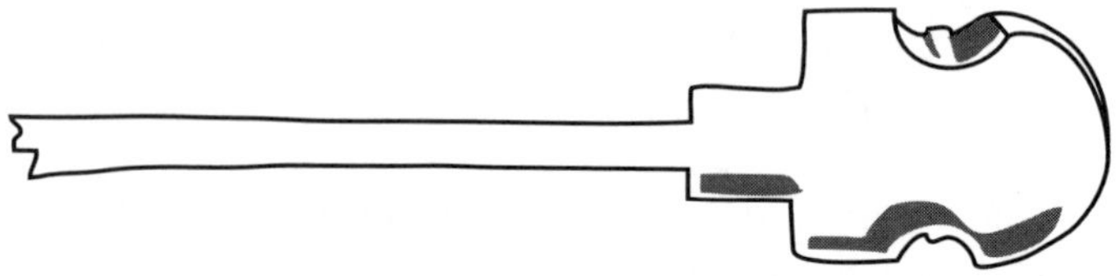

All these instruments were made of one piece, only the necks of the larger examples were elongated by pieces of extension, and all the instruments were provided with numerous frets.

It is from an ancient instrument of this kind, sometimes called *cithara/kithara*, that the modern name guitar (chitarra) has been derived.

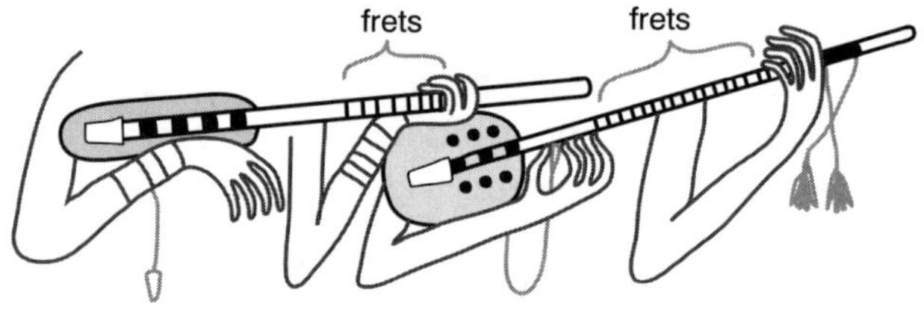

Two types of Ancient Egyptian guitars are depicted in a music scene from the tomb of Nebamun [Ta-Apet (Thebes), 15th century BCE, now in the British Museum]. One is a long-necked guitar with long almond-shaped resonator, and one with a rounded resonator.

Both instruments [shown above] are provided with fingerboards. One has 8 visible frets, which begin halfway down the neck. The other has **17 visible frets**, indicative of the ability to perform narrow-stepped scales.

3. The Twin Horns/Trumpets

Horns/trumpets were known in Ancient Egypt since its very early times. Generally, trumpets in Ancient Egypt always appeared in pairs. With the typical two horns: one was sounded at dawn, the other at dusk.

The more or less conical horn *(al-buq)* has survived in the Spanish terms: ***alboque***, ***alboquea***, or ***albuquea***. **Buq/buk** is an Egyptian (not Arabic) word that means *mouth*.

The Egyptian trumpet was straight, like the later Roman tuba, or the present-day trumpet. Ancient Egypt had a variety of trumpets. They were generally 2 to 3 ft [60-90cm] long, and made of brass or bronze, with mouthpieces, and with flares or "bells" at the other end.

4. Castanets

Spain, like Ancient Egypt, is one of the few countries in which the castanets have developed into a high art, a total musical instrument that has literally become part of the dancer's body in musical expression. Many of the regions of Spain use various types of castanets for their individual folk dances, some have different names—***postizos, pulgaretes, palillos***.

Tiny fingertip pairs of cymbals were in use in Ancient Egypt. They are known as *castanets* because they were made of (or look like) chestnut (***castaña***).

These small-type cymbals, 2" to 3" [5-7.5 cm] in diameter, are played between thumb and middle finger up to this day. Castanets—called ***crotala***—are used in pairs, and are struck together while dancing. The term *castanets* is used here in the narrower sense of clappers, the striking faces of which are hollowed out to give a fuller resonance.

Egyptian castanets existed in two forms: 1) shaped something like a very small wooden boot, cut in half, lengthwise, and grooved in the leg part, while the tapering foot part served as a handle; 2) nearly the shape of modern Spanish ***castañuelas***, but it was less flat and looked like the chestnut, ***castaña***, for which it was named.

Numerous Egyptian castanets were found in Ancient Egyptian tombs, and are now scattered throughout the museums and private collections worldwide.

The religious significance of castanets is shown in the musical scene of four musicians with castanets, depicted in the **Apet** procession at the Luxor Temple, from the time of Tut-Ankh-Amen [c. 1360 BCE].

Rhythmic Hand-Clapping—The Egyptian clapping with hands and stamping with feet has turned at an early time into a finely graded, dynamic and varied means of expression, and thus acquired an additional significance in Egypt where it turned into a high art in their culture of music.

Rhythmic clapping of two groups of men and women from the tomb of Tuthomosis (Tomb 342), **Ta-Apet** (Thebes) [18th Dynasty, now in the British Museum]

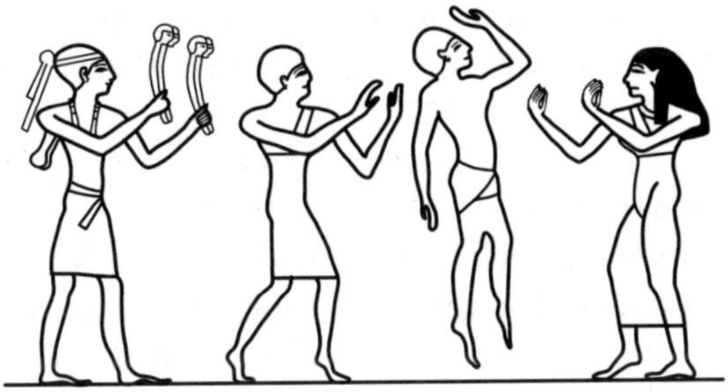

Egyptian clapping, foot stamping, and finger snapping consisted of rhythmic beats, whether simple or complicated rhythms, tonally nuanced, and dynamically well balanced. The tonal differences were produced in such a manner, that clapping used to take place as in Spain with ***palmas sordas*** or with ***palmas brillantes***, i.e. with hollow or flat hands. In addition, and since primeval times, all possible other forms of body beats existed.

Rhythmic Dancing

In Ancient Egypt. there were priestess-dancers who bear a quite striking resemblance to flamenco dancers. The upraised arms, and the evident grace and movement of these four Egyptian dancers remind us strongly of their modern counterparts. The famous snake priestess from Ancient Egypt wears a similarly flounced skirt, holds her snake-extended arms aloft as a dancer does, and wears a transfixed expression on her face. The sinuosity of snakes and the sinuosity of the arms and hands in flamenco are analogous.

As noted earlier [chapter 8], the Egyptian origin of the Romany dancing was noted by Voltaire and Richard Ford.

Ecstatic dancing formed an integral part of the rites of **Auset** (Isis) and **Ausar** (Osiris). Dances and songs were performed by the Pharaoh himself—as part of the temple rituals. The Pharaoh was, as such, the *Lord of the [Song and] Dance*. In the Hall of Offerings, at Dendera Temple, a song celebrating the taming of the lioness, goes:

The Pharaoh comes, to dance.
He comes, to sing.
Mistress, look, how he dances!
Het-Heru, look, how he jumps!

The **netert** (goddess) **Het-Heru** (Hathor) herself was lovingly referred to as the **Mistress of Dance** and the **Mistress of Music. Ausar** (Osiris) was also referred to as "**...fond of music and dance**".

Dancing is much more than sensation and pleasure. It is life and unity with nature. The proper rhythm of the dance elevates the dancer to a higher realm. The goal of the exhilaration dance is the attainment of a state of ecstasy in which the dancer transcends the human and physical and achieves ecstatic liberation from the self. His/her body becomes a medium which, through connecting to the ancestors, becomes the bearer of all the forces of nature. The dancer, possessed by his deified ancestor, is being transformed into this spirit, and is drawn into the circle of those supernatural forces in charge of the operation of fertility, victory, and the course of the stars.

The Ancient Egyptian temples maintained dancers of both sexes as a special class. We find them over and over again, either in the quiet dance, with gentle steps and with arms outstretched in rhomboid form, or in the most daring acrobatic positions.

Egyptian women participated in the performance of temple rites that included singing, instrument playing, and dancing. These female performers were generally daughters of the priests and nobles of the society—a reflection of the high regard for this profession.

The Iberians are a dancing people and have been famed as such from earliest times to the present. E. Louis Backman, in *Religious Dances*, notes that *"...Spain is the country in which the religious dance flourished...abundantly and...most vigorously."* There were dances associated with baptisms, weddings, and death rituals. There were hymns to invoke divine aid against illness and hymns to commemorate saints' feast days.

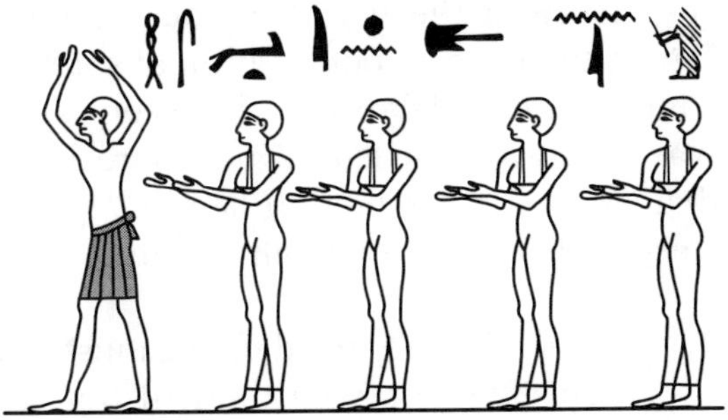

Man dancing a solo to the sound of the hand. Tomb near the Pyramids.

The link between the dances of the Gaditanae and flamenco is mostly a rhythmic ecstatic mime: the beat, the cadence, the measure marked by handclaps, by castanet, tambourine, or drum; the upraised arms in constant and sinuous motion; and the head aloof, thrown back even, always fixed between the archways of the arms. And finally there is the ecstasy—the overpowering emotion, exultation, transport, or rapture. Flamenco is complete with passion, delirium, and frenzy. The masters of flamenco are the (Egyptian) Romany—the descendants of the Ancient Egyptians.

The Musical Activities

For the (Egyptian) Romany of Hispania, as well as for the Ancient (and present-day Baladi) Egyptians, music was/ is an integral part of their daily life. To stay in harmony with nature, the Egyptians—throughout the ages—utilized music and dance in all aspects of their personal earthly voyage—from the cradle to the grave. For them, music is not just a way of life, it is life itself. It is as natural, critical, and vital as breathing.

Sound related activities were the means to communicate with the supernatural forces of the universe. The vocal voice of the Ancient Egyptian priests and the musical orchestras were sounding bridges between the macro- and the micro-cosmos—between the world of **neteru** (gods) and ancestors—and the world of the earthly living. In Ancient Egypt, the proper coordination of sound production (words, song, music, and dances)—between earth and the heavens—was clearly acknowledged and appreciated in Plato's collected dialogues, such as *Laws II* [656c-657c], as well as in *Laws VII* [798e–799b], which highlights that:

1. Music, singing, and dancing must be performed/selected according to a well thought out selection of melodies that are appropriate for the different occasions.

2. The Egyptians have had established melodies for all kinds of occasions.

3. Egypt was the ideal model for such rules and practices.

The Ancient Egyptian musical profession has comprised the whole range of representatives of the temples and other societal activities. There were various and well trained groups of singers and dancers who learned and practiced the set performance rules, suitable for the various occasions.

In Ancient Egypt, temples were commonly provided with recitation priests (chanting), and a complement of male and female musicians, singers, and dancers—all of whose task it was to participate in the various daily and seasonal cycles of rituals, so as to attune to the universal harmony. At the religious ceremonies and processions, certain musicians attached to the priestly order were employed for the exclusive service of the temple.

Many musicians in present-day Egypt belong to the mystical Sufi groups. They perform in weddings, circumcisions, folk saints' festivals, funerals, etc. They are all well disciplined musicians, dancers, reciters, and singers—just like their ancestors.

Singing and dancing were/are common at religious processions and pilgrimages throughout Hispania—particularly where the (Egyptian) Romany live. Likewise in Egypt, music was/is an essential part of pilgrimage and folk saint festivals. At the head of the present-day Sufi procession is one of the most venerable of the fellowship, playing the Egyptian *nay* (a sort of flute). In Ancient Egypt, the procession was also usually headed by a flute-player, according to Herodotus. Other members of the procession play other musical instruments. In these festivals, music was required in the ritual performances, just like modern times, and was, according to Apuleius, of a spiritual character.

Ancient Egyptian tombs show choirs of male and female singers approaching the shrine of a folk saint. The female singers wave sistra and necklaces; the male singers mark the measure by clapping their hands. The lord of the shrine awaits the choirs, who sing songs ending with special recitations.

During the festivals, the Egyptians perform ecstatic singing and dancing. A group of trained mystical seekers (Sufis) would perform this special practice, by chanting, rhythmic gestures, dancing, and deep breathing. While performing their ritualistic dance, the group repeats words and phrases accompanied by a well-trained choir performing instrumental and vocal music. The accompanying singing of well-composed musical rosaries helps achieve the trance. The music sets the rhythm (beat), which is altered by the conductor/guide to achieve the trance conditions needed to achieve ecstatic visions. The bodily movements of the participants are linked to a thought and a sound or a series of sounds. The movements develop the body, the thought focuses the mind, and the sound fuses the two and orients them towards a consciousness of divine contact.

Musical and dancing rituals had/have an important role in the seasonal round of agricultural activities, such as the sowing of seeds, threshing, and harvesting. Several scenes that date back to the Old Kingdom (4,500 years ago) mark the ritual singing for the first or the last sheaf. In several of these tombs, there are portrayals that show the corn harvest, accompanied by music.

Singing and dancing also accompanied the pressing of grapes, as depicted in several tombs in Sakkara, since the Old Kingdom era.

Music and dancing also played/play an important role, during and after the funeral procession. An example is depicted in the tomb of Ti [5th Dynasty, i.e. c. 2400 BCE], where the usual dance escort of the burial is shown. Likewise in Galicia and throughout Iberia, the populace has had ritual dances and songs at funerals. Ritual chanting and dancing make it possible for the soul of the deceased to find his/her way from our earthly realm—to the higher heavenly realms.

The Heavenly Muses

The iconography of dancing in Hispania goes back to prehistoric times. There is a paleolithic rock painting from Cogul, near Lerida (Catalonia), representing nine women dancing around a young man. This is reminiscent of the Ancient Egyptians' model musician—**Heru** (Horus) **Behdety**, whose Greek rendering is *Apollo*. Diodorus of Sicily wrote about **Horus Behdety** and his nine muses—well trained in various arts associated with music, in *Book I* [18, 4-5]:

> *Osiris was laughter-loving and fond of music and the dance; consequently he took with him a multitude of musicians, among whom were **nine maidens** who could sing and were trained in the other arts, these maidens being those who are called **the Muses**; and their leader (hegetes), as the account goes, was Horus Behdety (Apollo), who was for that reason also given **the name Musegetes**.*

Diodorus' account provides us with two interesting points:

1. The title of **Heru** (Horus) **Behdety** is noted as **Muse-gete-s**, which is an Egyptian term, meaning *musician*. **Muse-gete/Muse-kate** is not an Arabic word.

2. The concept of nine muses is of Egyptian origin.

We find the Muses described in the holiest of the Ancient Egyptian books, waiting at the gates of heavens. Jerez de la Frontera, "*City of the (Egyptian) Romany*", is located in the very heart of the flamenco country and has nourished some monumental figures in the history of ***cante jondo***. Above them all towers the legendary, Pharaonic Manuel Torres, ***"Niño de Jerez."***

Jerez de la Frontera means *guardians of the frontier*. Next to Jerez is a heavenly gate—***Puerto de Santa Maria***. From the holy Cádiz to Jerez de la Frontier to Puerto de Santa Maria, the (Egyptian) guardians maintain the ancient traditions, as other (Egyptian) Romany continue to do—from the delta of the Guadalquivir to the delta of the Ebro River, and beyond.

For you, the (Egyptian) Romany of Hispania—the guardians of old traditions and in the flamenco spirit—celebrate the passage [§§1972, 1975b] of the **Unas Transformational** (so-called *Pyramid*) **Texts** [c. 2350 BCE], describing the muses welcoming the successful resurrection and arrival of Unas to a higher realm.

The double doors of heaven are open....The Souls of Buto dance for thee, they clap their hands for thee, they let loose their hair for thee, they beat their thighs for thee. They say to thee, Osiris N: 'Thou art gone, thou art come, thou sleepest, thou art awake, thou landest, thou livest.'

Long live the spirit of the past so as to light the future ahead.

Appendices

Glossary

Almohad— a Berber movement that was established by Ibn Tumart in the early 12th century. The Almohad dynasty came to control much of western North Africa and Andalusia. They withdrew from the Iberian Peninsula in 1223.

Almoravid— North African Moslem Berber dynasty ruling in Andalusia from 1086 until 1147.

Animism— the concept that all things in the universe are animated (energized) by life forces. This concurs, scientifically, with the kinetic theory, where each minute particle of any matter is in constant motion, i.e. energized with life forces.

antiphony— two different and alternating sounds, such as a response sung between a single voice and group of singers, or between two groups of singers, etc.

Baladi— local, a term used to describe those who settled in Iberia before the coming of the Syrians in 741. The same term—Baladi—applies to the present native silent majority in Egypt, which adheres to the Ancient Egyptian traditions, under a thin layer of Islam.

BCE— **B**efore **C**ommon **E**ra. Noted in many references as BC.

CE— **C**ommon **E**ra. Noted in many references as AD.

cent— a standard unit for measuring musical intervals. An octave is equal to 1200 cents.

copla— an anonymous lyric poem three or more verses in length to be sung in a great variety of rhythms and melodies.

cosmology— the study of the origin, creation, structure, and orderly operation of the universe, as a whole and of its related parts.

Dhimmi— (Arabic) Christians and Jews living under Islamic rule.

Jews and Christians living in Moslem lands were/are subject to special restrictions and taxes. Also see *jizya* and page 27.

Duat/Tuat— (Ancient Egypt) the Underworld, where the soul goes through transformation leading to resurrection.

Fifth, Perfect— can mean either: 1) the natural sound of the fifth tone of an ascending diatonic scale, or a natural tone four degrees above or below any given natural sounding tone in such a scale—dominant. 2) the interval between two such natural sounding tones, or a combination of them.

enharmonic— designating a ¼ step/note or less.

fret— narrow, lateral ridges fixed across the finger board of a stringed instrument, such as a guitar, etc., to guide the fingering.

Gitana/Gitano— see pages 21-30.

Heb-Sed— Ancient Egyptian festival associated with the rejuvenation and spiritual and physical renewal of the Pharaoh.

interval— can mean either: 1) the ratio of the number of vibrations between two different tones. 2) The distance separating two consecutive musical notes.

Islam— Islam means submission. The Moslems believe in Allah as the sole God, AND that Mohammed is his messenger. Allah is an Arabic word, meaning *who has everything*. According to Islamic traditions, Moslem followers are encouraged to spread Islam by the sword, if preaching Islam does not "convince" people to convert.

jihad— Moslem holy war to spread Islam.

jizya— A special tax paid by Dhimmi—Christians and Jews living under Islamic rule.

matriarchy— a society/state/organization, whose descent, inheritance, and governance are traced through the females. It is the woman who transmits political rights, and the husband she chooses then acts as her executive agent.

matrilineal— a society whose descent, inheritance, and governance are based on descent through the maternal line.

Morisco— see pages 21-30.

Mozárab— see pages 21-30.

Mudéjar— see pages 21-30.

musammat/muwashshah— a strophic poem. Each stanza may contain as many as eight parts.

mysticism— consists of ideas and practices that lead to union with the Divine. Union is described more accurately as togetherness, joining, arriving, conjunction, and the realization of God's uniqueness.

neter/netert— a divine principle/function/attribute of the One Great God. (Incorrectly translated as *god/goddess*).

papyrus— could mean either: 1) A plant that is used to make a writing surface. 2) *Paper*, as a writing medium. 3) The text written on it, such as "*Leiden Papyrus*".

Romaní— see pages 21-30.

samaa— an Ancient Egyptian term meaning to unite (through music), and as such is indicative of the means of transmission and intermediation between the human and Divine.

seguiriyas— the most ***jondo*** (*hondo*) of flamenco rhythms.

sierra— mountain range, hills.

stanza— a group of lines of verse forming one of the divisions of a poem or song. It typically has a regular pattern in the number of lines and the arrangement of meter and rhyme.

stele (plural: *stelae*) — stone or wooden slab or column inscribed with commemorative texts.

Taifa kingdoms— small kingdoms that formed in Andalusia following the breakup of centralized Umayyad rule in 1031. The Taifa period lasted until the arrival of the Almoravids in the Iberian Peninsula in 1086.

Selected Bibliography

Acquaroni, J.L. *Andalusia*. Madrid, 1964.

Arnaiz-Villena, Antonio, editor. *Prehistoric Iberia: Genetics, Anthropology, and Linguistics*. New York, 2000.

Baines, John & Málek, Jaromír. *Atlas of Ancient Egypt*. Oxford, 1994.

Baldi, Philip. *The Foundations of Latin*. New York, 1999.

Baramki, Dimitri. *Phoenicia and the Phoenicians*. Beirut, 1961.

Bendiner, Elmer. *The Rise and Fall of Paradise*. New York, 1983.

Blackman, Winifred S. *The Fellahin of Upper Egypt*. London, 1968.

Bleeker, C.J. *Egyptian Festivals: Enactments of Religious Renewal*. Leiden, 1967.

Borrow, George. *The Zincali: An Account of the Gypsies of Spain*. New York, 1923.

Bowman, Alan K. *Egypt after the Pharaohs: 332 BC – AD 642 from Alexander to the Arab Conquest*. Berkeley, CA, 1996.

Brett, Michael & Fentress, Elizabeth. *The Berbers*. Cambridge USA, 1997.

Brockett, Clyde Waring Jr. *Antiphons, Responsories and other Chants of the Mozarabic Rite*. New York, 1968.

Brody, Aaron Jed. Edited by Machinist, Peter. *Each Man Cried out to his God*. Georgia, USA, 1998.

Budge, Sir E. A. Wallis. *Egyptian Language: Easy Lessons in Egyptian Hieroglyphics*. New York, 1983.

Budge, E.A. Wallis. *The Gods of the Egyptians*, 2 volumes. New York, Dover, 1969.

Budge, Wallis, *Osiris & The Egyptian Resurrection* (2 volumes). New York, 1973.

Butt, John. *The Oxford Spanish Dictionary & Grammar*. New York, 2001.

Castro, Maríe Cruz Fernández. *Iberia in Prehistory*. Cambridge USA, 1995.

Chapman, Robert. *Emerging complexity: The later prehistory of south-east Spain, Iberia and the west Mediterranean*. NYC, 1990.

Chase, Gilbert. *The Music of Spain*. New York, 1959.

Chejne, Anwar G. *The Arabic Language: Its Role in History*. Minneapolis, Minnesota, USA, 1969.

Condor, C.R. *The Tell Amarna Tablets*. London, 1893.

Conrad, Barnaby. *La Fiesta Brava: The Art of the Bull Ring*. Boston, Mass., USA, 1953.

Corbin, J.R. *The Anarchist Passion: Class conflict in Southern Spain*, 1810-1965. U.K. 1993.

Culican, William. *The Ancient Levant*. New York, 1966.

Cunliffe, Barry. *The Ancient Celts*. Oxford, 1997.

Daniels, Peter T & Bright, William. *The World's Writing Systems*. Oxford, 1996.

Devijver, H. & Lipinski, E., editors. *Studia Phoenicia x Punic Wars: Proceedings of the Conference held in Antwerp from the 23rd to the 26th of November 1988 in cooperation with the Department of History of the 'Universiteit Antwerpen' (U.F.S.I.A.)*. Belgium, 1990.

Diodorus of Sicily. *Books I, II, & IV*, tr. By C.H. Oldfather. London, 1964.

Dorey, TA & Dudley, DR. *Rome Against Carthage*. London,

1971.

Entwistle, William J, M.A. *The Spanish Language: Together with Portugues, Catalan and Basque*. London.

Erman, Adolf. *Life in Ancient Egypt*. New York, 1971.

Erman, Adolf. *The Literature of the Ancient Egyptians*. Tr. By A.M. Blackman. London, 1927.

Fear, A.T. *Rome and Baetica: Urbanization in Southern Spain c.50 BC—AD 150*. Oxford, 1996.

Fischel, Walter J. *Ibn Khaldûn in Egypt: His Public Functions and His Historical Research (1382-1406): A Study in Islamic Historiography*. Berkeley, 1967.

Flynn, Maureen. *Sacred Charity: Confraternities and Social Welfare in Spain, 1400-1700*. Ithaca, NY, USA, 1989.

Gadalla, Moustafa. *Egyptian Cosmology: The Animated Universe - 2nd edition*. USA, 2001.

Gadalla, Moustafa. *Egyptian Divinities: The ALL Who Are THE ONE*. USA, 2000.

Gadalla, Moustafa. *Egyptian Mystics: Seekers of the Way*. USA, 2003.

Gadalla, Moustafa. *Egyptian Rhythm: The Heavenly Melodies*. USA, 2002.

Gadalla, Moustafa. *Exiled Egyptians: The Heart of Africa*. USA, 1999.

Gadalla, Moustafa. *Historical Deception: The Untold Story of Ancient Egypt – 2nd edition*. USA, 1999.

Gadalla, Moustafa. *Pyramid Handbook – Second Edition*. USA, 2000.

Gardiner, Sir Alan. *Egyptian Grammar: Being an Introduction to the Study of Hieroglyphs, 3rd ed*. Oxford, 1994.

Gibson, John C.L. *Textbook of Syrian Semitic Inscriptions: Volume I: Hebrew and Moabite Inscriptions*. Oxford, 1971.

Gibson, John C.L. *Textbook of Syrian Semitic Inscriptions: Volume II: Aramaic Inscriptions including inscriptions in the dialect of Zenjirli*. Oxford, 1975.

Gilmore, David D. *Aggression and Community: Paradoxes of Andalusian Culture*. New Haven, CT, USA, 1987.

Gilmore, David D. *Carnival and Culture: Sex, Symbol, and Status in Spain*. New Haven, 1998.

Gilmore, David D. *The People of the Plain: Class and Community in Lower Andalusia*. Columbia NY, 1980.

Gilsenan, Michael. *Saint and Sufi in Modern Egypt*. Oxford, 1973.

Goedicke, Hans. *The Report of Wenamun*. Baltimore, USA, 1975.

Hale, Edward Everett & Hale, Susan. *The Story of the Nations: Spain*. New York, 1907.

Handloff, Robert E, editor. *Mauritania: A Country Study*. Washington DC, 1990.

Heather, P.J. *Goths and Romans, 332-489*. Oxford, 1991.

Heather, Peter, editor. *The Visigoths from the Migration Period to the Seventh Century: An Ethnographic Perspective*. San Marino, 1999.

Heather, Peter. *The Goths*. Cambridge, MA, USA, 1996.

Hecht, Paul. *The Wind Cried: An American's Discovery of the World of Flamenco*. New York, 1968.

Hemingway, Ernest. *Death in the Afternoon*. New York, 1960.

Herodotus. *The Histories*. Tr. By Aubrey DeSelincourt. London, 1996.

Ibn-Arabi. *Sufis of Andalusia*. Tr. By RWJ Austin. Berkeley & LA, 1971.

Issawi, Charles, tr. *An Arab Philosophy of History: Selections from the Prolegomena of Ibn Khaldun of Tunis (1332-1406)*, tr. and arranged by Charles Issawi M.A. London, 1958.

James, T.G.H. *An Introduction to Ancient Egypt*. London, 1979.

Jones, Donald W. *External Relations of Early Iron Age Crete, 1100-600 BC*. Philadelphia, 2000.

Josephs, Allen. *White Wall of Spain: The Mysteries of Andalusian Culture*. Iowa, USA, 1983.

Josephus, Flavius. *Against Apion*, tr. H. St J. Thackeray. London, 1926.

Kamen, Henry. *The Spanish Inquisition: A Historical Revision*. New Haven, CT, USA, 1998.

Kapitan, Tomis, editor. *Archaeology, History and Culture in Palestine and the Near East: Essays in memory of Albert E. Glock*. Georgia, 1999.

Kennedy, Hugh. *Muslim Spain and Portugal: A Political History of al-Andalus*. New York, 1996.

Khaldûn, Ibn. *The Muqaddimah: An Introduction to History*, tr. From the Arabic by Franz Rosenthal, abridged and edited by N.J. Dawood. Princeton, 1969.

Khell, Vera and Hellmut. *The Great Pilgrimage of the Middle Ages: The Road to St. James of Compostela*. London, 1966.

King, Joan Wucher. *Historical Dictionary of Egypt*. London, 1984.

Lane, E.W. *The Manners and Customs of the Modern Egyptians*. London, 1836.

Lane-Poole, Stanley. *The Moors in Spain*. New York, 1888.

Lathrop, Thomas A. *The Evolution of Spanish: An Introductory Historical Grammar*. Delaware, 1986.

Leibold, John. *This is the Bullfight*. London, 1971.

Maddox, Richard. *El Castillo: The Politics of Tradition in an Andalusian Town*. 1993.

Mahdi, Muhsin. *Ibn Khaldûn's Philosophy of History: A Study in the Philosophic Foundation of the Science of Culture*. London, 1957.

Mandel, Miriam B. *Hemingway's Death in the Afternoon: the Complete Annotations*. Lanham, MD, USA, 2002.

Mateus, Maria Helena & d'Andrade, Ernesto. *The Phonology of Portuguese*. Oxford, 2000.

Maugham, W. Somerset. *Andalusia: Sketches & Impressions*. New York, 1923.

Melczer, William. *The Pilgrim's Guide to Santiago De Compostela*. New York, 1993.

Meyerson, Mark D. & English, Edward D, editors. *Christians, Muslims, and Jews in Medieval and Early Modern Spain: Interaction and Cultural Change*. Notre Dame, USA, 1999.

Michener, James A. *Iberia: Spanish Travels and Reflections*. New York, 1968.

Mierse, William E. *Temples and Towns in Roman Iberia: The Social and Architectural Dynamics of Sanctuary Designs from the Third Century B.C. to the Third Century A.D.* Berkeley, CA, USA, 1999.

Mitchell, Timothy. *Blood Sport: A Social History of Spanish Bullfighting*. Philadelphia, 1991.

Mitchell, Timothy. *Flamenco Deep Song*. Yale, 1994.

Mitchell, Timothy. *Passional Culture: Emotion, Religion, and Society in Southern Spain*. Philadelphia, PA, USA, 1990.

Mitchell, Timothy. *Violence and Piety in Spanish Folklore*. Philadelphia, PA, USA, 1988.

Morag, Shelomo. *The Vocalization Systems of Arabic, Hebrew, and Aramaic: Their Phonetic and Phonemic Principles*. Jerusalem, 1962.

Morca, Teodoro. *Becoming the Dance: Flamenco Spirit*. Iowa, USA, 1990.

Nelson, Harold D, editor. *Algeria: A Country Study*. Washington DC, 1986.

Nelson, Harold D, editor. *Libya: A Country Study*. Washington DC, 1979.

Nelson, Harold D, editor. *Morocco: A Country Study*. Washington DC, 1986.

Nelson, Harold D, editor. *Tunisia: A Country Study*. Washington, DC, 1986.

Peckham, J. Brian S.J. *The Development of the Late Phoenician Scripts*. Cambridge USA, 1968.

Penny, Ralph. *A History of the Spanish Language, 2nd ed*. Cambridge, 2002.

Perini, Mário A. *Modern Portuguese: A Reference Grammar*. New Haven, CT, USA, 2002.

Pitt-Rivers, J.A. *The People of the Sierra*. Chicago, 1963.

Plato. *The Collected Dialogues of Plato including the Letters*. Edited by E. Hamilton & H. Cairns. New York, USA, 1961.

Plutarch. *Plutarch's Moralia, Volume V*. Tr. by Frank Cole Babbitt. London, 1927.

Pohren, D.E. *The Art of Flamenco*. Spain, 1962.

Rawlings, Helen. *Church, Religion and Society in Early Modern Spain*. New York, 2002.

Read, Jan. *The Moors in Spain and Portugal*. New Jersey, USA, 1975.

Ribera y Tarrago, Julian. *Music in Ancient Arabia and Spain: Being La Música de las Cantigas*, Tr. and abridged by Eleanor Hague and Marion Leffingwell. London, 1929.

Romant, Bernard. *Life in Egypt in Ancient Times*. Italy, 1986.

Roth, Norman. *Jews, Visigoths and Muslims in Medieval Spain: Cooperation and Conflict*. Leiden, 1994.

Ruiz, Arturo, and Molinos, Manuel. Translated from Spanish by Turton, Mary. *The Archaeology of the Iberians*. Cambridge, UK, 1998.

Salisbury, Joyce E. *Iberian Popular Religion 600 BC to 700 AD: Celts, Romans and Visigoths*. Lewiston, NY, USA, 1985.

Shah, Idries. *The Sufis*. New York, 1964.

Siculus, Diodorus. Tr. by C.H. Oldfather. London, 1964.

Solsten, Eric & Meditz, Sandra W, editors. *Spain: A Country Study*. Washington, DC, 1990.

Solsten, Eric, editor. *Portugal: A Country Study*. Washington, DC, 1993.

Sordo, Enrique. *Moorish Spain: Cordoba Seville Granada*. New York, 1963.

Stalls, Clay. *Possessing the Land: Aragon's Expansion into Islam's Ebro Frontier under Alfonso the Battler 1104-1134*. Leiden, 1995.

Stanislawski, Dan. *Portugal's Other Kingdom: The Algarve*. Austin, TX, USA, 1963.

Stanton, Edward F. *The Tragic Myth: Lorca and Cante Jondo*. KY, USA.

Steen, Garth L., ed. *Alexandria: the Site & the History*. New York, 1992.

Strabo, *The Geography of Strabo*, Tr. By Jones, Horace Leonard. London, 1917.

Taggie, B.F., & Clement, R.W. *Iberia & The Mediterranean*.

Thompson, E.A. *The Visigoths in the Time of Ulfila*. Oxford, 1966.

Trend, J.B. *The Music of Spanish History to 1600*. Oxford, 1926.

Trend, J.B. *A Picture of Modern Spain Men and Music*. New York, 1921.

Turner, Victor & Turner, Edith. *Image and Pilgrimage in Christian Culture: Anthropological Perspectives.* Columbia, NY, USA, 1978.

Vassberg, David E. *Land and Society in Golden Age Castile.* Cambridge, 1984.

Warmington, B.H. *Carthage.* New York, 1969.

Webster, Susan Verdi. *Art and Ritual in Golden-Age Spain: Sevillian Confraternities and the Processional Sculpture of Holy Week.* Princeton, 1998.

Weill, Raymond. *Phoenicia and Western Asia: to the Macedonian Conquest.* Tr. By Ernest F. Row. Chicago, 1980.

Wilkinson, Sir J. Gardner. *The Ancient Egyptians: Their Life and Customs.* London, 1988.

Zagona, Karen. *The Syntax of Spanish.* New York, 2002.

Numerous references written in Arabic.

Sources and Notes

The author is extremely knowledgeable in several languages, such as the Egyptian and Arabic tongues. He is also very knowledgeable in Islam, being born-Moslem in Egypt and subjected to Islamic studies all his life.

References to sources in the previous section, *Selected Bibliography* are only referred to for the facts, events, and dates—not for their interpretations of such information.

1. The Romany (Gypsy) Essence of Hispania

The Egipcianos of Iberia – Borrow (129, 191, 206), Josephs (18, 97); Kaplan (34-5) re. meaning of Roma, Erman (*Life in Ancient Egypt*, 32).

The Egyptian-Iberian Fugitives –
Meaning of flamenco: Pohren (40-1).
Concept of land ownership in Egypt: Gadalla (*Egyptian Cosmology*), Gardiner.
New Land Policy in Spain: Gilmore (14), Josephs (21), Vassberg (6-7).
Religious cleansing: practically all references on this historic period, especially Josephs (15-6), Read (184).
Racial/ethnic cleansing: practically all references on this historic period, especially Borrow (332), Rawlings (23).

The Cultured Romany/Gitanos – Josephs (85, 98, 97-9), Stanton (78-9).

The Most Religious –
Religiousness of the Romany: Borrow (132), Stanton (85).
Festivals in Spain and Egypt: Gadalla (*Egyptian Mystics*, 94), Josephs (120-1), Stanton (79).

The Timeless Egyptian-Hispanic Culture – Herodotus (*Book 2*), Josephs (5-6, 51).

Secondary references on this chapter – Corbin, Kamen, Stanton, Turner.

2. Our Heavenly Mother

The Ascension of the Queen –

Egyptian Practices: Gadalla (*Egyptian Mystics* re. Egyptian festivities), Plutarch (*Moralia Vol V*).

Iberian Practices: Trend (*A Picture of Modern Spain Men and Music* re. Elche festival).

Gadalla (*Egyptian Rhythm* re. the two Marias).

Gadalla (*Historical Deception* re. the meaning of the name Maria).

Lady of Sorrow – Gadalla (*Egyptian Mystics*) after Plutarch (*Moralia Vol V*) re. the story of Isis and Osiris, Budge (*Osiris Vol II*, 276) re. Isis as the Lady of Sorrow.

The Virgin Mother with the 10,000 Names – Gadalla (*Historical Deception, Egyptian Cosmology*), Flynn (27) re. the many names/titles of Maria in Spanish confraternities, Josephs re. Maria's many names in Romany festivals.

Matrilineal/Matriarchal Society – Gadalla (*Egyptian Cosmology*).

The Ama Rules –

Egyptian Practices: Gadalla (*Historical Deception, Egyptian Cosmology*)

Iberian Practices: Gilmore (*Aggression and Community*, 146-148, *People of the Plain*, 181).

The Revered Ama –

Egyptian Aspects: Diodorus (*Book 1*).

Iberian Aspects: Flynn (28, 29, 125, 126).

The Bull of His Mother –

Egyptian practices: Budge (*Osiris Vol I*, 13, 397, 398), Diodorus, Gadalla (*Egyptian Mystics*), Herodotus, Strabo, Wilkinson (210, 294, 300).

Iberian Practices: Conrad (20), Josephs (135), Mitchell (*Violence and Piety in Spanish Folklore*, 130, 169).

Secondary references on this chapter – Conrad, Hemingway, Leibold, Mandel, Mitchell (*Blood Sport, Passionate Culture*), Pitt-Rivers.

3. Out of Egypt

The Mirages of Iberia – practically all references, especially Castro.

The Egyptian Romany Colonies – Diodorus (*Book 1*), Gadalla (*Egyptian Rhythm*), Herodotus (*Book 6*).

The Egyptian Influence in the Eastern Mediterranean – Diodorus (*Book 1*), Herodotus (*Book 1*), Steen (21-22).

The Spread of the Egyptian Religion – Budge (*Osiris, Vol II*, 286-287, 294-297, 307), Diodorus (*Book I*), Herodotus (*Book 2*), Plutarch (*Moralia Vol V*).

The Twin Sisters – Practically all references agree to the characteristics of the newcomers.

4. The Egyptian-Hispanic Alloys

The Egyptian Knowledge of Metallurgy and Metalworking – Erman (*Life in Ancient Egypt*, 460), James (187, 222, 226), Wilkinson (84).

The Golden Silver Alloy (Electrum) – Erman (*Life in Ancient Egypt*, 461,464).

The Copper and Bronze Alloys – Erman (*Life in Ancient Egypt*, 460, 461), James (34, 225).

The Glazing Alloys – Erman (*Life in Ancient Egypt*), Gadalla (*Historical Deception, Pyramid Handbook*), James, Wilkinson.

The Egyptian Mining Experience – Erman (*Life in Ancient Egypt*, 465-469, 472-475), James (220), Strabo (*Geography Vol 3*).

Fortifications of Isolated Communities – Diodorus (*Book 1*), Gadalla (*Exiled Egyptians*), Wilkinson (407-409).

5. In the Beginning – Almeria

The Sirets and Petrie Archeological Connections – Arnaiz-Villena (137,149), Castro (33, 371), Chapman (19, 21). Map was compiled from above references.

The Telling Tombs – Chapman (22, 178), Arnaiz-Villena (137, 171-2), Castro (28), Gadalla (*Pyramid Handbook*), James (187).

Dry-Weather Farming – Arnaiz-Villena (155), Castro (14,15), Chapman (265), James (24).

The Early (New) Settlers – Arnaiz-Villena (1, 149, 151), Castro (70, 87, 369), Chapman (21, 25-6, 32, 160, 163, 166, 167), Cunliffe (134).

6. Masters of the Seas

The Egyptian Ships – Practically all related references on the subject matter.

Khufu's ship: Gadalla (*Historical Deception*, 295).

Size of Egyptian boats: Romant (117).

Types and details of ships: Erman (*Life in Ancient Egypt*, 480-7).

Ships of war: Wilkinson (*Vol I*, 411-12).

Egyptian Goods – Bowman (222-3), Wilkinson (*Vol I*, 147-50, *Vol II*, 60-1, 70).

The Egyptian Geodesy –

Pavilion of Senusert: Gadalla (*Historical Deception*, 316).

Astronomy in Ancient Egypt: Gadalla (*Egyptian Rhythm*, 19-20, 41)

Patrons and Shrines of the Seafarers –

Practices in Ancient Egypt: Wilkinson (*Vol I*, 415).

The Ancient Egyptian concept of God as the ALL being the ONE: Gadalla (*Egyptian Divinities*).

"Names" of gods: Weill (69), Josephs (112).

Deities: Gadalla (*Egyptian Divinities*).

Astarte as an Ancient Egyptian deity: Erman (*Literature*, 169-170).

Our (Holy) Mother of the Sea –

The Two Marys: Gadalla (*Egyptian Divinities*, 65-6).

7. Merchants of the Seas

The Phoenicians' Homeland – Baram (3,4,6), Kapitan (273), Weill (15).

The Egyptian-Phoenician Connection – Baram (19-25), Culican (22-3), Weill (71).

The Egyptianized Phoenicians –

Religious Practices: Baram (64, 68, 69, 78), Weill (78).

"Proto-Sinaitic" inscriptions: Culican (125), Weill (167-8).

Moabite scripts: Daniels (95).

The Seafaring Phoenician/Carthaginians – Baram (37), Castro (239), Culican (110), Herodotus.

The (Non-) Phoenician Iberian Colonies – Castro (191), Culican (108-9), Josephs (11), Warmington (62).

Secondary references on this chapter – Condor, Geodicke, Warmington.

8. Canopus and Cádiz: A Tale of Two Harbors

The Gitano Dancers of Cádiz –

Josephs (75-7, 85, 89).

Egyptian Fishing Techniques at Cádiz –

Spanish practices: Josephs (53, 55, 58, 63-4).

Egyptian practices: Romant (82), Culican (110), Wilkinson (*Vol I*, 241, *Vol II*, 188).

The Many (Egyptian) Names of Cádiz –

The geographic description: Castro (178-9).

The many "names" of Cádiz: Entwistle (42), Gadalla (as an expert in Arabic language).

The holiness of the name: Erman (*Life in Ancient Egypt*, 279).

The Immortal Hercules: The Egyptian Lord of Travel –

Herodotus and Diodorus, as indicated in the text; also Baines (129).

The Egyptian Herakles' statue at Cádiz: Brody (35,40).

The Greater Canopus Harbor (Alexandria before Alexander): Maiden of the Seas – Bowman (218-20), Steen (26, 28-30, 36-8).

The Foundation of Cádiz –

Lack of Phoenician evidence: Castro (179).

The "Tin Route": Cunliffe (42), Warmington (24).

Analysis of Strabo's account: Castro (176).

The lighthouses of Pharos (Alexandria) and Cádiz: Strabo (*Geography*), as referenced in the text of this book.

The Lost Temples of Cádiz –

Herakles as represented in many "names": Brody (33).

Herakles' statue's Egyptian origin: Brody (35, 40).

The temple priests: Fear (234-5), Josephs (108).

The temple of Hathor/Astarte: Castro (181).

9. The Assyrian Devastation and Aftershocks

The Assyrian Assaults –

The Assyrians and Egypt: Erman (*Life in Ancient Egypt*, 50).

Changes in the Mediterranean Basin: Castro (239), Cunliffe (46).

The Egyptian Exodus –

Characteristics of new population in Iberia: Castro (192, 374).

Issues regarding Carthage: Devijver (149).

Turdetania Urbanization – Castro (183-8, 262, 376). Map was compiled from Castro's various chapters.

The Persian Rampage of Egypt –
The Persian history in Egypt: Gadalla (*Egyptian Rhythm*, 206).
Corresponding demographic changes in Iberia: Castro (248-9).

Secondary references on this chapter – Dorey, King.

10. Romanticizing the Romans

Romanticizing the Romans – Strabo (*Geography*), as referenced in the text of this book.

The Fictional Romanization of Iberia – Fear (249, 250, 256, 267), Josephs (51), Mierse (1).

The (Non-) Roman Temples and Tombs – Fear (188-9, 192, 240-2), Josephs (11), Mierse (70, 121).

Secondary references on this chapter – Baladi, Dorey, Heather (3 references), Warmington.

11. The Moors and the Egyptians

The Identification of the "Moors" (The Moabi Brothers) –
The cultured status of pre-Moorish Iberia: Josephs (9).
Common origin of three "languages/dialects": Chejne (35).
Moabite references in Iberian records: Roth (46-7, 50).
The role of the Jews: Lane-Poole (24), Roth (45, 146).

The Nomadic Moorish Rulers –
Ibn Khaldun: Fischel, Khaldun.
Moors' history in Iberia: Kennedy (18-25), Lane-Poole (52), Solsten (*Spain*, 9-13).

The Civilized Populace –
The Egyptian immigrants: Gadalla (*Exiled Egyptians*, 107-8), Kennedy (17, 26, 51, 107). Roth (45).

The Egyptian Green Revolution –
Conditions in Iberia: Kennedy (107), Roth (152).
Egyptian farming excellence: Diodorus, Herodotus, James (24), Strabo, Romant (91-5).

The Egyptian-Hispanic Arts and Crafts – Read (185), Sordo (28).
Egyptian style decorations: Erman (*Life in Ancient Egypt*, 78,

97, 102).

The Egyptian Housing and Gardens of Iberia – Erman (*Life in Ancient Egypt*, 195-6), Romant (40-1), Sordo (12), Wilkinson (Vol I, 5, 18-9).

Secondary references on this chapter – Acquaroni, Bendiner, Brett, Fischel, Hale, Handloff, Heather (3 references), Ibn-Arabi, Issawi, Kamen, King, Mahdi, Maugham, Meyerson, Nelson (*Algeria, Libya, Morocco, Tunisia*), Read, Solsten (*Spain, Portugal*), Sordo, Stalls, Stanislawski.

12. The Origin of the Hispanic Languages/Dialects

The Egyptian Source of Arabic Language –

Lack of "Arabic" language influence in Spain: Entwistle (107), Zagona (4).

History of "Arabic" language: Chejne (28-35).

Spoken Language in Egypt: Gadalla (being a native Egyptian).

Sound Shifts and Linguistic Studies – Practically all references in linguistic studies.

The Distinction of a Language –

The four pillars: Khaldun (433).

Word order in Ancient Egypt: Baines (200).

The Intimate Egyptian-Hispanic Tongue – Borrow (332), Butt (325), Stanton (85).

The Divine Mother Language –

The Egyptian language as the mother of several language families: Baines (199), Plato, Plutarch.

Characteristics of Semitic languages: Chejne (31-6).

The acrophonic principles and the Ancient Egyptian system of writing: Baines (200), Daniels (25).

Romancing the Mother Tongue –

Overview of Hispanic languages: Constable (180), Entwistle (8-9), Stern (150).

Basque language: Arnaiz-Villena (191), Hale (9-11).

Writing Variations and Linguistic Studies – Baladi (120), Culican (125), Daniels (95, 123, 261, 264), Erman (*Literature of the Ancient Egyptians*, xxxvii, *Life in Ancient Egypt*, 342), Peckham (3).

Iberian scripts: Arnaiz-Villena (167-191).

Secondary references on this chapter – Baladi, Budge (*Egyp-*

tian Language), Butt, Gardiner, Gibson (2 volumes), Lathrop, Mateus, Morag, Peckham, Penny, Perini, Solsten (*Spain, Portugal*), Zagona.

13. The Animated Religious Traditions

The Animated Cosmic Order – Gadalla (*Egyptian Cosmology*, throughout).

Iberian relics: Rawlings (93).

The Role of Saints –

Egyptian practices: Gadalla (*Egyptian Mystics*, throughout).

Iberian practices: Mitchell (*Violence and Piety*, 36), Rawlings (90-2), Salisbury (162-3).

The Cyclical Renewal Festivals –

Egyptian practices: Gadalla (*Egyptian Mystics*, throughout)

Iberian practices: Flynn (31), Mitchell (*Violence and Piety*, 31-2), Rawlings (92).

Egyptian Mysticism in Galicia (Priscillianism) –

Iberian practices and history: Chase (30), Salisbury (191-215, 265, 280), Trend (*The Music of Spanish History*, 38-9).

Egyptian concepts: Diodorus, Gadalla (*Egyptian Mystics*, 41-2, 58, and throughout).

Santiago de Compostela –

Egyptian practices: Gadalla (*Egyptian Mystics*, 95).

Iberian practices: Trend (*The Music of Spanish History*, 70-2).

The Egyptian/Iberian Mystical Societies –

Egyptian practices: Gadalla (*Egyptian Mystics*, 18-24, 145-7).

Iberian practices: Rawlings (95-6), Webster (15).

Secondary references on this chapter – Blackman, Bleeker, Flynn, Gilsenan, Ibn-Arabi, Khell, Lane, Mandel, Melczer, Shah, Turner, Webster.

14. The Egyptian-Hispanic Musical Heritage

The Egyptian Romany Muses –

Pre-Islamic history of music in Iberia: Ribera (7), Stanton (4), Trend (*The Music of Spanish History*, 38-9, 49).

The Music of Civilization –

Pre-Islamic history of music in Egypt: Gadalla (*Egyptian*

Rhythm, 210, and throughout).

The Heavenly Musical Forms –

Iberian practices: Chase (224-5), Ribera (88), Trend (*The Music of Spanish History*, 4, 30-2).

Egyptian practices: Gadalla (*Egyptian Rhythm*, 58-62, 67, 98-9, 157-8, 182).

Love Conquers All – Gadalla (*Egyptian Mystics*, 62), Hecht (163), Ribera (89-90), Stanton (6), Stern (83, 86).

Singing and Poetry –

Iberian practices: Borrow (292), Compton (xiii-xv, 3, 115, 123), Constable (180), Gilmore (*Carnival and Community*, x), Hecht (162), Stern (4, 50-1), Trend (*The Music of Spanish History*, 30).

Egyptian practices: Erman (*Literature of the Ancient Egyptians*, xxx-xxxi, *Life in Ancient Egypt*, 394-6), Gadalla (*Egyptian Rhythm*, 162-3).

Musical Instruments – Gadalla (*Egyptian Rhythm*, 97-152).

Rhythmic Dancing –

Similarities between Ancient Egypt and Iberia: Josephs (79-80, 85, 89, 94).

Egyptian practices: Gadalla (*Egyptian Rhythm*, 165-172).

Iberian practices: Chase (244), Josephs (79-80, 85, 89, 94), Salisbury (259).

The Musical Activities –

Egyptian practices: Gadalla (*Egyptian Rhythm*, 155-6, 172-3, 178-9, 185, *Egyptian Mystics*, 103, 150).

Iberian practices: Chase (33), Josephs (82), Salisbury (29).

The Heavenly Muses –

Egyptian traditions: Gadalla (*Egyptian Rhythm*, 152, 173).

Iberian traditions: Chase (245), Stanton (78-9).

Secondary references on this chapter – Brockett, Gilbert, Ibn-Arabi, Josephus, Mitchell (*Flamenco Deep Song*), Morca, Pohren, Stanton.

Index

A

Abbasids, 153, 155-6
Abd-al-Rahman I, first Umayyad emir of Andalusia, 153
Abd-al-Rahman II, Umayyad emir, succeeds to emirate, 153
Abd-al-Rahman III, first Umayyad caliph of Andalusia, 154
Abdera, 137
Adon, religious connotation, 103
ador, 212-13
Aegeans and Iberia, 56-7
Aelian, on bulls in Ancient Egypt, 51-2, 53-4
Agadir, *see* Cádiz
agriculture in Andalusia, 157, 159
Alcoy tablet, 189
Alexandria, *see* Canopus *and* Pharos
Algarve, 67, 84, 90
Al-Ghazali, 215-6
almadraba (fishing method), 118-9
Almeria
  culture, 84-92
  in Ancient Egypt, 125
  in Iberia, 67, 82, 83, 85, 89, 90, 92
  its Ancient Egyptian meaning, 82
Almohads, origins of, 154, 237
  invasion of Spain and Portugal, 154
  defeat at Las Navas de Tolosa, 154
Almoravids,
  first landing in Spain, 154
  rise to power in North Africa, 154, 237
Anat, an Egyptian deity, 104
Andalusia, chapter 11
  see also Turdetania *and throughout the book*
Animism/Animistic beliefs in Iberia and Egypt, 28, 32-3, 175, 191-6, 237, *also see* Priscillianism
antiphony, 212-14
  defined, 237
Apis, as the Ancient Egyptian bull-god, 49-52, 62-5, 124, 139, 203
Apollo, *see* **Heru Behdety**
Arabian music, 208-9
Arabic language, *see* languages, Arabic
Arabs, 14, 55-6, 149-54, 208-9, *and throughout* chapters 11 *and* 14, *also see* languages, Arabic
Argar (Argaric),
  burials, 83-7
  communities, 83-6
  farming, 88

fortifications, 83-6, 91
metallurgy, 83-6, 89-92
settlements, 83-6, 89-92
society, 83-6, 89-92
Arianism, 197
artistic styles in Ancient Egypt, 98-9, 162-4
Arius of Alexandria, 197
arts and crafts
in Ancient Egypt, 23, 69-75, 98-9, 162-4
in Iberia, 23, 162-4
also see music, dancing, *and under other related subjects*
Ascension Day festivities in Iberia and Egypt, 37-9
Assyrians
and Egyptian, 133-4
and Phoenicians, 133-4
Astarte,
as an Egyptian deity, 104-5
and temple of Cádiz, 132
Athenaeus (writer, 3rd century CE), on Egyptian musicians, 221
Augusta Emerita, 146, 147
Ausar, 32, 37-8, 40-1, 228
and **Auset**, 33, 37-8, 40-1, 44, 62-5, 117-8
and cyclic framework, 32-4
and farming activities, 50-1
and **Heru**, 197
symbolism of, 38, 49-54, 197
Auset, 32-4, 40-1, 145, 147-8
and **Anat**, 104
and **Ausar**, 32-3, 37-8, 40-1, 44, 62-5, 117-8
and her son (**Heru**), 32-4, 40-1, 47-8
and Mary/Maria, 39-41, 42-3, 47-9
and matrilineal/matriarchal society, 40, 43-6
meaning of name, 43
and **Nebt-Het**, 39, 40-1
symbolism of, 42-3, 50-1,64

B

Baal/Baalat, religious connotation, 103, 131
Baetis river, 147
Turdetania, 136-8
see also Guadalquivir river
Baladi (Egyptians/Hispanic), 15, 26-7, 35-6, 204, 237, *and throughout the book*
Baria (Villaricos), 137, 139-40
Basque language, *see* languages, Basque
Beni Hassan, tombs,
Ancient Egyptian forts, 81
Ancient Egyptian sheilds, 72
scenes of bullfights, 53
Berbers, 14, 29-30
rebellion of, 153, 154
role in the fall of the caliphate, 154-5
history in Moorish Spain, 150-4
in the Umayyad army, 150-1, 152-4
bohemian, 2, 21
meaning of word, 22
Borrow, George, regarding the one origin of ***Moriscos*** and ***Gitanos***, 29, 240

Bremner Rhind Papyrus, 197
bronze, 68, 70-2, 90-1
Bronze Age, *see under* Argar (Argaric) *and* El Argar
Budge, E.A. Wallis, 32, 240-1
buk-nunu (musical increment), 211-12
bulls,
  in Ancient Egypt and Iberia, 49-54
  running of (in Ancient Egypt), 52
Byblos, 40, 107-13

C

Cádiz, 31, 117-21, 128-32, 148
  temples and their Egyptian roots, 120, 123, 130-2
Canopus, 96, 123-27
cante jondo, 31, 210, 214
Cantigas, 207, 212
Carmo, Turdetanian town, 147, 148
Carthage, 111, 113-16, 134, 135
Carthaginians, and Iberia, 113-116
castanets, 225-6
Castro, Marie Cruz Fernández, 56-7, 114-15, 115-16, 241
  on the non-Phoenician evidence in Cádiz foundation, 128
cent, defined, 211-12, 237
chanting, 196, 214, 216, *also see* poetry *and* music
Christianity, and Ancient Egypt, 32-4, 40-3, 47-9, 52, 65, 197
clapping, 226-7
colonies, Copper Age, *see* Los Millares
  Bronze Age, *see* Argar *and* El Argar
Columbus' Santa Maria and Ancient Egyptian ships, 94-7
comma (the Egyptian musical unit), 211-2
  and **buk-nunu**, 212
confraternities, in Iberia, 13, 24, 43, 204-6
copla, 217, 237, *also see* poetry
copper, 67, 68, 70-3, 89, 90-2
Copper Age, in Iberia, *see* Los Millares
Córdoba (Corduba), 136-7, 150, 161, 162
  the Great Mosque of, 162
cosmology, 191-200
  in Ancient Egypt and Iberia, 62, defined, 237, *also see* Animism *and* Priscillianism
Counter Reformation, 48
Crete, and Ancient Egypt, 61, 62
cuneiform, 184
cymbals, 225-6

D

dancing, 227-34
  in Cádiz, 117-8
deities, 102-5
  of seafarers, 102-5
  see also **neteru**

Dendera, Temple of, 228
Dhimma, 26, 27, 237-8, *also see* jizya
Dhu-'l-Nun the Egyptian, 158, 204, 215-16
Diodorus, Sicilus (Sicilian historian 1st century BCE), 46-8, 50, 57-8, 60, 62, 82, 197, 241, 247
 on the Egyptian excellence in farming, and water management, 160
 on Egyptian muses, 233
 on Hercules being an Egyptian deity, 122-3
 on the Moabites, 150
Dor, 212-14
Duat, defined, 238

E

Ebro river (valley),
Egypt, *see under applicable subjects throughout the book*
El Argar, 83-6
 Bronze Age site, 83-8
 culture, 83-92
 gravegoods, 86-7
 settlements, 83-6
 settlers characteristics, 91-2
 society, 88, 90-2
 tombs, 86-7
electrum, 68-70
El Garcel, Copper Age site, 83
Elche, festival of the Ascension, 37-9, 106
enharmonic, 210-12, 238
Erman, Adolf, 121, 242
Erytheia, 120, 123, 131
Etruscans, 98, 135
Extremadura, 84, 90

F

farming,
 dry weather, in Ancient Egypt and Iberia, 88, 100, 159-61
and music and dance, 213, 232
Fear, A.T., 143-6, 242
fellowships, 13
 formation of, 204-6
 participation in festivals,206
festivals, of the Romany (and Ancient Egyptian equivalent), 33-4, 51, 63, 105-6, 194-6
Fifth, Perfect (music)
 and the Ancient Egyptian tonal system, 211-2
 defined, 238
fishing techniques at Cádiz and similarities to Ancient Egypt, 118-19
flamenco, 25, 31, 117-8, 227-9,
 Egyptian origin of word, 25
Flavius Josephus, on the Ancient Egyptian enharmonian, 211, 244
Ford, Richard,
 on Cádiz dances, 117-8
 on traditionalist Iberians, 35
fortification of settlements
 in Ancient Egypt, 80-82
 in Iberia, 83-4, 89, 90
fret, definition, 238

G

Gadalla, Moustafa, 1, 242, 268-271
Gades (Gadir, Gadeira), *see* Cádiz
Galicia, 73, 85, 89, 197-201
  also see tin *and* "Tin Route"
gardens of Ancient Egypt and Iberia, 164-6
Gitano, 21, 105-6, 117-8, 238
  meaning of word, 22-3
  as metal workers, 23-4, 29-31
  also see Romany *and throughout the book*
glazed objects/articles, in Ancient Egypt, 73-5,98-9
  in Iberia, 164-5
gods, goddesses, *see* **neteru**
gold, 70
Granada, 67, 90, 137, 151
Greeks,
  and the Ancient Egyptian sources of their heritage, 58-65
  and Egyptian goods, 98-9
Guadajoz river, 137
  settlements, 137
  towns, 137
Guadalquivir River (Baetis), 135-7, 142, *and throughout book*
  delta, 33, 54
Guadiana River (Anas), 136-7, *and throughout book*
guitar, 223-4
gypsies, 2,9
  the Egyptian origin of the word, 22
  also see ***Gitano***, Romany, *and throughout book*

H

handclapping, 226-7
Hathor, *see* **Het-Heru**
Heb-Sed, 49-50, 238
Heka, 202
Heracules/Herakles/Hercules, the Egyptian deity, 121-25
Herakleion, 123-5
Herakleopolis Magna, 122-3
Herodotus (c. 484-c.420 BCE), 32, 49, 58-9, 61, 63, 243
  on the **Dor-ians**, 58-9
  on Egypt and the Phoenician sailors, 113-14
  on Egyptian command of the seas, 101
  on Egyptians' strict adherence to their traditions, 35-6
  on Greeks, 57-9, 63
  on Hercules (Herakles) being Egyptian, 121-22
  on the River Nile, 159
Heru, 32, 34, 40-1, 42, 49, 62, 148, 197, 203, *also see* **Heru Behdety** *and* Herakles
Heru Behdety, 203
  and the nine muses, 233
Het-Heru, 104, 106, 117, 132, 139, 228
hieroglyphics, 112, 177-8, 185-7, *also see* languages, Egyptian
Homer, 60-1, 125, 126
  on the Egyptian origin of Heracules, 122
Horakles, *see* Heracules/Herakles
Horus, *see* **Heru**
Huelva, 84, 90

I

Iberian-Tartesian writing, 188-90
Ibn-'Arabi, 158, 215, 243
Ibn-Khaldun, 29, 141, 151-2, 208-9, 244
instruments of music, *see* musical instruments
interval (music), definition,238
irrigation, *see* farming
Isis, *see* **Auset**
Islam, defined, 238

J

Jerez, as *City of Gitanos*, 24, 31, 117-8, 233-4
Jews, in Iberia, *see* Moab/ Moabites
jihad, defined, 238
jizya, 26, 238
Josephus, Flavius, *see* Flavius, Josephus
jund, 156
Jundis, settlement in Iberia, 156-7

L

languages
  Arabic, 80, 167-70
  Aramaic/Syriac, 150
  Basque, 21, 182
  Berber, 30
  Egyptian, 14, 22, 25, 27-8, 33, 103, 104, 106, 120-1, 127, 150, 167-90, 211, 225
  Hispanic, 167-8, 172, 173, 174, 180-2, 188-90, 211, 225
  Iberian-Tartesian writings, 188-90
  Latin, 145, 174-5, 176, 180-1, 186-7
  Romance, 168, 180-1
  Semitic, 150, 176-80, 186-7
  sound shifts and linguistic studies, 171-2
  studies, 171-3
  writing variations in, 183-90
La Tene, the Egyptian meaning of the word, 22
Latin, *see* languages, Latin
Laurita tombs, 137-8
Livy, on Turdetanians, 35
Lorca, Federico Garcia, 9, 24, 30-1, 35, 45, 117
Los Millares, 83
  climate, 88
  Copper Age site, 83-6
  culture, 85-92
  farming activities, 86
  gravegoods, 86-7
  settlements, 83-6
  settlers' characteristics, 91-2
  society, 88, 90-2
love, divine, 214-16
lute, 222-3

M

Magna Graecia, 59, 62
Marcus of Egypt

and Arianism, 197,
and Priscillianism, 199, 200
Maria/Mary, Virgin, and
Auset (Isis), 39-41, 42-3, 47-9
and the meaning of Mary/ Maria, 39
also see Christianity and Ancient Egypt
matrilineal/matriarchal society in Egypt and Iberia, 40, 43-46, 238
Mazarrón (Little Egypt), 157-8
Melek, religious connotation, 103
Melqart (Heracles/Herakles),
religious connotation, 103, 131
and temple in Cádiz, 131, *also see* Hercules
metal ages and dating in Iberian (and other countries) history, 56
metallurgy,
in Ancient Egypt, 68-75
Mierse, W.E., 143, 146, 245
minerals, shortage in Ancient Egypt, 71
mining,
in Ancient Egypt, 68-9, 75-80
in Iberia, 67, 73, 90-1
Minoan, 183-4
Moab/Moabites, 149-51
Moors, 55-6, 75
definition of, *see* Moab/ Moabites
racial origin of, 149-51
Moriscos, 26-30, 37, 106, 158, 167
also see Romany *and throughout the book*
Mozarabes, *see* ***Mozarabs***
Mozarabs, 9, 26-7, 181
also see Romany *and throughout the book*
Mozarabic rites, 27, 214
and Catholicism, 27
Mudejars, 9, 26, 75, 163-4
also see Romany *and throughout the book*
Murcia, 24, 67, 90, 156-9, 167
muses, 233, 234
music
of Islam, 208-9
practices in Iberia and Ancient Egypt, *see* chapter 14
musical instruments in Ancient Egypt, 220-7
musical tradition in Egypt, 230-232
musicians in Egypt, 230-1
musmaat, 215, 219-20, 239
also see muwashshah(at/s)
muwashshah(at/s), 218-20, 239
mysticism, 204-5
defined, 238, *also see* Animism *and* cosmology
mystics, 204-6

N

neter/netert/neteru, defined, 15, 102-3, 239
"names" and religious

connotations, 103, 104, 106
also see under different names
Nile, 33, 37-9, 54, 82, 93, 95, 100, 159-61
noria (water wheel), 158, 161

O

offerings, 196, 200
ood, *see* lute
Orders, *see* fellowships
oud, *see* lute

P

Palermo, Stone of,
on Ancient Egyptian copper statues, 71
on imported lumber from Phoenicia, 108
on running of bulls in Ancient Egypt, 52
papyrus, defined, 239
Path, mystical, 199-200
patron saints, *see* saints
Pentecost,
and Ancient Egyptian origin, 34
and ***Gitano*** festival, 33-4
percussion instruments, 222, 225-7
Persia, invasions of Egypt, 139-40
Petrie, Flinders, and Ancient Egypt, 83-8, 112
Pharos (old Alexandria), 61, 124-6
Lighthouse, 130
Phoenicia, 11-2, 107-8, *and throughout* chapter 7
Phoenicians, 11-2, 55-6, 92, 101, chapter 7, *and throughout the book*
arts and crafts, 111
and Cádiz, 128-32
colonies (lack thereof), 115-6
and consonantal alphabets, *see* Proto-Sinaitic inscriptions
and dependence on Ancient Egypt, 107-13
in the Iberian Peninsula,55-6
Pillars of Heracles, 101, 113-4
seafaring, 101, 122, 129, *also see* Cádiz, Straits of Gibraltar, *and* Tin Route
Plato (428-347 BCE), 60, 64, 246
on Egyptian adherence to traditions, 36
on Egyptian festivals, 230
on Egyptian language, 177
Laws, 230
Pliny, on temples of Cádiz, 132
Plutarch, 50, 63, 64, 201, 246
on Ancient Egyptian alphabets, 177
poetry, in Egypt and Iberia, 212, 214, 216-20
poll-tax, *see* jizya
Priscillianism, 197-203
and Santiago de Compostela, 200-3
Proto-Sinaitic inscriptions, 112-3

R

Reconquest, 9, 21, 25-9, 30, 105, 154, 167
relics, in Ancient Egypt and Iberia, 192, 195
religious beliefs in Ancient Egypt, 102-3, *also see under* Animism, cosmology, *and throughout the book*
religious festivities, *see* festivals,
religious music, *see* music,
Reshef-Baal, as an Egyptian deity, 103-4
roads in Ancient Egypt, 77-9
Romans,
 Ancient Egyptian influence on, 63-5, 98-9
 in the Iberian Peninsula, 55-6, 141-48
Romany, 2, 9, 21, 65, 67, 90-1, 106, 117-8, 191, 194, 206, 207
 Egyptian origin, 21-4
 meaning of word, 22, 195
 and ***romeria (romertias)***, 33, 195
 also see throughout the book
romeria, its Ancient Egyptian meaning, 33, 195

S

saints role in Ancient Egypt and Iberia, 33, 191-2
samaa, 215-6, 239
 also see **musammat**
Santiago de Compostela, 106, 200-3
seafaring deities, 102-5
Segura River, 85, 157-8
Semitic language, *see* languages, Semitic
Serapis, 62, 64, 125, 148, *also see* **Apis**
Set (Seth), 34, 40-1
Seville, 117, 154, *also see* Triana
ships in Ancient Egypt, 93-7, 101, 102
shrines, 192-3
 visitation and rituals, 194-6
Sicilus, Diodorus, *see* Diodorus Sicilus
Sierra Morena, 89
 mineral ore, 89
Silius Italicus, on the priests at Cádiz temples, 132
silver, 67, 70, 89, 90, 92
Siret, Louis and Henri, 83-91,139
stanza, definition, 239
 also see poetry
stele/stelae, definition, 239
Strabo (geographer, c. 58 BCE-25 CE), 247
 on bulls in Ancient Egypt, 54
 on Cádiz, 128-30, 132
 on Egyptian excellence in water management, 160,161
 on Egyptian knowledge of astronomy and geography, 101
 on Iberia, 67, 73, 76, 142,144
Strait of Gibraltar (Calpe), 84, 118-9
 also see Pillars of Hercules, "Tin Route", *and* Cádiz
sound shift, 167, 171-2
Sufi/Sufism, 199-200, 204-6

Egyptian origin, *see* Dhu-'I-Nun the Egyptian
also see under mystics *and throughout the book*
Sufi Orders, *see* fellowships
Sufi Ways (Orders) in Egypt, *see* fellowships
Sufism, 199-200, 215-6
its relation to Islam, 204-6
the origin of, 158, 216
Syria/Syrians, 104

T

Taifas (kingdoms), 154, 239
Tajo (Tagus) River, ancient settlements, 84-5, 90, *also see* "Tin Route"
Tehuti Research Foundation, 1, 268-72
temples, near Egyptian mining sites, 76-7, 148
tin, 70-3, 84-5
bronze, 70-3, 84-5
resources, 73, 85, 89, 90
"Tin Route", 73, 84, 85, 128, 197
tonal system, 210-2
Triana, as home of Romany, 24
Trayamar and Ancient Egyptian finds, 137-8
Trend, J.B., on Santiago de Compostela, 202-3, 247
Tudmir, 157-8
tuna fishing at Cádiz, 118-9
Tunisia, 134, 151, 208, *also see* Carthage
Turdetania, 134-40

U

Umayyads, defeated in Syria, 153
founding of dynasty in Iberia, 153

V

Villaricos, *see* Baria
Visigoths, 151
Voltaire, on Cádiz dancers and Egypt, 31, 117

W

Way (Sufi), *see* Path
wine, its spiritual metaphor, 214-5
word-langage and music-language contrasted, 216-7

Y

Yemen, Arab tribal group, 153, 156, *also see* Moors

About TRF Books

Tehuti Research Foundation (T.R.F.) is a non-profit, international organization, dedicated to Ancient Egyptian studies. Our books are engaging, factual, well researched, practical, interesting, and appealing to the general public. Visit our website at:

http://www.egypt-tehuti.org
E-mail address: info@egypt-tehuti.org
eBooks can be ordered at: http://www.egypt-tehuti.org/gadalla-books.html

The books listed below are authored by T.R.F. chairman, Moustafa Gadalla.

Egyptian Mystics: Seekers of the Way

ISBN: 1-931446-05-9 (pbk.), 192 pages, US$11.95
eBook: 1-931446-15-6, 192 pages, US$7.95

This book explains how Ancient Egypt is the origin of alchemy and present-day Sufism, and how the mystics of Egypt camouflage their practices with a thin layer of Islam. The book also explains the progression of the mystical Way towards enlightenment, with a coherent explanation of its fundamentals and practices. It shows the correspondence between the Ancient Egyptian calendar of events and the cosmic cycles of the universe.

Egyptian Cosmology: The Animated Universe - 2nd *ed.*

ISBN: 0-9652509-3-8 (pbk.), 192 pages, US$11.95
eBook: 1-931446-03-2, 192 pages, US$7.95

This book surveys the applicability of Egyptian cosmological concepts to our modern understanding of the nature of the universe, creation, science, and philosophy. Egyptian cosmology is humanistic, coherent, comprehensive, consistent, logical, analytical, and rational. Discover the Egyptian concept of the universal energy matrix, how the social and political structures were a reflection of the universe, and the interactions between the nine universal realms, ...etc.

Egyptian Rhythm: The Heavenly Melodies

ISBN: 1-931446-02-4 (pbk.), 240 pages, US$14.95
eBook: 1-931446-14-8, 240 pages, US$9.95

Discover the cosmic roots of Egyptian musical, vocal, and dancing rhythmic forms. Learn the fundamentals (theory and practice) of music in the typical Egyptian way: simple, coherent, and comprehensive. Review a detailed description of the major Egyptian musical instruments, playing techniques, functions, etc. Discover the Egyptian rhythmic practices in all aspects of their lives. This book will make your heart sing.

Egyptian Harmony: The Visual Music

ISBN: 0-9652509-8-9 (pbk.), 192 pages, US$11.95
eBook: 1-931446-08-3, 192 pages, US$7.95

This book reveals the Ancient Egyptian knowledge of harmonic proportion, sacred geometry, and number mysticism, as manifested in their texts, temples, tombs, art, hieroglyphs, ...etc., throughout their known history. It shows how the Egyptians designed their buildings to generate cosmic energy, and the mystical application of numbers in Egyptian works. The book explains in detail the harmonic proportion of about 20 Ancient Egyptian buildings throughout their recorded history.

Egyptian Divinities: The All Who Are THE ONE

ISBN: 1-931446-04-0 (pbk.), 128 pages, US$ 8.95
eBook: 1-931446-07-5, 128 pages, US$5.95

The Egyptian concept of God is based on recognizing the multiple attributes of the Divine. The book details more than 80 divinities (gods/goddesses), how they act and interact to maintain the universe, and how they operate in the human being—*As Above so Below, and As Below so Above.*

Historical Deception The Untold Story of Ancient Egypt - 2nd Edition

ISBN: 0-9652509-2-X (pbk.), 352 pages, US$19.95
eBook: 1-931446-09-1, 352 pages, US$13.95

This book reveals many aspects of the Ancient Egyptian civilization in 46 chapters, with interesting topics, such as: deities, the role of the Pharaoh, temples, tombs, pyramids, Sphinx, music, literature, architecture, international trade, calendar, medicine, sciences, industries, art, Exodus, and much, much more.

Exiled Egyptians: The Heart of Africa

ISBN: 0-9652509-6-2 (pbk.), 352 pages, US$19.95
eBook: 1-931446-10-5, 352 pages, US13.95

Read a concise and comprehensive historical account of Egypt and sub-Sahara Africa for the last 3,000 years. Read about the forgotten Ancient Egyptians, who fled the foreign invasions and religious oppressors. Read how they rebuilt the Ancient Egyptians model system in Africa, when Egypt itself became an Arab colony. Read about the Ancient Egyptians' social, economical, and political systems, and their extended application into sub-Sahara Africa. Find out how the Islamic jihads fragmented and dispersed the African continent into endless misery and chaos. Discover the true causes and dynamics of African slavery.

Pyramid Handbook - Second Edition

ISBN: 0-9652509-4-6 (pbk.), 192 pages, US$11.95
eBook: 1-931446-11-3, 192 pages, US$7.95

A complete handbook about the pyramids of Ancient Egypt during the Pyramid Age. It contains: the locations and dimensions of interiors and exteriors of the pyramids; the history and builders of the pyramids; theories of construction; theories on their purpose and function; the sacred geometry that was incorporated into the design of the pyramids; and much, much more.

Tut-Ankh-Amen: The Living Image of the Lord

ISBN: 0-9652509-9-7 (pbk.), 144 pages, US$9.50
eBook: 1-931446-12-1, 144 pages, US$6.50

This book provides the overwhelming evidence from archeology, the Dead Sea Scrolls, the Talmud, and the Bible itself, that Tut-Ankh-Amen was the historical character of Jesus. The book examines the details of Tut's birth, life, death, resurrection, family roots, religion, teachings, etc., which were duplicated in the biblical account of Jesus. The book also reveals the world's greatest conspiracy and cover-up, which re-created the character of Jesus, living in another time (Roman era) and another place (Palestine, Israel).

Egypt: A Practical Guide

ISBN: 0-9652509-3-0 (pbk.), 256 pages, US$8.50
eBook: 1-931446-13-X, 256 pages, US$5.95

Quick, easy, and comprehensive reference to sites of antiquities. Detailed plans and descriptions of all major temples and tombs in Ancient Egypt. Tips are included to help understand both the modern and ancient Egyptian cultures. This pocket-sized book is informative, detailed, and contains an illustrated glossary. A no-nonsense, no-clutter, practical guide to Egypt, written by an Egyptian-American Egyptologist.

Tehuti Research Foundation

Ordering Information (Paperback Books)

Name ____
Address ____
City ____
State/Province _____________________________________
Country _________________ Tel. (_____) _____________

______ *books* @ $16.50 (*Egyptian Romany*)	= $	
______ *books* @ $11.95 (*Egyptian Mystics*)	= $	
______ *books* @ $11.95 (*Egyptian Cosmology*)	= $	
______ *books* @ $ 8.95 (*Egyptian Divinities*)	= $	
______ *books* @ $11.95 (*Egyptian Harmony*)	= $	
______ *books* @ $19.95 (*Historical Deception*)	= $	
______ *books* @ $19.95 (*Exiled Egyptians*)	= $	
______ *books* @ $11.95 (*Pyramid Handbook*)	= $	
______ *books* @ $ 9.50 (*Tut-Ankh-Amen*)	= $	
______ *books* @ $ 8.50 (*Egypt: Pract. Guide*)	= $	
______ *books* @ $14.95 (*Egyptian Rhythm*)	= $________	
Subtotal	= $	
North Carolina residents, add 7% Sales Tax	= $	
Shipping: (U.S.A. only) $1.00 each book	= $	
Outside U.S.A. (per weight/destination)	= $________	
Total	= $	

Payment: [ ] Money Order or Check
[ ] Visa [ ] MasterCard [ ] Discover

Card Number: ____

Name on Card: _________________________________ Exp. Date: ___/___

Tehuti Research Foundation
P.O. Box 39406
Greensboro, NC 27438-9406 U.S.A.

Call TOLL FREE (within USA) and order now 888-826-7021
Call to order (outside USA): 336-855-8111
Fax (within USA): 888-202-7818
e-mail: info@egypt-tehuti.org